Durham Centennial Book

Pride In The Past,
Faith In The Future

In this commemorative book is information on the Santa Fe Trail, which passed through Durham, and at this writing, is being considered by Congress for designation as a National Historic Trail.

Those interested in the detailed history of Durham will find that material, as it was carried in the 60th anniversary booklet entirely reproduced on pages 110 - 123.

An early day promotional pamphlet is reproduced on pages 45 - 48, giving information on early day businesses.

The update, "In Recent Years", and information of current businesses starts on page 203.

DEDICATION

Dedicated to those who went before us, whose memories are treasured and commemorated in this book, and to present residents whose generous assistance in compiling material, information and photographs was invaluable in helping to recapture our town's past.

Attention, Readers!

The compilers of this book would like to thank all those who responded to our published pleas for information and photographs. We ask the reader's understanding of any oversights, especially in light of so expansive a project, requiring as it does the reconstruction from memory of so many facets of the past.

Copyright 1987
by
Martha Pat Vogt and Christina Vogt
A compilation of Durham, Kansas
ISBN No. 0-931515-20-3   Typesetting by Kathy Trudgen

Home Folks. 1
Welcome. 2
Memories of a Childhood in Durham. 6
Early History. 10
The Santa Fe Trail Connection. 11
Artifacts From The Trail. 18
Early Day Cook's Story. 20
Early Durham. 23
The Crane Ranch. 24
Santa Fe Trail Ruts. 37
The Chisholm Trail. 38
The Railroad. 40
Promotional Pamphlet. 45
Early Settlers. 49
First Newspaper 60
Incorporation. 61
Memories of the 1930's. 66
"The Faith" - Churches and Cemetery Rosters. 67
Mayors of Durham & Ordinances of Interest. 83
Durham Logo. 88
"We're all equal". 88
Places and Faces. 89
Bridges. 100
Durham Buildings. 102
Saturday Night in Town. 106
A Visitors View. 107
60th Anniversary. 110
Sports. 124
Leisure Time Activities. 135
Social Life · 140
Home Circle Club. 143
The First Airplane. 144
Humor and Hi-Jinks. 146
Schools, Students and Teachers. 148
Graduates of Durham High School. 174
Floods and Fires. 179
Farming and Ranching. 189
In Recent Years. 203
Durham Businesses Today. 204
Consider Durham for Retirement. 210
The Wagon Bridge. 214
Centenaria. 219
Senior Citizens. 220

HOME FOLKS

Home folks – love 'em, well I guess,
Hearts just made of real kindness;
Miss 'em – I should say I do,
Don't find many folks as true.
Seems like now I just can hear
Home folks words of love and cheer,
Knowin' I've a welcome there
Truer an' warmer than anywhere.

Home folks ain't just family kin,
They're the folks with whom you've been
Reared and raised for years an' years,
Minglin' all your smiles and tears
Till they seem a part of you
From your childhood clear on through,
Standin' by you, lose or win,
Same as real blood, kith an' kin.

Makes no difference what you do,
Seems like homefolks stay still, stay true;
Overlookin' wayward ways,
Just rememberin' happy days,
Or when praise is but your due
Fer some thing you've tried to do,
Home folks hands are quick to clasp
Yours in proud an' hearty grasp.

Stranger folks are pretty nice,
Distant things lure and entice,
but I like home folks the best!
Bein' with 'em's like a rest.
When death comes an' I must go,
Wish that I could only know
That there'd be some home folks nigh,
Sorta watching, lingerin' by.
                    Ruth Yoland Shaw

View of Durham from the old Wagon Bridge.

Welcome to the Durham Centennial!

The Centennial Committee, all Durham Citizens, and the Publishers of this Commemorative Book hope that you will enjoy the festivities, the reunions, the reminiscing with old friends and the various activities of this special three-day event of July, 1987, marking Durham's 100th birthday.

This centennial book represents a collection of photographs, old letters and documents, and personal recollections that will help the reader better understand Durham's special place in Kansas history. Durham, located on the old Santa Fe Trail, which was said to span "from Civilization to Sundown," was later the site of one of the largest privately owned cattle ranches ("Durham Park") from which Durham got its name, and finally, located on the Main Line of the Rock Island Railroad. . . all these facets of Durham's history are explored.

But it's the people who make a town what it is, and every effort has been made to secure a full panoramic view of those people, in photographs obtained from many sources. Together with interviews and old documents, through which has been re-created, the scope of Durham's community and school life. We apologize in advance for any omissions and errors. But we hope the book will provide you with some heartwarming memories as you read about and see the places and faces that we all cherish and hold dear.

Two previously published booklets about Durham, one printed in 1903 as a promotion for the town, and the other in 1947, for the town's 60th anniversary celebration, are reprinted in their entirety within these pages, as they are not accessible to many readers otherwise, and because they give a perspective of the town from the times they represent. Also within these pages are never before printed letters about life in and around Durham. This book makes no claims to be the comprehensive history of the town, but rather a celebration of its highlights, its people, its times.

Centennial Committee Members

The Centennial Committee, includes, from left, 1st row, Tom Donahue, Kent Becker, Curtis Frick, Ben Goertz, Dudley Donahue, Anna Mae Goertz, Joan Donahue and Arlene Pankratz. Second row, Jim Hein, Rhonda Donahue, David Hein, Jim Donahue, Geraldine Frick, Lin Boucher (designer of the Durham Centennial logo) and Ruby Yauk. Bob Gordon, chairman of the committee, is pictured separately.

The General Centennial Planners: seated, left to right, Arlene Pankratz, Anna Mae Goertz, Jean Oblander, Geraldine Frick, Lin Boucher, Ruby Yauk, Bob Gordon; standing, left to right, Melvin (Cocky) Frick, Ona Donahue, Dudley Donahue, Joan Donahue, Ben Goertz, Jim Hein, Glennon Crowthers, Jim Donahue, Tom Donahue, Richard Dirks, Dave Hein, Curtis Frick, Willie Popp, D. D. Regier, Harvey Yauk. Not pictured are Dorman Becker and George and Vernedda Klein.

Ben Goertz is the present mayor of Durham, shown with his wife, Anna Mae.

Quality, Not Quantity...

What makes a town a town? Its a spirit, its honesty, its integrity and courage, in the strength, friendliness and vitality of its people, traditions, heritage.

That is why, small as it is, Durham holds a valued place in the pages of Kansas history. Noteworthy because of its historical connection with the Santa Fe Trail, the Crane and Moore Ranches, and railroading, it is also important to us as individuals. . . the place where many of us got our start, came to understand and our own identity. We learned usefulness, faith, ("world view") how the world was, based on what we saw, heard and felt, there in our early days.

As Ben Goertz, the present mayor, says; "I believe Durham was unique in that it was so varied, it was not just mainly one denomination of people, or one ethnic group. It was a real melting pot. . . of many kinds of peoples and faiths and backgrounds, and in that diversity there was built a harmony, and a much broader view than was to be found in many of the larger towns, even though we were smaller. We were really less provincial, or in-grown, than other towns, and that is an advantage."

Goertz added that his father was in business in Durham since 1927, "and he did business with everyone, and it was all done by agreement, and trustworthiness and integrity were constant and dependable."

Bob and Velma Gordon. Bob is chairman of the Durham Centennial Committee.

How Durham Got It's Name

In 1872, when Albert Crane bought the Moore Ranch and created a huge ranching empire (laid out like a park), he named the ranch "Durham Park", after the Durham cattle imported from the British Isles. The ranch was the first post office in the county and when Durham became a town, the post office was moved there, and the name shortened to Durham.

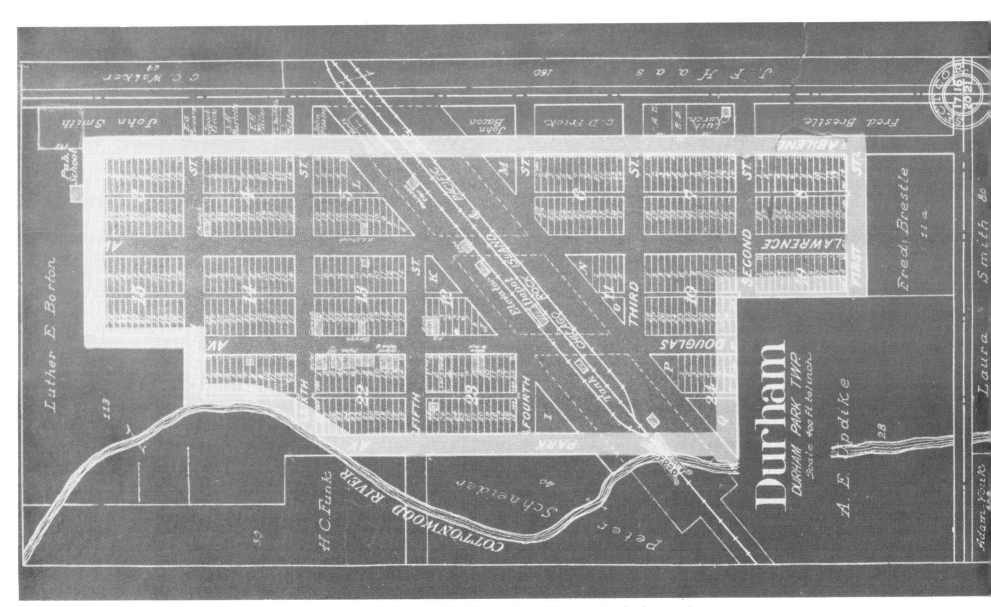

Anyone who has ever lived in Durham will recognize the layout of
the town, with the railroad tracks cutting through the business area
and the river skirting the town.

Memories of a Childhood in Durham

Fondly Remembered
Growing Up In Durham

By Pat Nelson Vogt and Norman Dean Nelson

"The skies are bluer, and the grass is greener, over at Durham!"

So said our mother, Mrs. Dwight (Anna) Nelson, back in 1946, when she returned from a drive in the countryside, to report that 1) she had found a wonderful place for us to move, and 2) it was a very special little town, and we would love it.

So, we moved from Manhattan KS, to Durham, where our parents spent the next 10 years, before moving on to Galva, Kansas. Thus, our growing up years, those formative years when you realize your own identity by bouncing it off of different experiences were spent in this very special small town. We respectfully submit these recollections of those days.

"The Durham Kid Experience"

As kids growing up in Durham, we and our friends all knew that we were living on the very ruts of history, those of the Santa Fe Trail, and this was very much a part of our heritage, our identity. Every school child was mindful that we were in the location of an important part of the Western Migration, and so we were somehow "beyond Durham", a part of the very heart of life's adventures, even though we were "in Durham" and loving it.

Anyone who was a student of Miss Frances Jones (later Mrs. John West) was thoroughly immersed in the historical significance of this community. Miss Jones' father had worked on the famed Crane Ranch, which was preceded by the Moore Ranch on the Cottonwood Crossing of the Santa Fe Trail, and at our impressionable age of 5th and 6th graders, she opened our eyes and minds to the history all around us.

This forever changed the world view of many students, so that they have maintained a lifetime fascination with American history.

The pace was slower in a small town, and there seems to have been an exceptionally charitable attitude prevailing among the persons in the community. Present day officials looking back and asked to comment about that environment, say they believe that it was because Durham was a "melting pot" of many denominations, ethnic backgrounds, and different cultures, a real variety of people who

had learned to accept, respect, and to cooperate with one another, so that there had come to be a "kinship in diversity", far surpassing the prevailing provincial atmosphere in many other small towns.

Durham always seemed a friendly place, and the "town kids" and the "country kids", were distinguised only by their location of their residences, and the proximity to various things of interest.

Growing up in or around Durham was a delight for most children, for there was a freedom, an easy lifestyle that allowed for differences and similarities.

The Big Eye of television had not yet made its appearance, back in the 40's, when we were there, and our entertainment was that of the previous generations of kids in Durham, home-made. Fishing from the little bridges, exploring the creek banks, always dreaming that we'd somehow find the cannon that the "old soldiers, almost a century before us, had spiked and thrown into the Cottonwood, to keep the Indians from getting it," according to legend.

The "Past" enlarged and transcended our "Present" as we became figures in history, young and obscure as we were. The river was always the focus.

In the earlier years, Durham was an entity unto itself, and the merchants looked after our needs, the volunteer fire department

was ready to respond to the alarm of the ringing of the downtown fire bell. (However, on at least two occasions, the old Maxwell Fire Wagon failed to start, and had to be towed to the scene of a fortunately minor house fire).

Nearly everyone farmed in those days (now only 2% of America is family-farm), but morning and evening chores were a part of life, and required a very early arising, so that school could come after work.

Farming was what started Durham – (the Moore Ranch and the Crane Ranch, as well as providing services – Moore's on the Santa Fe Trail) and the tendency to be hospitable and helpful and to entertain was as strong in Durham as in any community I've ever known.

Because it was a farm community, and most farm boys learned to drive equipment as well as vehicles at a very young age, and because you could get a "school permit" at age 14, there was an awful lot of youthful driving, if only around the block. Many a youngster remembers being taught to drive by their parent's instruction, in the family car, driving along the country roads, and learning to make a turn-around on the country road, staying between the ditches without benefit of power steering. But owning a car was a different matter.

Cars? Some had them, some didn't, and mainly a car was not essential to your lifestyle if you lived in town (although country kids had to drive in to school). Town kids could walk or ride a bike to school, as the town was small enough that your feet could take you wherever you wanted to go.

For children, your life was what it was, determined by your parents, and your own preferences for entertainment and activity. You could put together a Hallowe'en party for friends, and lead them through a dark barn in which you had cleverly devised creepy surroundings.

You could play "horse", a form of basketball that required fewer participants than were usually available for a full-scale game, under the circumstances of fewer kids in a small town, available at a moments notice.

Boys and girls played ball together, particularly baseball and football, also with revised rules. Teams of kids threw their enthusiasms toward a number of activities, most of it wholesome, unsegregated, and not unlawful, as we tested the waters of independence.

Dress up your cats in doll clothes, teach tricks to your dogs, go hunting with bb guns, build a cave on the river, or, if you dreamed of being another Roy Rogers or Dale Evans, you could borrow a horse and go riding.

During the late 1940's, George Weins, the town blacksmith, owned a black shetland pony named Dixie, who although she was mean-tempered and usually uncooperative with her variety of inept riders, gave us a chance to learn some real "horse-sense."

Fishing was always an option, because the creek was so close, (too close, when it flooded), and swimming was something to be done either in the river or a farm pond. (Later, we got rides to the Municipal Pool at Abilene for swimming lessons and acquaintance with chlorinated water, and without fish and turtles for swimming companions).

Ben Goertz, elsewhere in this book, recollects the swimming done down by the railroad bridge, in the deeper parts of the Cottonwood, by groups of boys on summer days during the 30's.

But speaking of farm ponds, as we were, that was another thing about Durham. Baptisms, for those of the faith requiring immersion as proof of their conversion, were performed at farm ponds or rivers.

This was always a sober occasion, and the ministers as well as the convert needed to wade into the water for the convert's ceremonial dip. (See photo elsewhere in this book). This practice of baptism was consistent from Durham's earliest days until at least the 1950's, when those churches with immersion regulations acquired baptismal fonts, or alternative methods.

This was another reminder to children of the pioneers' way of doing things, of carrying out their amenities using whatever conditions and resources were at hand.

Country kids had more farm chores than town kids, although most town kids were responsible for chicken flocks, an occasional pig or cow, as well as other expected chores. We had not come to the era where children were so under-valued as help that they became "decorative", or worse yet, "guests" requiring entertainment and special care. We kids were on our own then.

The Indians had a saying that tornadoes never hit river areas, (being lowlands); thus Durham, on the Cottonwood, was prone to floods, but not tornadoes. Fires took a toll at times, but it was the threat of floods that made people cringe when black storm clouds lowered in the skies.

Floods provided a source of interest as well as frustration and danger, and when flood water came into your house, it was a gigantic job to remove the silt that settled on the floors, and stains on the walls, once the waters receded. But you couldn't say it was dull.

The cooks at the Durham school made an impression on us. Durham was and is known for its wonderful cooks, dating back to

Every generation of Durham kids enjoyed adventures on the
Cottonwood River, from fishing and exploring, to this attempt at
Cave building in the creek bank.

Molly Hoop's valiant efforts to feed folks at Moore's Ranch (see
related story) and many a bride nowadays could benefit from the
gift of one of the old Home Circle Club's cookbooks (see history of club
elsewhere in book). Not only were our mothers, and our friends'
mothers, (and dads, too) very good cooks, but the school system
served a fare far above the average lunch program.

The school was of course, the old red brick two-story structure,
which housed all 12 grades in the same building, and the cafeteria
was in the basement. The school lunch program, like all others,
operated on a close budget, and with some government subsidies,
but the cooks turned out really superb meals: kolaches, light rolls,
custards, mashed potatoes with beef and gravy. . . the list could go
on and on.

Some of the hungrier ones often dropped by the cooks' kitchen
during morning recess to ask "What's for lunch?" and the cooks
would tell us, and we could look forward to it. At that time, school
lunches were 35¢. Among the cook over the years, we remember,
Maud Haas, Alma Mueller, Lydia Klein, Blondie Frick and Bernice
MacDowell, and others, but they most certainly set a high standard
for culinary achievement.

Not enough praise can be heaped upon those teachers who served
in the Durham school system. It was a small school, and salaries
were not impressive, yet it could be said that kids then didn't create
the major discipline problems, by and large, which developed in
some larger schools as the permissive generation came in later.

Other recollections of Durham include the patience of the local
merchants, their consideration to us as customers, even though we
were juveniles, and the prevailing spirit of charity and concern that

was seen, over and over again, in the area.

As school girls, we did a lot of lending and borrowing of clothing, (something today's kids apparently aren't so prone to do), but in this way, we learned generosity, while enhancing our school wardrobes with someone else's borrowed sweater, skirt or jacket.

The telephone office was also fascinating, with one person operating all the switches to connect one phone with another. Martha Zimmerman, the long-time operator, would put out "line rings" whenever some major news event happened, or when a local merchant paid to advertise a special shipment of merchandise such as produce. She also made a line ring when an accident or illness took the a life of a town resident. Such personalized service surpassed radio or (later television) news breaks.

Two other items as remembered by children are worth noting. The Trinity Lutheran Church, like many churches, had a custom of tolling the church bell whenever a church member had just died. When the slow tolling began, everyone paused in their activity around town to count the number of times the bell was rung, because each toll represented a year of that person's life, and the longer the bell rang, the more we were aware that some old-timer whom we knew, had passed on. Shorter tolls usually meant an accident to a young person.

The bell's last usage for tolling a death was at the time of Lydia Kerb's passing, which was in 1959. Shortly thereafter, a windstorm knocked the steeple and bell from the church top, and it was not replaced, and the custom was discontinued. But Hemingway's novel, For Whom The Bell Tolls, could not have more profoundly affected our emotions and our concern for our fellow Durhamites, in the way that just hearing that bell start to toll, did. And as John Donne said, "Do not send to know for whom the bell tolls, know that it tolls for thee, " reminding us all, with each incident, of our own mortality, our own limited time on this earth.

In a more adventurous vein, we must not fail to mention the famous, now vanished, Durham Jail. It was built of cement blocks, and was a one-story flat-topped square building, located not far from the elevators in Durham. It was no longer in use when we lived there, but kids of all eras of Durham were fascinated by its eerie silence, its small confines, the criminal element it had represented.

The post office and the railroad depot were two points of great interest to most young people in Durham, for they were links to the world at large. . . bringing, as they did, our mail to the little boxes to be opened by dialing the correct combination, and whisking the trains through town, showing us the world beyond our scope.

During the era of trains, there was a constant and reliable delivery of goods to merchants via the "local" which brought everything from machinery to groceries to the local merchants. The Rock Island passenger trains were an ever-present reminder to us kids that there was a big world out there, and lots of places, that when we got ready, or brave enough, or old enough, or rich enough, we'd go and see.

But during our time as youngsters in Durham, it was a cherished experience. Like being part of a big family, you were safe in this town, you were known, you were probably liked, and you had an identity and a calm source. . . Durham.

Two bathing beauties in the "old-time swimming pool"

Early History

The east side of Main Street about 1908.

The Santa Fe Trail Led Through Durham Area

"From Civilization To Sundown"

Durham – A stop on the Santa Fe Trail

There is no way to celebrate Durham's past without making note, and giving thought and space, to Durham's first reason for being; that is, as one of the major outposts, or "stops", on the historic Santa Fe Trail, so vital a link in the settlement of the West.

The Santa Fe Trail ruts are still visible in three places near Durham; in the area of Durham's predecessor, the Moore (later Crane) Ranch; ruts can also be seen north of town, and at a spot on the horizon, several miles west of Durham near Waldeck.

The Moore Ranch was a trading post in the 1860's, located just west of the present town of Durham, and was an important stop during the last two decades of the Santa Fe Trail's historic operation. There, westward travelers, and freight wagon crews stopped and prepared for the hazardous passage over the North Cottonwood River, and entry into the wilderness of buffalo and Indian country.

This stop, known as "Cottonwood Crossing" on the Santa Fe Trail, was actually a farm home turned into a trading post, inn and wagon camp, and it represented a last link with civilized life for those heading westward; and re-entry into safer, civilized land, for those freight wagons and persons returning eastward on the trail.

By the 1860's, Cottonwood Crossing was on the edge of the frontier, although earlier in the Santa Fe Trail's history, Council Grove, some 40 miles eastward, had been the "jumping off spot". There travelers would see the last white people, (and incidentally, any

trees large enough from which to hew an ox yoke, should a yoke break enroute) before they faced the vast expanse of lonely, dangerous, prairie wilderness leading to the Southwest.

In the 1850's, more than thirty years prior to Durham's actual settlement in 1887, as the frontier pushed west, a man named George Smith had set up a "way station" at the Cottonwood River Crossing, and went into the business of supplying travel needs to traders on the Trail. The story of Smith and those who followed him will be taken up a little later; but first, a look at the setting in which Kansas, and the Durham area, played a part in the dealings of the Santa Fe Trail.

It is noteworthy to observe that Kansas was the only state which was crossed end-to-end by the Santa Fe Trail. In addition, the Trail had two-thirds of its length in Kansas. Highway 50 through Kansas roughly traces the route of the Santa Fe Trail.

First, it is helpful to look at the Santa Fe Trail in its general context. The Trail originally began at Franklin, Missouri, and stretched some 950 miles as a primitive "highway of commerce" into present New Mexico. The Santa Fe Trail flourished for about 60 years, from 1821 to 1880, and contrary to the popular idea that all trails west carried immigrants, it was largely a trade roadway for goods and supplies, although many immigrants also crossed over the pathway.

Over the years, many hundreds of traders made their way to Santa Fe and gathered on the crowded Santa Fe plaza, selling cloth, hardware and other manufactured goods in return for Mexican silver, furs and donkeys. Jacks were then brought back east. Legend holds that the Mexican Jacks formed the stock for the famous Missouri mules.

But to understand the reason for the desperate and dangerous journey by wagon through wilderness, mountains and Indian country for nearly 1,000 miles, one must study the history of the early 1800's in America.

Missouri was, in the early 1800's, on the American western frontier and suffering an economic depression. Its merchants naturally looked westward to bolster Missouri's flagging economy. Officially, a Missouri merchant named William Becknell, carrying saleable merchandise, blazed the pathway from Franklin, Missouri to Santa Fe in 1821, but roots of the idea of trade with the Spanish southwest reach well back before that achievement.

Several circumstances set the stage for the creation of the Trail. While Santa Fe was still a part of the Spanish empire, Spain had strictly forbidden its colonies from trade with the United States, even the remote and northerly town of Santa Fe, a settlement on El Camino Real 600 miles away from any other Spanish commercial center.

When Zebulon Pike was exploring the newly-acquired United States land encompassing most of the western U.S. and known as the "Louisiana Purchase", he was arrested in 1806 by Spanish soldiers for traversing their region. After his release, he recalled many of his observations about Spanish territory in his journal. Upon publication of Pike's journal in 1810, the opportunity for very profitable trade with Santa Fe sparked much commercial interest. It was evident that Santa Fe was hungry for trade goods, and would be an excellent market for American trade.

So, in 1821, when Mexico became independent from Spain, it opened trade with the United States, and those who dreamed of the opportunities in Santa Fe had only to wend their way there. Becknell had returned with thousands of dollars in profits from his first trip Southwest, and others determined to also travel this route of trade.

The Trail played an important part in the war with Mexico. During the Mexican War, 1846-47, military supplies were clogging the Santa Fe Trail. In 1846, General Steven Watts Kearney led his troops over a portion of the Trail, arriving in Santa Fe August 18, 1846, taking the city without firing a shot. While this ended the international era of the Trail, commerce flourished and by the early 1850's, regular mail and stagecoach service moved on the Trail. Increasingly, it became a military road for troops fighting to suppress Indians. (See Molly Hoop's account elsewhere in this book).

The collection of Santa Fe Trail relics of Claude Unruh is fascinating to visitors.

After the treaty of Guadalupe-Hidalgo was signed with Mexico in 1848, Santa Fe became an American city, but the Santa Fe Trail still enjoyed brisk traffic, especially since the Forty-Niners began using the trail after the discovery of gold in California in 1848. In addition, 10 years thereafter, the Colorado mining camps lured more travelers down the Trail, when Gold-Rusher's went to Colorado.

Much could be written about the hardships of the trail, the dangers of being in a wilderness, in event of injury, illness, or nature's extremities such as windstorms, blizzards, drought, intense heat, flash floods, or prairie fires. And much could be said of the continuing presence and threat from Indians, who resented white men trespassing their lands, and also wanted the horses the white men had. Suffice to say that not everyone who started out on the trail, survived to see the wonders of Santa Fe. Some who died lie yet in unmarked graves along the route. Wagons were customarily locked wheel to wheel to encircle against Indian attack, and trail users eventually used more oxen than horses to pull their wagons, as Indians were less interested in oxen. All along the trail, great dangers existed, but that is another story.

With the historical setting clear, Durham's place on the Trail can be put into perspective. Unlike some stops further east of Durham, the Cottonwood Crossing (Durham) developed into a very active and important stop on the trail for several reasons.

Even today's reader can appreciate the significance of the Durham stop as being well-equipped, as evidenced by the list of Marion County stops, in the Western Journal of Commerce, published in Kansas City, November 6, 1858 has:

> "Lost Spring. . . 13 miles from Diamond Spring. . . has buffalo chips, water and grass. Little Muddy Creek (Tampa). . . 10 miles from Lost Spring. . . buffalo chips, water and grass. Cottonwood. . . 7½ miles from Little Muddy Creek. . . Mail station, entertainment, corn, hay, wood, water, grass, provisions."

It must have seemed heavenly to the weary travelers to know that such a variety of comforts awaited them at Cottonwood Crossing. As for the word, "entertainment", there is no clear definition, but it is presumed to have taken the form of gambling, drinking, and perhaps music.

The traveler would find many supplies there on the banks of the Cottonwood. In addition to wood from which to carve an ox yoke, it was possible to repair weakened wagon wheels or tongues. Travelers knew it would be disastrous to begin the long trek across the treeless prairie without insuring a solid yoke and secure wagons.

In 1831, before the development of Moore's Ranch at Cottonwood Crossing, Josiah Gregg, the first historian of the Santa Fe Trail, wrote of the team hostler's departure from civilization and the critical need for wood.

> "Early on the 26th of May, 1831, we reached the long looked-for rendezvous of Council Grove, where we joined the main body of the caravan. . . On the day of our departure from Independence, we passed the last human abode upon our route; therefore, from the borders of Missouri to those of New Mexico not even an Indian settlement greeted our eyes. . .
>
> "During our delay at the Council Grove, the laborers were employed in procuring timber for axle-trees, and other wagon repairs, of which a supply is always laid in before leaving this region of substantial growths; for henceforward there is no wood on the route fit for these purposes. . . The supply procured here is generally lashed under the wagons, in which way a log is not unfrequently carried to Santa Fe, and even sometimes back again. . . "

Thus, even though the town of Durham still lay sleeping as a germ yet to grow into a community, the activity in the very same area made it important to thousands of travelers on the Trail, who passed by the future town, and partook of the help and sustenance available from the natural resources and persons then in the area. (The 1860 census counted only 74 persons in all of Marion County).

Durham took a step closer to development when, in the 1850's, George Smith's way station began doing volume business in booze and supplies. In 1859 two brothers purchased the station from Smith. Smith went on to the little town of Lost Springs while the two brothers, Ira Moore and Abraham Atlantic "Lank" Moore took over the operation. Ira is not mentioned in other history records, but Lank Moore continued to operate the trading post and inn for another 13 years. The late 1850's were the busiest years on the Santa Fe Trail with 50-100 oxen-pulled wagon trains east and west-bound through the area each day.

The increased traffic during the 1850's is evident from a Cottonwood Falls, *Kansas Press* article from July 25, 1859:

> "We are indebted to S. M. Hays and Company of Council Grove for a statement of the Santa Fe trade through Council Grove from June 28th, 1859 to July 15th, 1859, a period of 17 days. There passed the Grove,

during this time 415 men, 289 wagons, 56 horses, 744 mules, 2,251 oxen and 23 carriages engaged in this trade, and they transported over the plains over 1,700 tons of freight.

"Add to those previously reported and this season have passed 1,970 men, 1,510 wagons, 361 horses, 3,707 mules, 14,515 oxen, 51 carriages and transported over the plains 4,920 tons of freight, amounting to a total of $1,263,112. Then there is the wages of 1,970 men, incidental expenses, which swell the amount to at least $1,400,000 or enough to build 140 miles of railroad at $10,000 per mile."

A detailed firsthand account is carried elsewhere within this book, where the then cook, Molly Hoops, describes her attempts to feed guests (including U. S. soldiers protecting from Indians), at the Moore Ranch.

When A. A. Moore's wife, Nancy (Waterman) Moore became seriously ill, events combined to result in the last Indian scalping in the area. Evan Hoops, husband of the Moore's cook, Molly, was sent to Cottonwood Falls for a doctor and Edgar Miller was sent to Turkey Creek in McPherson County to fetch the family members of Nancy. Miller was killed by Cheyenne Indians before reaching his destination. (See related story).

Moore moved to Marion Center in 1861 after buying a grocery store there. He operated the ranch at Cottonwood Crossing through a tenant until he sold it to Albert Crane in 1872. (Crane's wife, like Moore's, had the maiden name of Waterman, but there is no record about a relationship between the two).

Moore became a prominent figure in Marion County government. By the time he sold the ranch, he was already County treasurer when the county was founded in 1865. He was the first postmaster in the county at the ranch (which was the first post office in Marion County), and the first state representative and first state senator from the County.

As the railroad progressed westward, the Santa Fe Trail's eastern point also moved westward and other roads fed into it. The railroad had entered Marion County in 1871, the year before Moore sold the ranch to Crane, and travel along the Santa Fe Trail had all but stopped by then. Still, it wasn't until the 1880's that The Railroad reached the Cottonwood Crossing area.

Compared to the rigors of the trail, a railroad line far surpassed wagon travel in efficiency, safety and economy, so with the coming of the railroads, The Santa Fe Trail, this primitive trail of commerce

stretching "from Civilization to Sundown", rich in lore and legend, and important to the development of the United States, came to an end.

As we close out this report putting Durham in perspective on the Santa Fe Trail, we note that this daring, courageous era of history lent to others a wanderlust and a longing for the open spaces, (such as Durham), that is felt by many Kansans. It was put into words, 'way back in the 1840's, in a book <u>Commerce of the Prairies.</u> When Josiah Gregg found city life difficult to abide after his final trek across the Santa Fe Trail, he wrote this:

"Since that time, I have striven in vain to reconcile myself to the even tenor of civilized life in the United States. Scarecely a day passes without my experiencing a pang of regret, that I am not now roving at large upon those western plains."

"The Santa Fe Trail Crossed Here" reads a sign west of Durham, near the Cottonwoon Crossing, famous in early days of the Santa Fe Trail.

The Drama of the old journey is still very much alive.

According to George Stone, history professor at Sterling, Kansas, "The American dream was really exemplified in the Santa Fe Trail. These people have given us a sense of hope that drives us on like few other cultures on earth, a sense that there's a better life just over the next hill. "

There are various places to view artifacts and see trail ruts, along the Santa Fe Trail's old route, including the Santa Fe Trail Center in Larned, Kansas, Bent's Old Fort National Historic Site, near LaJunta, Colo. , and seven places in New Mexico: Pecos National Monument; Pigeon's Ranch, Glorieta, N. M. ; San Miguel and San Jose del Vado, N. M. ; Las Vegas, N. M. ; Fort Union National Monument, N. M. ; Wagon Mound, N. M. ; Cimarron, N. M. ; Clayton, N. M. ; not to leave out our city of Durham.

Facts about the Santa Fe Trail

Spain prohibited its colonies from trade with the U. S. , so Santa Fe, although far from the rest of the Spanish empire, got manufactured goods from markets down in Mexico, 600 miles south.

But when trade was finally allowed, Becknell made the first successful commercial trip to Santa Fe, with five men and some mules, on a fur trading mission. Returning with saddlebags of silver, he planned a trip the following spring, with 21 men and wagon trains using oxen. He also planned to avoid the mountain route, going by way instead, following the river from Great Bend through Raton Pass, later known for the "toll passage" of Dick Wootton, the only place on the Santa Fe Trail where a toll had to be paid.

Santa Fe Trail traders traveled in the spring and the fall, when temperatures were moderate, and grass and water were available, so they didn't endure the sufferings of other immigrants.

Many died enroute, and were buried along the Trail, without markers, to prevent Indians from discovering and mutilating their bodies. Diseases also took a heavy toll.

However, a trip across the prairies often was prescribed by doctors as a tonic for ailments medicine couldn't cure. Captain Francis Aubry, Army officer at Leavenworth, Ks. , is quoted as saying, "Many an invalid I have had in my caravans, but before they reached Santa Fe, they were eating buffalo meat raw and sleeping soundly under their blankets. " Perhaps this was the first idea that a change of climate could cure illnesses.

Buffalo chips were used for cooking fuel.

In 1828, the federal government called in the military to defend the trail, with two companies of Infantrymen ordered out to protect caravans.

Two additional artifacts from Durham's early history are in the Marion County Historical Society building at Marion. Mrs. Phyllis Melton, historian, says that there is one shipping label to the Crane Ranch, and the axle from one of the large covered freight-wagons is there, although there is not room to display it prominently at present.

How To Find The Santa Fe Trail Ruts

If you want to see the actual path of the Santa Fe Trail, here's how.

From Durham's Main Street, turn west onto 5th Street, proceeding over the bridge, and follow the road as it curves north one mile. Where the road curves west, continue north on a dirt road, across another bridge. Then look to the west for the marker placed by Durham school children in 1906.

To the right, up the hill going east, the trail is also visible and a road marker indicates "Santa Fe Trail Route. "

To reach the D. A. R. marker, go south on the dirt road, over the bridge, and join the paved road as it turns west. A short distance from this point, look on the north side of the road and see the D. A. R. marker right beside the road, among the weeds.

At this same point, look south across the field and see the actual ruts of the Santa Fe Trail, fanning out into 4 lanes, pictured against the horizon.

From here to the Waldeck ruts, continue west down the paved road to the Lehigh-Waldeck road. Turn south on the way to Lehigh. Just after you cross a railroad track, look west and just to the south of the railroad tracks, you can see the deep indentations of the Santa Fe Trail on the horizon, as it wended its way across Kansas.

Ed Miller, Indian Casualty

The grave of Edgar Miller, see related story.

How Ed Miller Died

The following letter was written many years ago. All of the pioneers mentioned have since passed on, but the historical interest remains, as to the actual details of this tragedy.

In July, 1864, Lank Moore, owner of Moore's ranch of the Santa Fe Trail, was in Marion with his family for a brief stay. While here they were living in the house later occupied by Mr. Western Martin, just south of Central Park. Mrs. Moore's health was very poor and she was anxious to have her mother come and see her. Her mother, Mrs. Waterman, was living three miles south of the present town of Galva, in McPherson County. Mr. Waterman was the proprietor of the Big Turkey Creek Ranch of the Santa Fe Trail at that place.

There was a man by the name of Miller who lived on Mud Creek about two hundred feet from the later residence of W. H. Carpenter. Mr. Moore went to see him to ask him if he would not send one of his boys to the Turkey Creek Ranch to bring Mrs. Moore's mother to Marion. Mr. Miller agreed to send one on the errand, his son, Edgar, who was a boy about eighteen years of age.

The young man left his home and went to French Frank's Ranch on the Santa Fe Trail where he ate his breakfast and then left there about eight o'clock in the morning for the Turkey Creek Ranch which was down the trail about ten miles southwest.

Al Bichet, a young man who was working for French Frank's on the ranch, accompanied young Miller for about three miles and was the last white man who saw him alive. About half an hour later, Miller and Bichet parted company. Later, Watermans at Turkey Creek Ranch saw a lone horseman coming rapidly along the trail from the east. Just a short time before they had seen a party of about twenty Cheyenne Indians killing a cow near the Trail and only a mile or so east of the ranch.

Suspecting that the Indians were hostile and that the approaching horseman was someone of their friends, they hastened to the top of their house, and through a field glass got an unobstructed view for several miles east along the Trail. The Miller boy, (for it proved later to have been he) was coming rapidly along the Trail and did not seem to scent any danger until he was about two hundreds yards from the Indians.

There had been up to this time no hostile demonstration on the part of the Indians. Suddenly they began to gather up their weapons and to mount their horses. The lone horseman halted and for a moment seemed to hesitate and then he wheeled his horse and started down the trail east with the Indians in full pursuit.

As nearly as the watchers at the ranch could tell he was holding his own in the race with the Indians when all disappeared in a cloud of dust. Two days later, the Watermans became so uneasy because they had heard nothing from their daughter, Mrs. Moore, who they knew was sick, that they decided to come to Marion.

When they reached Marion the first question that was asked them was, "Where is Ed Miller?" They had seen nothing of young Miller but told the story of the lone horseman, and the heart-broken parents needed no futher proof that their son had been killed by the Indians.

On the following day, Henry Roberts, Jack Griffith, Roddy Coble and Evan Hoops started in search of the body of Ed Miller. They went northwest to the Santa Fe Trail and then followed the Trail to French Frank's Ranch where they secured further information. They followed the Trail west and when about four miles west they found the mutilated body of Ed Miller.

Henry Roberts was sent back to Frank's Ranch to get tools and when he returned a grave was dug on a beautiful little mound near the Trail and the body laid tenderly away. Ed Miller was the only white man killed by Indians in the settlement of Marion County.

On Friday, December 8, 1911, more than forty years later, Henry Roberts, Taylor Riddle, H. P. Paddock and Lewis E. Riggs went along the old Santa Fe Trail to endeavor to locate the grave.

Ed Miller's grave is two miles east of Canton, just inside of McPherson County. It is on the southwest quarter of section 24, twp. 21, range 1 west. It is on land owned by Mr. M. M. Jones and is about three hundred feet south of the Santa Fe railroad track.

Henry Roberts, mentioned in this article, later purchased a beautiful black granite tombstone to be placed at the grave of Ed Miller, giving his age, date of death and by whom killed.

By an old settler

Claude Unruh
Collector of
Santa Fe Trail Artifacts

Arrowheads, bird points, and tools shown in Unruh collection.

Claude Unruh, of Durham, whose property northwest of Durham is intersected by the Santa Fe Trail route and who has lived in the vicinity of the old trail for about half a century, has probably found more artifacts and treasures from the by-gone era of the trail than almost anyone else. He has assembled with great care a very comprehensive collection of historically significant items.

During his years farming on the property that gracefully slopes to the Cottonwood River, just west of Durham, Claude has unearthed many greatly varied artifacts. They reveal a segment of our history, reflecting the Indian, Anglo and Hispanic cultures that made their mark on this land.

The Indian relics include items of war, such as war arrowheads and tomahawks, and items of daily living, like tiny, delicate bird points fashioned for shooting game and birds and working tools of flint and sharpening rocks. And, reflective of the warring between two cultures is the presence of cavalry soldier's buckles and bullets.

There are also remnants of the trade coursing over the Santa Fe. Claude says one of his favorite items is a Spanish coin from the mid-1800's showing that the owner had been to trade in Santa Fe and apparently lost the coin on the return trip through Cottonwood Crossing.

Another of his finds is a religious medal inscribed in Latin, "Mater Dolorosa" (Our Lady of Sorrows).

"It was probably carried by a Santa Fe or Mexican trader; it's a reminder of the Hispanic influence of the Trail," says Unruh.

The novice historian is drawn to the especially large horseshoes, assuming they are shoes for oxen. "No, they're mule and workhorse shoes," corrects the historical expert, "oxen have cloven feet, so their shoes are made in two half-crescents, like these," he says indicating two smaller pieces of metal.

One gets a true respect for early day ingenuity by perusing the collection. "Just hold this," Claude says, handing the visitor a flattened rock about 4 inches long and curved, and sharpened as a knife

– on one edge. "You see how naturally it fits between your thumb and forefinger. It was well-suited for its purpose for scraping animal hides."

Claude's property encompasses the land where the Durham school children from District No. 57 erected a marker to the Cottonwood Crossing. Dedicated in 1906, it was the first in Marion County to mark the Santa Fe Trail. Long ago, Claude put up a fence around the marker to keep the cattle back and also to create a little picnic area with table and swings and shade, to commemorate the importance of the Cottonwood Crossing on the Santa Fe Trail.

Claude was told the stone came from the Cottonwood River and that when set, placed within its base were a Bible, the names of the children involved, and historical matter of the locality.

The same year, 1906, the D. A. R. also marked the crossing south of the river. Later, John Borton enhanced the marker on Claude's property with two bronze plaques.

Standing at this crossing that presented such hazards to early day travelers and seeing actual remnants of their lives, history speaks clearly.

Ox shoes and horse shoes, tomahawks, and tools from the Claude Unruh collection of artifacts of early Durham and the Santa Fe Trail, in his home on the Cottonwood Crossing.

Early-Day Cook at Moore's Ranch had Troubles...

When Molly Hoops and her husband, Evan, who later became the county's first sheriff, arrived in this area in 1864, they hired out to Moore's Ranch at $40 a month to get a start that first winter they had claimed their homestead. Her own fascinating account of life at the Ranch on the Santa Fe Trail follows. Molly originally compiled these memories for a local newspaper article in the 1880's.

"We had not been there long, " writes Mrs. Hoops, "until we had the name of setting the best table from the Missouri River to Santa Fe. The stage came in twice a week with from six to 10 passengers. Government grain teams went through twice a week. They were hauling grain for the stage mules and horses. Often we had other customers. Sometimes the owners of trains and wagon bosses would have meals with us. "

Families traveling in the wagon trains camped out, cooking their own meals on camp fires or small stoves which they set up for long stops when baking and washing was done. A camp ground at Cottonwood Crossing was provided but when trains arrived the Ranch was a busy place of trading and talking.

"About the last of November of 1864, " Mrs. Hoops continues with her narrative, "we had 21 soldiers for three days. They were returning from California and until they passed the Fuller farm on Doyle creek the day before they got to our Ranch, they had not seen a woman for three years.

"When the soldiers stopped and asked for supper, Mr. Moore came in and said, 'Molly, can you get their supper?'

"I told him that I could. He warned me that they looked rough, but that they would be 'gentlemanly. '"

"In an hour it was ready. I had cookies already baked and plenty of good sauce and some bread and butter. I always kept the coffee ground and in a tight tin can. I also had cold beef to slice. I had mince meat ready to use. I made some pies quickly. While they were baking I made hot biscuits for the whole lot and sent Evan to the storehouse to cut buffalo steaks. Mrs. Moore set the table.

"In they came with their belts full of bowie knives, scabbards and a double-brace of revolvers. Their spurs were jingling. They were long-haired, long-whiskered, but kindly looking – every one of them.

"They looked at Mrs. Moore and me as though we were beings from another sphere. It was not a bold look, but as though we were next best to seeing their own women kin.

"One poor fellow commenced on mince pie and finished on mince pie. He ate nothing else. When they were through, they went into the office and each laid down a dollar and declared they never had had a meal equal to that. Having known the hunger of a homesteader when fare is meager, I knew their appreciation.

"That night we saw our first Kansas blizzard. The soldiers had to stay three days.

"While we were at the ranch Mr. Moore cleared $3000. He often dealt with Indian traders, buying furs of different kinds and buffalo robes which he shipped east.

"Mr. Moore bought one load of flour that proved to be very old and wormy. Nearly all flour received in the West at that time was wormy, but this was worse. The first sack I opened was dreadful to behold. There were great worms an inch and a half long and down to tiny little ones. In horror, I called Mr. Moore and he said not to mind; pick out what I could see and let the rest go. 'I can't, ' I said, 'you go to Council Grove and get a sieve. '

"Until he could go and return, I hunted up an old pan and had Evan punch holes in the bottom, with a nail, this kept out the largest

A Pioneer Cook's Story

This marker was placed on the Santa Fe Trail's Cottonwood Crossing area in 1906 by School Dist. No. 57, Durham.

worms as I shook the flour through. The holes clogged badly and sifting enough flour to make bread for eight of us and all the other customers at our table was a tiring chore. I never rested from one meal to the next. We got a seive in a few days.

"All the dried fruits we got in those days were full of worms.

"Sometime in December a splendid mule train stopped at the station. That was the best outfit that crossed the plains that winter. Everything was new from the mules, horses, wagons, down to tin cups. All the equipment and the men were glistening. The new train was loaded with a quartz mill made in Pennsylvania which the train owner was delivering to Arizona. The owner had stopped at Council Grove to receive treatment for a bad case of neuralgia in his face. He came on the next day on horseback.

"Mr. Moore came to me saying, 'Molly, there is a sick man in the store, do you think you can do anything for him?'

"I assured him I could. I pulled the lounge up to the fire and put more fuel in the stove. I put some hops on to scald in vinegar. The poor fellow came in directly groaning with pain and cold. He said he had scarcely slept for a week. I gave him a good dose of quinine, then stirred corn meal in the hops and vinegar until thick enough to spread. I put it in a flannel bag and applied it to his face. I covered him with a blanket and a buffalo robe and he was soon asleep. In half an hour I renewed the corn meal poultice. He slept until late the next morning. When his train was ready to move on he came in to say goodbye and to thank me for treating him. He wished us all good luck and laid a $10 bill on the stand for me.

"After he was gone and I realized that the $10 was mine, I cut up some lively capers — I assure you. I began to think what I could do with it. Should I save it to buy a bedstead, or a table or a set of chairs, or just what? I finally made up my mind to buy a heifer."

DID YOU KNOW

Moore's Ranch and way station, located on the Santa Fe Trail northwest of Durham, was the site of the first attempt to hold Marion County elections. The election board met at the ranch and opened the polls for voting. Then the board realized that unless Indians were included, there were not enough men available to fill the offices. They stopped the election, deciding to postpone it until the county population was larger. The Moore brothers then opened their tavern to ease the disappointment.

The D.A.R. Places First
Markers For The
Santa Fe Trail

Four monuments to be erected by
Daughters of the American Revolution.

The following from the Durham Journal – Thursday, October 4, 1906

Four monuments to be erected by Daughters of the American Revolution.

Marion, Kansas, September 25, W. D. Armstrong, Durham, Kansas.

Dear Sir:

I received a letter this morning from Hon. G. W. Martin, Secretary of the State Historical Society, of Kansas saying that the Daughters of the American Revolution want to plant three or four monuments as markers of the Santa Fe Trail in Marion County. In my letter to Martin, I have suggested that four monuments should be placed in this county to mark the sites of Lost Springs Ranch, Moore's Ranch, French Frank's Ranch and one near the west line of the county, as nearly as possible to mark the place of the massacre of Ed Miller, of our settlement, (the Marion settlement). I suggested these places because of the historical incident connected with them. For instance, the history of Lost Springs Ranch is great and of much interest, and while it has never been written and put in permanent form, it is still a matter of tradition. The old Cottonwood Crossing, afterwards known as Moore's Ranch, was the location of the first post office in the county, which was named after the name of the ranch. It is also the only place where fortifications were erected by the United States. There within the limits of French Frank's Ranch is where a traveler was massacred by the Cheyenne Indians in 1865. These being historical places I thought best that the definite location of these be kept. Hence I suggested them.

Now the Santa Fe Railroad will haul these stone monuments any place on their line where desired for the purpose of having them placed, free of charge. I have suggested to Martin to see if the one placed at Moore's Ranch cannot be sent over the Rock Island to Durham, and that those to be placed at French Frank's Ranch and on the west line of the county, cannot be sent over the Rock Island also to Waldeck or Canton, as parties interested may suggest. I had a talk with John Smith to-day after receiving the Martin letter and he suggested that I write to you. He further said he would furnish free of charge cement blocks for a foundation to those three monuments. You being one of the first settlers in the vicinity, is, I suppose the reason Smith thought of you, thinking for that reason you would be interested.

Now I wish you would write and tell me what you wish to do, what if any public demonstration you wish in connection with this matter. If any, after a consultation with your people, I will write B. F. Dole, relative to the placing the two west of Durham. I am willing to give any assistance I can in finding the locations or in any other way.

Yours truly,
Alex E. Case

PS.   I think the papers prepared and read at the placing of the monument, set this summer by your people, should be filed with the State Historical Society, thus making them a matter of State history. I think it is important.

(See History of Durham, next page).

The following account was taken from the Durham Journal, dated
Thursday, September 13, 1906

History of Durham

Following is a history of Durham read at the first real marking of
the Santa Fe Trail one and one half miles north-west of Durham,
Kansas, on Friday, April 20, 1906.

In August, 1872, Albert Crane bought from Moore four townships
which were united in one as a consolidated township and was named
Durham Park. The reason it was so called was because of the
Durham Shorthorn Cattle that were bred there. L. A. Reed was the
first overseer of this ranch.

In February, 1887, the town of Durham was platted by the Golden
Belt Town Co; and the following June the Chicago, Rock Island and
Pacific railroad was built through the town. Early in the same year
Funk City was started on the land adjoining Durham on the east,
south of the railroad, and a number of business houses and
dwellings were erected.

J. A. Stephenson was appointed town agent.

The first dwelling erected in Durham was by Fred Auschwitz, on
lot 21, block 8, south of railroad. J. A. Stephenson built the first
dwelling north of the railroad.

T. L. Wardrop built the first blacksmith shop.

In June 1888, J. A. Stephenson was appointed postmaster and the
post office was moved from the White House (Crane Ranch) one and
one-half miles to Durham.

During the spring population began to increase rapidly, and Frank
Peaslee, of Glen Elder, Kansas, opened the first dry goods and
grocery store, and Theodore Smith the first lumber yard.

Geo. Crawford erected a dwelling on the corner of Sixth Street
and Lawrence Avenue and opened a hardware store on Main
Street.

Richard Ross and David Ehman erected the first carpenter shop.

In 1888 the school district voted to change the location and build a
two-story four-room building. The proposition carried and the
building was contracted and completed by Theodore Smith on the
northeast corner of Lawrence Avenue and Eighth Street.

Dr. P. H. Bartells contracted with Ross & Ehman for the erection
of a two-story dwelling on the southeast corner of Sixth Street and
Lawrence Avenue, and upon the completion of the building moved
his family here.

The first teacher employed was Mrs. J. P. Gardenier who taught
three terms in succession.

Durham, 1904.

7143. BIRD'S EYE VIEW OF DURHAM, KANS.

During this interval David Whitman, John Heidel, Henry
Weident, Herman Luck and Fred Reisig all erected dwellings south
of the railroad, and Frank Baker, R. Richard Ross, Thomas Bell,
Ella G. McArthur, Conrad Shaffer, and others all erected dwellings
north of the railroad.

About this time C. J. Dyck, who had a large building and stock of
dry goods and groceries in Funk City, was persuaded to move his
improvements and stock of goods to Durham, this being done, the
people of that town all moved their buildings to Durham, among
them was Conrad Stebens, who started the first livery stable and
hotel in town.

The Crane Ranch

Marion County Record, June 25, 1875
Durham Park
The Pride of the West
(An account of a trip to the ranch made by E. W. Hoch and Tom Reed.)

In the genial company of Mr. T. W. Reed, Merchant, we visited for the first time, Durham Park, on last Saturday.

This magnificent estate is situated on the Cottonwood River in Marion County, Kansas, eighteen miles from Marion Center (county seat). It contains 10, 000 acres of choice land, upon which Nature has exerted her finest touches, and Art has added its perfecting polish.

It is the property of Mr. Albert Crane, a wealthy Chicago gentleman, who has invested in this farm about $300, 000 - though the land itself cost him perhaps not one-tenth of that sum. The rest expended in improvements and stock.

Mr. Crane is the Alexander of the West, the Van Meeter of Kansas. He is a man of fine sense, good culture, and affable manner. His grey hair and whiskers betoken age, but his sparkling eye, firm, quick step and animated speech, seem to deny the fact.

Major D. W. Crane devotes his whole time to the short-horn herd. And he seems master of his profession.

The present proprietor of the Park bought it in 1872. It was then a wild waste. The Park residence is built upon a beautiful knoll, commanding a splendid view of a very large part of the farm. It is a comfortable two-story dwelling, with veranda all around it, and observatory on top.

Scattered about the farm, are various other buildings, the abodes of forty persons employed on the farm.

Forty-odd miles of fencing - half board and half wire - have been constructed. The lumber used for the various purposes on the farm, required the full capacity of fifty cars for its transportation.

Fifteen hundred acres of ground are under cultivation. Six hundred acres of sod have been broken this season, and twelve breaking teams are still running.

Grains and grasses raised this season: Rye, 150 acres; Hungarian 150; oats 200; corn 800; all promising crops.

Seven hundred acres of blue grass have been sown, but as it was simply sown on prairie sod, it has made but little progress, as yet, in rooting out its firmly entrenched, native rival. A luxuriant growth of the beautiful blue grass, in the yard, which withstood last summer's suns and the rigors of last winter, proves that it will do well here if it only has half a chance. A large orchard has been set out and is doing well. Also quite an area has been set in forest trees - the mere beginning of an extensive work in this line, for which they are preparing.

Another object of interest is a sheller and grist mill, with a capacity of two hundred bushels of corn per day.

None but thoroughbred bulls are kept on the place. There are fifty five of these, all very fine. Six of the finest are kept for use in the shorthorn herd consisting of eighty-four splendid cows. The whole number of cattle on the place is 2, 400 - 150 thoroughbred shorthorn, 250 "high grades, " the rest Texans and half breeds. There are some exceedingly fine thoroughbred yearlings. The principal families represented are the Bates and Booths of pure blood. Besides these, there are Rose of Sharons, Louans Young Marys, Susans, Brides, Jubilees, Groynnes, Carolinas, etc. "Booth" one of the only two in the United States, the other being Kentucky; is nearly four years old, weighs 2, 500 pounds, valued at $5, 000.

Lord Abraham is six years old, was bred in Lincolnshire, England, and imported in 1872; in color he is a strawberry roan; weighs 2, 450 pounds.

Lord Bates second is a pure "Bates" eight months old, weighs 800 pounds, was bred in Kentucky; is pronounced by everybody a perfect beauty.

Maiden, pure "Booth" bred by J. R. Booth, Yorkshire, is certainly one of the very finest of her species. Her large shapely form symetrical neck and head, silken hair, and lustrous, almost human eyes, together with her docile disposition, are marks of excellence that would make her conspicuous in any herd.

Duchess of York the 9th is a remarkable fine cow, strawberry roan, weighs 1, 900 pounds. There are sixteen cows in the herd.

We were surprised to learn that the first sale of a thoroughbred bull to resident of Marion County, was made only a few weeks ago to Rev. A. H. Lackey, of Peabody. The reason is two-fold, of which the hard times is one, and the general but erroneous belief that the prices are above the ability of the ordinary farmer, the other. It would do all such persons good to go and examine the stock and learn the prices. Mr. Lackey's enterprise in initiating the new era, is commendable. Besides the cattle, there are several hundred head of fine hogs on the place. Seventy five horses are used on the farm.

In addition to their other stock in trade, the managers also deal extensively in politeness and good edibles of which companion Reed and ourself hereby stand up to testify.

And this is a very imperfect description of Durham Park, and can convey no adequate idea of the extent of the concern. Go and see.

MEMORIES OF THE CRANE RANCH
By David I. Day

(From the Milking Shorthorn Journal - May 1941)

A dozen years ago in Chicago during the International Livestock Exposition, discussion with a number of progressive Milking Shorthorn breeders veered to the historic Crane Ranch of pioneer days in Kansas. Other dual-purpose herd owners entered into the conversation. Finally two or three prominent figures in beef Shorthorn circles expressed their opinion. All agreed that some action should be taken to salvage all possible facts and figures. Since then I have constantly been on the alert for material bearing upon this fabulous adventure in cattle.

The facts and figures were found buried deeper under the years than I had thought. It was my idea that a man like Albert S. Crane, rich enough to finance a reputed three million dollar ranch, and to spend more than $20,000 each for individual Shorthorns, would loom large in the written records of Chicago where he lived and made his fortune. So far as my investigation has proceeded very little has been learned about him. Possibly some who read this article may possess additional information, and if so, we shall be glad to hear from them.

The best indications are that Mr. Crane was the son of Hunter and Maria (McMullen) Crane and a native of western New York. It is reported that the father of the capitalist was for some years a merchant in Sackett's Harbor, Jefferson County, New York, and that he died in Oswego, New York, in 1859. Some years before the Civil War, Albert Crane came to Chicago and acquired a large fortune in Chicago real estate. Information from another source says that he was active more or less in religious work, serving as a warden of Christ Church, (Protestant Episcopal) about the time he became interested in establishing the ranch which attracted wide attention to him.

Someone has called the Crane Ranch "the western outpost of the almost unbelieveable speculation in Bates Duchess cattle in the 1870s". I have not learned how Mr. Crane first became interested in Shorthorns, or, for that matter, in ranching. Many conflicting tales are told as to why he chose to select the fertile land near the headwaters of the Cottonwood River, in Marion County, Kansas, as the scene of operation.

It must be remembered however, that this was a period when millions upon millions of Longhorn cattle were being driven up the trails from Texas to market at the Kansas railhead towns. As the railways pushed westward, the popular markets for cattle shifted.

Many men of many kinds were financially interested in this greatest movement in livestock in all the history of humanity.

Probably Mr. Crane was, in some ways, financially interested in this business. Through some of his contacts, he heard of Moore's ranch, tavern, and trading post in which some old-timers say a man called Calen had acquired an interest. It was a well-known landmark on the Old Santa Fe Trail, having been established by A. A. Moore in 1859.

At any rate, the Chicago capitalist bought the property in 1872 and continued to hold the title until 1885. He called the place Durham Park Ranch. The surrounding township derived its name from the ranch. A post office named Durham Park was established.

Some who knew the ranch say that William Hallowell, one of the ranch managers was postmaster. Others recall a man named Janfrey as serving in that capacity. It is reported that a bank was established there early. Around all these ranch activities grew up a little town of Durham, so called first in 1887 and this is still a little trading town of 245 population.

As the tale of the ranching venture unfolds, the name of William Hallowell appears and reappears until the close of the chapter. Like Mr. Crane, he appears to be a man of mystery, upon whose life and other activities besides the ranch, facts and figures seem hard to find. I have found no one who knows where he went after the ranching bubble burst, how he fared later in life, or where his family may be at the present time. A grapevine message came to me in 1940 that a daughter lived in Waukegan, Illinois, but I was unable to get a trace of her.

A few years ago, I read a paragraph of a letter yellowed with age. It was dated May of either 1875 or 1876, the figures being faded. It said, "The ranch of Crane's is an eighth wonder of the world. I saw great heards of Longhorn cows, said to number more than 3,000. There were calves in all directions, more than 1200 of them. I understand these Longhorns are crossed on Shorthorn blood, so the calves are immeasurably better than their dams. These mixed-blood calves will be sold in many instances as range breeding livestock. I saw hundreds of very good red and roan heifers and older cows, said to have been brought from Illinois for breeding purposes. Aside from these common cattle, Mr. Crane owns cows he paid more than $20,000 for. . . and one of his bulls was brought over the sea from England at a cost of $25,000; so valuable that they padded the stall on board ship so the rolling of the waves would not injure him. "

Other old letters tell of seeing 1100 acres of Kansas sod plowed and seeded to bluegrass, some of which failed to come up for six or seven years, of seeing mixed pastures composed of timothy, bluegrass and clover, something like many mixed pastures of the present time.

All of this frontier ranching glory was created and passed into history in thirteen years. No doubt it meant a financial loss, some due to exorbitant prices paid for cattle, some due to the financial depression, which engulfed the country after the Civil War. But out of the collapse came a certain amount of livestock improvement as many homesteaders obtained excellent Shorthorn blood from this establishment. Certainly it launched a mass of tradition which has penetrated every corner of several states.

My attention has been called to the discrepencies as to the size of this great ranch. Old histories say 17,000 acres. Some Marion County people have said 4,160 acres. The records of the abstract office say 5,760 acres. This can be reconciled by the fact that memories may not be too exact after the passage of three score years. And, further, water rights was the controlling factor in the cattle country. A moderate amount of land along a live stream might carry with it the control of many additional acres of land back from the water.

Now there were others active in the ranch management for Mr. Crane who deserve the attention of the inquisitive historian. As I have said, William Hallowell is more or less an elusive figure. More so is a man named Watson who was in a position of responsibility there. But even more interesting will be the story, when told, of Louis A. Reed, declared by many old-timers to have been first in command, quite generally regarded as Crane's lieutenant on his immense property.

All over the countryside folks spoke of Reed in the old days as an "English Lord." He quickly gained the name "Porcupine", but where he came from or what his family connections were have not been definitely determined. The indications are that he was a "remittance man" – a younger brother, or relative of some English noble, a class of young men fairly common then in this country and in Canada, always recieving regular cash remittance from the Estate overseas.

At any rate, it appears that Hallowell and Reed remained on the ranch property most of the time and that Mr. Crane was there but seldom. When Crane sold out in 1885 and started ranching on a reduced scale in Missouri, the deed went to the two ranch managers.

MORE CRANE RANCH MEMORIES
By David I. Day
Taken from Milking Shorthorn Journal
June, 1941

Clarification and Correction: As we anticipated, after the publication of the first installment of the Crane story in the May issue, much additional information has come to hand. It appears that Mr. Crane was born at East Bloomfield, New York. He studied law and graduated from the law department of Harvard University in 1842. He married Anna Waterman on August 13, 1846, at New Bedford, Mass., and lived there for a time. His first child, Daniel W. Crane, remembered by Marion County old-timers, was born there on July 22, 1847. Soon afterward, the family moved to Detroit and five sons and two daughters were born. One son, Arch M., was born at Pittsfield, Mass., in 1855, presumably while his mother was there on a visit. The last children born during the Detroit residence were twins, Walter and Anna W., born May 28, 1865. After moving to Chicago, a daughter Esther W., was born on February 27, 1867. For those particularly interested in the Crane family, we suggest the Genealogy Of The Crane Family by Ellery B. Crane, published about 1900. The name of Albert S. Crane, lawyer and real estate man, appears in the Chicago directory until 1898 and the records of Harvard University say that he died in that city in 1899.

More information is at hand as to the land upon which the Crane ranch house stood. Ira E. Moore, brother of Atlantic A. Moore, received a patent to this land on May 1, 1861, but doubtless had occupied the site as a tavern for some time previously. The Moores deeded this land to A. W. Collins, May 16, 1870. Mr. Collins deeded it to Crane on May 18, 1872. Note: In the first installment, we mentioned the name "Calen" -- as taken from old letters. Evidently, the name, "Calen," is merely a mis-spelling of Collins and that Collins instead of being a partner with the Moores in the tavern and trading post may have been a successor in the ownership of the property.)

So far we have taken most of the "mystery" out of Albert S. Crane. We have found where he was born, educated, married, lived, and died. The door is now wide open for a more exhaustive study of this remarkable man. The Crane book of genealogy has been located and this work combined with the records of Harvard University, the newspapers of Detroit, and of Chicago, and possibly records of Chicago real estate organizations, the Chicago bar, Christ Episcopal Church, and other points of direct contact with the Crane career may reveal many fascinating facts. So far as the history of the ranch itself is concerned, we believe we have most of the documented facts. We have arranged to file permanently the correspondence and interviews gathered for our two articles. This material will be placed in the A. E. Case Memorial File, Marion

City Library, Marion, Kansas, for the use of better historians – who may start where we quit.

The time may come when men of the ability of Dr. James T. Malin of Kansas State University and many skilled in historical research who are active in the Kansas State Historical Society may join hands in painting a complete picture of the old ranch and of the fine Shorthorns it brought to the Sunflower State. A book-length story can easily be developed now and it could tell the tale of the ranch itself and introduce many sidelights of the decades in Kansas immediately after the Civil War – the longhorn trailing up from Texas, the grangers settling on the prairies, the conflicts between the two and with drouths and many other handicaps of homesteading in the old days.

Still living at Durham but spending the winters with a daughter in Ramona where she teaches – is Charles W. Jones, one of the old-timers who worked on the Crane Ranch. He is confined to his wheel chair but he recalls the days when cattle purchased at fabulous prices were brought out to the new country, now comprising Marion county. As Mr. Jones remembers it, the big house on the ranch was called by the natives "the House of Lords" and there were stories going the rounds that only members of the English nobility were entertained there. This was all at a time when L. A. Reed, reputed to be a younger member of some English noble family, was active in the management.

"As I recall it," said Mr. Jones in a letter in 1940, "the ranch also had a 70-room boarding house, cattle sheds 300 feet square – with hay barns in the center each holding 300 tons of hay, and a large feed grinder. Approximately 180 head of valuable Shorthorns were haltered and kept in those sheds. There were seven tenant houses, about 40 men employed to care for the cattle, and 22 miles of 4-board fence confining some 500 head of stock cattle. The rest of the ranch was farm land and meadow."

Mr. Jones in his declining years likes to talk also of other things besides cattle which made up life in Kansas when the Crane Ranch was in its heydey. There were Indians, buffalo, deer, and prairie chickens. In one conflict between the soldiers and the redskins, the latter must have had a little the better of the argument as the soldiers spiked a cannon and dumped it into the Cottonwood River. After that, this place was called Cannon Hole and many years later an attempt was made unsuccessfully to retrieve the big gun.

Another old-timer still alive who knew the ranch in its glory is Ad Spaugh, Manville, Wyoming, hero of Frazier Hunt's book entitled The Long Trail From Texas. This book appeared serially in *The Country Gentleman* and is a masterpiece of narrative and description.

making the old cattle trails live again. Our interest here in Mr. Spaugh is that he started his long career as a cattleman, as a herder on the Crane Ranch. The lady who taught the country school mentioned in the story lives next to the city library in Marion, Kansas – and the hotel where his sister Clara worked is just across the street from the library. Only one error in Mr. Hunt's story is that he failed to comprehend properly the term, "the Cottonwood" – and so spells it with a small c. As a matter of fact, the river is a branch of the Neosho River – and is truly the Cottonwood River.

Now, to some more memories, these in the mind of Rosse Case of Marion and information he gathered from old settlers, some of it recently from J. L. Jones who worked on the ranch but not for Mr. Crane. He was employed by a contractor who put up hay for winter feed. According to these recollections, the ranch house was popularly known as the "White House". It was so called, it is said, because it was probably the only painted house in Marion county at that time. As such, it was alone worth going to see in a land of log cabins and sod shacks. Said Mr. Case: "It was erected on a knoll probably fifteen feet high on a beautiful quarter-section of level bottom land. It was a two-story building containing probably about eight rooms, and with a wide porch all around it. I think the whole ranch was fenced as at that time it was necessary to fence all land to be used for farming or for the hay because this was then an open range country. I understand that Mr. Crane had 135 head of purebred Shorthorn cattle, some of the animals imported.

"The ranch house was surrounded, except on the front side, by cattle barns, all the purebred cattle were kept in the barns at night. In order to keep their hides looking well, only smooth wire was used for fencing. These animals were groomed thoroughly daily and kept in a condition like show cattle are today. There was one strip of land called 'The Lane' about a mile long and board-fenced on both sides. The fence was high, the boards close together with a smooth wire between them. The only purpose of this lane was to lead the bulls on for exercise when weather permitted. To show the labor expended in building the wire fence on the ranch, remember the cedar posts were set deep in the ground, ten holes were bored through each post, and the smooth wire was run through the holes. No staples were used whatever."

It is recalled that nearly all the corn raised in Marion, McPherson and Saline counties, and in Dickinson county, too, was hauled to the ranch for sale and many say that Mr. Armstrong was often in difficulties to find enough feed for the cattle. In the corrals at the ranch property were built numerous racks and Mr. Case thinks they were from 15 to 20 feet wide and from 25 to 30 feet long. They were filled with hay from the first cutting and after it had settled, the second cutting would be stacked on top.

"The ranch always kept on hand some Texas longhorn cows which were grazed outside the fenced land," continued Mr. Case. "The idea was to breed them to the purebred bulls and thus improve the stock. I am told by J. L. Jones that all the Shorthorns on the ranch were reds and roans except one massive white bull named 'Horace Greeley' and which weighed 3,300 pounds. Mr. Jones says the bull was over five feet tall and so wide that a man could have made a bed on his back."

All the old-timers admit that the post office was established at the ranch house with the mail brought in from Abilene on the Union Pacific Railway but there are small discrepancies. Some say the postmaster was William Hallowell, others that the postmaster's name was Janfrey or Palfrey. Quite likely Hallowell had the commission and that Janfrey, Palfrey, or whatever his name was merely worked in the office when there was mail to handle. This is a matter, however, which can readily be reconciled and straightened out from the post office records and the newspaper files of Marion.

To illustrate the great mine of information contained in all good local newspaper files is a little investigation by Mr. Case in the files of the Marion Record. In the paper of September 7, 1872, is mention of the ownership of the ranch by Mr. Crane and of the hay contracts he had let – prairie hay, too. In the issue of July 11, 1874, the editor tells of a nice catalog received of the Durham Park herd and how the herd had been attracting the attention of the country and how large newspapers had sent their correspondents to see the property and write about it. This alone indicates the existence of old stories and old photographs we have not located yet. The first step, of course, is to learn what newspapers these correspondents represented.

In March, 1875, the census was taken and the report says that Mr. Crane then had 1920 acres under fence. This fence, as we have already said, was rather expensive to build and should have stood a lifetime. Old-timers say that prairie fires took some of them probably and they hint that the need of the first settlers for lumber was hard on the fence, too.

In June, 1875, the Marion Record warms up to the importance of the ranch and the editor made his first visit there. He is properly impressed by the vast estate and he sets the figure at 10,000 acres. While most of the pioneers still living invariably refer to Mr. Crane's holdings as a "$3,000,000 ranch" – ye editor on his official check-up says it represented an investment of $300,000. Possibly, he forgot to add the final zero and if so, it was bad proof-reading.

However, he did one thing for us – he describes the appearance of Mr. Crane. Said he: "Mr Crane is the Alexander of The West, the Van Meeter of Kansas. He is a man of fine sense, good culture, and affable manner. His gray hair and whiskers betoken age but his sparkling eye, firm and quick step and animated speech seem to deny the fact."

The editor of the Marion Record tells us that when he visited the ranch there were approximately 2,400 head of cattle there. There were 55 purebred Shorthorn bulls, six of the finest being used exclusively on the registered cow herd of 84 head. The rest of the sires were used in breeding up the commercial herd of Texas and cross-bred cows. He says all the principal families of the Shorthorn breed were represented in the registered herd. Among the best bulls he mentions Lord of The Lake, four years old, weighing 2,500 pounds, valued at $5,000; Lord Abraham, six years old, bred in Lincolnshire, England, imported in 1872, weighing 2,450 pounds; and Lord Bates 2d, a Bates-bred calf, weighing 800 pounds at eight months. Among the most impressive cows he mentions Maiden, an imported cow; Duchess of York, a strawberry roan, weighing 1,900 pounds, and some sixteen cows, he says, are imported matrons. He states that the first Marion county resident to purchase a purebred Shorthorn bull from Mr. Crane was a minister – the Reverend A. H. Lackey of Peabody.

So we close the yarn of the cattle adventure of Albert Sears Crane. Closed for me but – just opened, I hope, for others. We admit the grave possibility of errors both of commission and omission. Yet maybe the object sought has been achieved. Have we revived interest in Crane and his cattle? Have we laid the foundation for a more worthy narrative? Have we paid sincere tribute to a notable but half-forgotten man? Have we given pleasure to the old boys and girls who were part of the thrilling days when, as one letter quotes it, "there was no law west of Abilene, no God west of Dodge?" If so, we are repaid – and we dedicate the effort to the Milking Shorthorn men of Kansas, to the admirers also of the red, white, and roan cattle of all types and strains, wherever they may be!

Note: Mr. T. B. Armstrong has memories of Mr. Crane at a little later period after the Kansas ranch was sold and Mr. Armstrong's father managed a ranch in Missouri for Crane. He says: "Mr. Crane was a very aristocratic gentleman and a strict disciplinarian. If fact, he gave me quite a lecture one evening after supper because I looked through the dining room window where he was eating with my father and mother. He had the habit of wanting to know everybody's name prior to meeting them and would always have my father give the surname as well as given-name of ranch hands, tenants, and neighbors.")

An old letter from the Crane Ranch

Durham Park Marion Co Kansas
October 8th, 1877

Col. John B. Anderson

Junction City, Kansas

Dear Colonel:

I shall be absent from home from tomorrow until night of Oct. 15th. I have an offer for the heifers offered to you and if you do not take them before Oct 21st I shall accept the offer I have or withdraw them from sale, probably the latter--

I don't wish to dictate to you by any means but have been waiting patiently for a visit from you-- I don't like to 'throw you overboard' on them without warning -- would not like it done to me but cannot hold open offers so long--

Respectfully yours,

Daniel W. Crane

For Albert Crane
Owner--

The actual Santa Fe Trail ruts can be seen. The ridges are known as "swales".. west of Durham.

Elgin, Nebraska
XT Ranch, Apr. 2, 1941

Mr. David I. Day
Richland, Indiana

Dear Mr. Day;

This is to acknowledge your kind favor of last March 8th, nearly a month and truly regret not answering sooner in regards to your inquiries concerning "Crane's Ranch" on the Cottonwood River in Kansas. I very much regret that I am not in position to give you very much information in regards to Crane's Ranch because of the fact that I left there with my father when Mr. Crane sold his Kansas ranch. As no doubt you know my father went down into Howell County Missouri to run a ranch there for Mr. Crane.

As my memory serves me, Mr. Crane was a Chicago realestate man and as I was probably 4 or 5 years old when we left Kansas for Missouri, I do not remember anything about him in Kansas. Tho I do remember him a trifle in Missouri as I have a distinct recollection of someone cleaning and oiling a double-barrel shot gun for Mr. Crane as he was coming down to the Ranch from Chicago and he was going to hunt quail and wild turkeys. It is my opinion that he was not at the Ranch at Durham Park very much as I think he left active management to his subordinates. As to Mr. Crane's biography, personality and when and where he passed beyond, I know nothing. Just in passing tho, I remember my father once remarking about Mr. Crane and Mr. Chisholm, seems tho these 2 gentlemen were both in a gateway, one was leaning against a post and the other man was leaning against the other post and father had to ask them to please remove one of their feet as their feet took up the entire width of gate. So be it.

Well now, about "Porcupine Reed". I seem to think L. A. Reed was an English Lord tho I have no direct evidence to substantiate this idea but I do remember him oft referred to as a Lord. I have sometimes thot that it might be that Mr. Reed was a "Remittance" man from England. There are many of them in Canada, men who have been induced by their relatives for some reason to leave England and go to Canada to live and then there would be funds sent them every so often from the English estate. I was interested in "Porcupine" some and a short time ago possibly 6 or 7 months, I sent a letter to the Chamber of Commerce at Abilene Kansas asking their Secretary to please go into the cemetery and see if a tombstone was there erected to the memory of L. A. Reed. If there was none there, I was thinking of maybe erecting one to his memory myself, even tho I had no recollection of ever seeing him. Memory serves me better

now. I asked the Secretary of Chamber of Commerce there to wait till frosty weather was past before going to the cemetary so you see it has been over a year since I wrote him. The Secretary never answered my letter. I wanted him to give me whatever inscriptions there was on his tombstone too. I would suggest to you if you are interested in his final resting place that you write the Cemetary Sexton. Also you might get further information from the House of Lords, London, England. Possibly 2 years ago a piece, serial, was published in *The Country Gentleman*. Just a minute, – This story was entitled, THE LAST FRONTIER, by Mr. Frazier Hunt and the first issue was December 1939. In case you have not read it, you might do so and possibly could lead you to new leads of desired information. The story freatures a Mr. "Ad Spaugh" who now is a rancher and real estate man whose address is, Manville, Wyoming. Mr. Spaugh remembers my father quite well as he started his ranching career by driving cattle over the Old Chisholm Trail, Texas to Kansas. I won't be sure but it may be Mr. Spaugh was born on the Cottonwood on Crane's Ranch. I believe it would pay you to even make a trip to Wyoming and see Mr. Ad Spaugh in person as it might be he would not feel inclined to write very much because he is I think over 80 years of age so you see he is nearing End of the Trail. I also think Ad Spaugh has a brother now in Chicago who might give you some information but I know not anyways near what Ad can.

Concerning Mr. Hallowell, I remember father speaking about the good appetite of Mr. Hallowell and his wife as they could sit down to dinner and the 2 of them would easily eat a fried chicken with the trimmings. I am of the opinion that Mr. Hallowell was on the Ranch pretty steady and do not think that he was on the staff of Natl. Live Stock Journal. Possible tho it may have been a brother.

Now about the size of the Ranch: I see you have 17, 000, 4160 and 5760 acres. Well I am sure I do not know but the Records of Marion Co. say 5760 acres which even today is a small parcel of land for a ranch and is only 9 sections. The 17, 000 acres would only figure some 26 sections. When I was a kid 19 years old I taught a country school on Mud Creek in Marion County and so happened to board with a Marcus Jones who was a brother of Charles Jones. I happened to notice that his farm was very irregular in shape and asked, "Marcus, how come that your farm is so irregular in shape and does not take in any good land but instead just follows the creek?" "Well sir, " Marcus replied, "when we came here to Kansas it was the practice for a cowman to take just land along the banks of a stream of water so that he could control the water for his cattle" and that accounted why Marcus Jones Ranch was so irregular and skirted the Mud Creek shoreline. Now, Mr. Day, this may account for seeming discrepancies in the size of Crane's Ranch, thus 5760 acres really could control 50, 000 acres or even 100, 000. This point can be verified today in New Mexico and Arizona where large ranch companies hold the water holes and thus control the range.

Mr. Watson was oft spoken of by father tho I do not remember him nor his conncetion with the Ranch. By the way, father had a ranch partner on the Cottonwood River at one time by the name of Clarence Lewis and believe he or his children live around Canton, Kansas and you could drop a letter there to "Any Pioneer Who Knows Anything About Crane's Ranch" at Durham Park.

Ranch Buildings? No I do not remember of any fires and fires in buildings even today are not of spontaneous origin but start when someone sets off a burning match. Even today I think Mr. F. D. R. at Washington thinks our Defense fires are started that way by friends of Adolph and FDR sits still like the boy who stole the apple.

I remember one set of buildings which was in form of a square about the size of an ordinary city block, maybe 400' square. The edges of this square was built around on all 4 sides with a small shed of lumber construction, the shed was possibly 16' or 18' wide maybe more, I don't know, but it was divided up all the way along with stalls and grain rooms. It is possible that there were quite a number of these shed squares scattered over many miles but as to the truth of this supposition, I am unable to say. At one time I knew of 7 tenant houses that I saw when father returned from Crane's Missouri Ranch and there may have been many more. Let's see, I was age about 12 at that time and I'm now 63. That would make it 1891 when I saw the mentioned tenant houses. With the coming of barb wire and homesteads, the large ranch holdings were simply broken up and disappated and as I think the buildings were of wood material. They offered no resistance against the wreckers who desired to remodel or rebuild and so I think these old structures were just wrecked or moved so that even the original tenant would not know the old house they once lived in. And I do not imagine the buildings were so very fancy or elaborate either as ranch buildings are mostly pretty simple structures and seems like 70 years would be a long time to survive.

Photographs? I know of none tho I did have some of the house I was born in on the Ranch but it was destroyed in a livery barn fire. This particular house I believe still stands and is about 2 miles west of Durham and is or was known as the Bob Smith house, as Bob Smith lived there, now dead.

Breeding purpose? I surely do not know and did not know that he had purchased 2 cows in Canada at over $2, 000 each tho I heard father speak about a bull purchased in England at cost I believe of $25, 000 and that the bull was brought over in a padded stall aboard the ship.

When I was a youngster I thot my Dad was a slow poke and was not much alive but guess he was head and shoulders ahead of me but it has taken me a lifetime to comprehend his worth. I could have had a world of gold in information concerning early frontier life if I had but asked him about it, and would have gladly passed it on to you and the world but that stage setting is forever gone and the voiceless lips tell us nothing.

Mr. William J. Armstrong
Star Route West
Elgin, Nebraska

Taken from Marion Record Special Phamplet published in 1876 by E. W. Hoch.

"Durham Park"

This magnificent estate, the largest of the kind west of the Mississippi, is the property of Albert Crane, of Chicago, and is situated in the northwestern part of Marion County, on the Cottonwood River, twenty three miles from Marion Centre, and thirty miles from Peabody, by section lines, or about eighteen miles from the former and twenty-five miles from the latter, by traveled road.

Of the early history of this Ranch, historian Williams has spoken in these pages, and we need not repeat. We speak of it only as we find it today. It comprises ten thousand acres of land, mostly under fence, and several thousand acres under cultivation. Full fifty cars were required for transportation of the lumber used for various purposes on the farm. —

AETNA
Federal Savings
and Loan Association
Topeka, Kansas

February 26, 1941

Mr. David I. Day.,
Feature Writer,
Richland, Indiana.

Dear Mr. Day:

Re: Albert - Crane's Ranch,
Durham Park, Marion County, Kansas.

There is at this time few people left who can give a graphic description and account of the old ranch together with the many historical and frontier anecdotes that should have been recorded long ago, however, it is my judgement that there are still a few left, one in particular a very warm friend of our family, Charles W. Jones who is an ex-merchant of Durham, Kansas, and who as I understand it worked under father when he was a boy at the Ranch. Mr. Jones and Father William D. Armstrong, were fast friends and confidents for probably 50 years.

William Wright, "Old Bill Wright," now called "Grandpa Wright" of Canton, Kansas, was another man who worked for Father both on Crane's Ranch at Durham and later on the Crane's Ranch in Howell County, Missouri. I think he could furnish many side lights on the old ranch days.

My older brother William J. Armstrong, an ex-civil engineer and now a Hereford breeder and rancher, at Elgin, Nebraska, c/o Star Route West, XT Ranch, undoubtedly can furnish much more information than the writer, as I am of the opinion that he has gathered some data relative to the Ranch.

Several months ago, I called on Charley Jones at his home in Durham, Kansas, he had been seriously sick for several years but at the time was using a wheel chair. We talked some about the old ranch days and he said if a stenographer would come to his home he would be most glad to dictate considerable information and anecdotes of the Ranch in the old days of its prime, information that had long since been forgotten and little known to the present generation. I had expected to do this, however, I have been transferred to the State of Oklahoma and it now seems impossible – I am wondering Mr. Day if you can not arrange to spend a day there with a stenographer, I am certain that it would pay big dividends in the matter of getting a large store of accurate and historic information,

together with most of the names of all important personages connected with this particular ranch and the exact type of information that you desire.

William D. Armstrong who apparently was second boss on the ranch use to tell about his long horse back trips over the country buying feed for the ranch. About broadcasting hundreds of acres in blue grass on the ranch that it did not come up for years. About a pony express rider taking the place one morning of a rider by the name of Hank Roberts the relief rider was captured and murdered by Indians before sun down that day near Canton, Kansas – I have forgotten the name of the rider that was murdered. Also about hanging of horse thieves in the early days.

There are still the markings of the Old Santa Fe Trail where it crossed the ranch, and I am not certain but that the excavations on the river bank may show where the Soldiers had their crude fortifications. Just where the Indians had their camps and their numbers can be procurred from Mr. Jones, also there is to be had information on Jesse Chisholm who drove thousands of cattle up from Texas to Wichita, to Abilene, and west to Dodge City, Kansas. I think this man Chisholm is still alive, that he had dealings with both Crane and Father on the ranch. I also think Crane had a goodly number of feeders or ordinary cattle on the ranch which can be cleared up thru Mr. Jones.

I am enclosing herewith a copy of a letter written by Chas. W. Jones to my brother Wm. J. Armstrong at Elgin, Nebraska, under date of Feb. 8, 1940. It speaks for itself and you will note that Mr. Jones of Durham, Kansas, is the one man who has valuable information. In this letter, he just scratched the surface.

I will attempt to pave the way for further information for you by writing both Chas. W. Jones and Wm. J. Armstrong – today. Sorry that I have delayed since sending you the Western Union message recently. I also wish to advise that I had or that our family had a great many pictures of Albert Crane, Reed and Mr. Hallowell and several others connected with Crane's ranch that were burned up in a fire at Durham some years ago, whether Mr. Jones has any or knows where they could be procured I do not know. I have a picture of both Father and Mother taken about the time the ranch was sold and at which time they took over in Missouri that I am having copied and will enclose, also one of Father's buggies and a fine team. If you can use them they are yours to handle as you see fit.

I know that Crane was a resident of Chicago at one time and that is where he probably died. His estate should be located and from it many pictures and relics could be procured for your article. Crane was immensely wealthy.

Finally, Mr. Day, when your article is finished and published, I will greatly appreciate 5 copies for preserving of the Old Days. I was Sheriff of Marion County 4 years, it looks like I personally should know more about the Ranch. I want you to call on me for any other information that is possible for me to furnish and I am certain if you find it convenient to go to Durham that you will get all that you desire.

Yours very truly,

T. B. Armstrong

Old store in Durham that burned down. Bill Armstrong and Charley Jones, with customers.

Bill Armstrong, who built the Valley Hotel in Durham, with his daughter in the wheelbarrel. Taken about 1903.

Durham, Kansas
February 8, 1940

Dear Will:

Albert S. Crane purchased in 1872 six and one-half sections or 4,160 acres of land from Moore and Calen in the Cottonwood River Valley, Marion County, Kansas, and started the ranch with a capital of three million dollars. It was the largest ranch west of the Mississippi River under control of one man.

He built a large house called the "House of Lords" and no one was allowed to enter it but English Lords. He also built a large rooming and boarding house of 70 rooms. He also built 10 miles of cattle sheds 300 feet square with hay barns in the middle of the sheds with a capacity of 300 tons of hay. He had a very large feed grinder to grind feed for the cattle, and kept 180 head of cattle haltered and stalled in those sheds. He had 40 men hired to take care of them. He had 7 tenant houses on this ranch. He built 22 miles of 4 board fence and kept 500 head of stock cattle. Balance of the ranch was farming and meadow land.

Crane bought all the corn and oats in the country at that time. The cattle in stalls cost all the way from $500 to $30,000 per head. This ranch was on the "Old Santa Fe Trail," 186 miles southwest of Kansas City. This trail ran from Kansas City to California. In the late 40s and 50s, the trail was used for a freight and transportation line across the country. These overland freight outfits would have 60 to 100 wagons, with 8 to 10 yoke of cattle to the wagon, almost 1000 head of work cattle or oxen to pull the caravan; some of the wagons in this train held a half car-load of merchandise. Generally these outfits or wagon trains carried 100 to 150 passengers too. It usually took from 6 months to 8 months to make the trip across the country.

Well, back to the ranch story. I saw two hogs on this ranch that weighed 3,200 pounds. The largest cattle weighed 3,200 pounds and they were all Red, Roan and White "Durham Cattle."

This ranch had a bank and post office. The name of the office was "Durham Park Post Office." The post-master's name was Janfrey. The first manager boss was an English Lord named L. A. Reed; this is the man they called "Porcupine". He died in Abilene, Kansas and was buried there.

There was two First Bosses, Watson and Halowell. Your father William D. Armstrong, was Second Boss and Purchasing Agent at the ranch, whom I have known for 65 years, a loving friend of mine. Your father, after Crane sold his ranch at Durham Park, went to Brandsville, Howell County, Missouri, where he supervised and was Superintendent of another large ranch containing about 20,000 acres, thoroughbread cattle and farming was conducted on this ranch for about 6 years at which time Crane sold this ranch to Mayor Hayes of Kansas City. Hayes attempted to interest your father in continuing there as superintendent but he quit and returned to Kansas, later buying a 320 acre farm on the Cotton wood which was originally in the Crane ranch.

I am the last and only one left here that was here when the ranch was a going concern. I can say that there are very few left anywhere that was here at that time but it is not going to be many years until there is no one left, here I am 78 years old at this time.

When the ranch was here we had plenty Indians, buffalo, deer, antelope and prairie chickens. All of this is now past and gone forever. At one time the government had a company of soldiers stationed here from Fort Leavenworth to hold the Indians down, but one day the Indians came down the trail and took in after the soldiers so strong the soldiers "spiked" their cannon and dumped it into the Cottonwood at a point which was later known as the "Cannon Hole." In later years after this episode an attempt was made to recover this cannon but after spending considerable money the attempt was given up.

Will, I can't walk a step anymore but I hope to sometime again. Your folks were always dear to me.

Your mother was cook on the Crane's ranch when your father met and married her.

Well, Will, I have given you a little history of the old ranch. I hope it will be of some benefit to you

With best regards to you and your loving wife,

Charles W. Jones
Durham, Marion County, Kansas

Dear Mr. Day: April 25, 1941

Your favor of the 18th inst. received. Hope you will pardon me for long delay in writing but my son who is my partner in business has been out of town for nearly two weeks and I have had everything I could possibly do to handle things in the office.

I will try to give you what little information I can in addition to what Frank Hagans and Tom Armstrong have given. Perhaps you would be interested in a little of the history of the nucleous of this ranch on the SE quarter of Sec. 7, Twp. 18, Range 2, Marion County, Kansas, before Mr. Crane got it.

Ira E. Moore, brother of Atlantic A. Moore, received a patent to this land May 1st, 1861. I believe that no one now knows when the Moore boys started this trading post on the Santa Fe Trail Wagon Road. The government did not survey this county and divide it into sections until 1857 and 1858. The probabilities are that the Moore boys operated this trading post before that date and supposedly homesteaded the land as soon as it was surveyed, making their filing early in 1858 immediately after the land was surveyed and they then received their patent approximately three years after filing their homestead papers. The Moores' deeded this land to A. W. Collins May 16, 1870. Collins deeded it to Albert Crane May 18, 1872 and Albert Crane at that time established this ranch.

Mr. Crane spent very little time here. Lived in Chicago and came out here very seldom. The ranch was operated by a man by the name of Hallowell and a Mr. Reed. Albert Crane had a son called "Major" Crane who spent considerable time here on the ranch but he had no part in the operation of the ranch. Simply spent his time riding horseback around the country. Seems to me that Mr. Crane kept this ranch some ten or fifteen years, then sold it to Hallowall and Reed, the whole thing finally winding up in a big lawsuit, the details of which, however, I have forgotten.

What follows is partly what I know, partly what I have heard from early settlers, and quite a little of it being what I just got from an interview with Jimmy Jones who, while he did not work for Crane, worked on the ranch for a contractor who put up hay for winter feed. Jimmy Jones is J. L. Jones and is a step-brother of Barzilla "Buff" Jones.

The Crane's ranch contained 5760 acres which largely surrounded the original SE quarter of Section 7. A lot of this land was fine Cottonwood River bottom land, balance being good upland. The SW quarter of Section 7 was a beautiful quarter of level bottom land on the east side of which, however, there was a knoll probably fifteen feet high. On this, Mr. Crane built his ranch house which was known all over the country as the "White House". It was a two story building containing probably eight rooms, having a wide porch all around it. It was probably the only painted house in this country at that time and it alone was a sight worth seeing for the people who lived in log and sod and adobe houses around here. I think the whole ranch was fenced as it was necessary at that time to fence any land which you wanted to use for farming or for the hay as most of this country was an open range. Mr. Crane had one hundred thirty-five head of thoroughbred cattle, some of which were shipped here from England or Scotland and at that time were called Durham cattle. The municipal Durham Park Township was named from this ranch. It was a large township comprising four congressional townships which made it twelve miles square.

Think that nearly all of the corn raised in Marion, Mc Pherson, Saline and Dickinson Counties was hauled to this ranch for sale. The ranch had a wind power grist mill with an output of forty bushels of ground corn per hour.

The ranch kept on hand a few hundred head of Texas longhorn cows which, however, were grazed outside of the fenced land, the idea being to breed these to the thoroughbred bulls to improve the stock. Mr. Jones says that all the cattle on the ranch were either red or roan except one white bull which Mr. Crane brought here from Kentucky. He mentions one bull, "Horace Greeley," which weighed 3300 pounds, was over five feet tall and in Mr. Jones' words "was so wide that he could have made a bed on his back".

In the corrals at the ranch house there were numerous racks built, each being 15 to 20 feet wide and 25 to 30 feet long. These were filled with hay from the first cutting and after it had settled the second cutting was stacked on top again.

The government established a post office at the ranch house and a man by the name of Palfry was the post master. Mail was brought to the post office from Abilene which is on the Union Pacific Railroad.

I cannot find anyone who ever saw Albert Crane, so it is impossible to get a picture of him or even a description. A number of the early settlers started their herds of shorthorn cattle with cattle from this ranch and kept their herds pure shorthorn herds as long as they lived, but all of these people have now passed away and I do not think there is a single one of these herds which has been kept intact. Do not know of anyone who has a picture even of the buildings on this ranch. We happen to have in our office a crayon drawing of the log cabin which the Moore boys used as a trading post where the Crane's ranch followed. Just happens that we have this as when the Union Pacific Railway came through Abilene, the business on the Santa Fe Trail Wagon Road of course was largely discontinued. My father bought this house and moved it here for a residence. I believe that I have given you all I can get on this subject and hope that it, together, with the information you have gotten from Hagans and Armstrong will help you.

Sincerely yours,
Rosse Case

Al and Charley Jones, figures in early Crane Ranch history.

Marion, Marion County, Kansas, Thursday, September 13, 1945

Charley Jones, Last of the Famous Cowboys of the Fabulous Crane's Ranch

(By Lucy Burkholder)

The passing of Charles W. Jones of Durham as reported in this paper last week, brings to an end the tale of a fabulous adventure in cattle of the 1870s. For "Charley" Jones, as he was familiarly known, was the last cowboy of that 'eighth wonder of the world – Crane's Ranch'. Another herder from the ranch, Ad Spaugh, made famous by Frazier Hunt's book, "Long Trail from Texas," died in December of 1943.

Crane's Ranch, later called Durham Park, was the successor to Moore's Ranche, a far-famed tavern and trading post on the old Santa Fe Trail at a point called Cottonwood crossing, now the Curvey farm west and north of the village of Durham. "Lank" and Ira Moore bought the place in 1859 and in 1872 they sold it to a Chicago capitalist named Albert Sears Crane.

According to the abstract records Crane owned 5,760 acres but Andreas' History of Kansas and other published histories, refer to 17,000 acres. This apparent discrepancy is probably accounted for by the custom of allowing water rights to owners of land along waterways. On this estate Crane invested three million dollars in an unbelieveable speculation in pedigreed cattle.

Purebred Durham cattle, now called Shorthorns in the United States, were imported, in padded stalls, from England, Scotland and the Dominion of Canada. Many animals cost as much as $5000 and at least one cow cost Mr. Crane $23,600. The big house, called the "White House" because it was the only painted building in the entire country, was built upon a knoll overlooking the rest of the ranch. It was a comfortable two stroy dwelling with a veranda all around and an observatory on top. There were seven tenant houses; a bunk house with room for 70 hands; cattle sheds built in a 300 foot hollow square with hay barns in the center, each holding as much as 300 tons of hay; 22 miles of 4-board fence (an Easterner's idea of a fence) and 20 miles more of smooth wire fence.

When E. W. Hoch visited the ranch in 1881 to get a story for the Marion Record, there were 2400 head of cattle on the place and 1500 acres under cultivation. Practically all the corn grown in Marion, McPherson, Saline and Dickinson counties, was bought at the ranch where there was a wind-power grist mill capable of grinding 40 bushels per hour. * * *

Santa Fe Trail Ruts Preserved

On the actual Santa Fe Trail ruts ... Dennis Youk is appointed caretaker.

As the appointed caretaker of the famed Santa Fe Trail ruts west of Durham, Dennis Youk has a prestigious and important job. He helps to preserve and protect history in our midst. He was appointed in more recent years by the family who owns the ground to be its keeper, and he takes his duty seriously, sometimes even taking the curious on a guided and narrated tour.

As a soil conservationist, he has carefully sculpted a waterway in the fields encompassing the ruts, for drainage is very important to this area. Riding on the bermed earth, the visitor is almost surprised to turn north and out onto the wide place, marked by ditches where the trail actually wended its way out of the Cottonwood River lowlands. Approximately 75 yards wide, the still-visible portion of the Trail is comprised of four or more ditches, or "swales." One gets a tingling feeling, standing on the historic spot, and envisioning the varied people from all types of circumstances who traversed this place during the trail's long epoch.

Rather than moving along in one pathway, the wagon trains headed west generally fanned out to 3 or 4 abreast to reduce the amount of dust the traders in the rear had to "eat", and also to enable circling the wagons for defense. In addition, there was often a need to cut a new path when there wasn't any grass near the trail, a necessity for feeding the livestock. While the historic soil has never been broken, it is still productive, feeding livestock today. Dennis bales the native longstem grass which is the same type of grass which lined the roadway during the Trail days.

Durham on The Chisholm Trail

The Chisholm Trail played an important role in the development of the cowboy as a figure in Western legend. Because the Chisholm Trail passed near Durham, the cowboy, as he is widely depicted, could be connected to actual people in the Durham area.

Deep in the American consciousness is a picture of the cowboy that actually came out of the Kansas cowtown. For a period of about 20 years, from 1867 to 1886, the Texas Longhorn trade took between five and seven million head of cattle from Texas into Kansas via several routes. The Chisholm Trail, which fed the Longhorns into the Kansas railheads, accounted for about three million head of cattle in the ten-year span from 1867 to 1877.

Following the Civil War, there was a severe shortage of beef in the East, but even though there was a surplus of Longhorns in Texas, they could not be brought to the Eastern markets for the lack of railroads into Texas. While the South struggled to recover from the War, the railroad did not seem likely to reach Texas for many years.

The railroad had, however, already reached into Kansas; if the Longhorns of Texas could be driven across the prairies, north to the Kansas railhead towns, they could be easily shipped to the eager Eastern markets, who were beef-hungry.

This solution still required overcoming several obstacles. In 1867, the Kansas legislature had passed a law prohibiting Texas cattle from entering Kansas during certain months because of the threat of "Texas fever." The Longhorns were immune to this destructive disease, but they could transfer it to vulnerable local herds by carrying infected ticks.

A Chicago businessman, Joseph McCoy saw the opportunities in trail drives and is credited as the first to organize one in 1867. He scouted various Kansas towns for his headquarters and chose Abilene, mostly because of its natural resources of grass and water.

Even though Abilene, just 30 miles north of Durham, was just inside the quarantine line, no one objected to McCoy's plans, the Governor gave his approval and Abilene was the first of the Kansas cattle centers.

Within a few months, what would later be known as a typical frontier town, was constructed in Abilene, including saloons and stockyards, transforming the quiet town. Arrangements were made with Texas drovers and what would later be called "the largest movement of domestic animals in the history of the world" was begun.

The first shipment of 20 carloads of cattle pulled out of Abilene on September 5, 1867 and by the end of that year, 35,000 head had moved through the town. In 1868, 75,000 head of cattle were driven into Abilene and shipped out and by 1869, the annual shipment of Longhorns was 175,000 head.

Three trails fed cattle into Kansas. The Shawnee was east of the Chisholm and lead into Baxter Springs, and the Western trail had Dodge City as its destination. The Chisholm Trail was the most popular route, however. 600 miles in length, it came from San Antonio into the central Kansas towns, following Jesse Chisholm's pathway. Chisholm, an Indian trader and part Cherokee Indian, had traced the route between his Wichita trading post and the Oklahoma territory.

Originally used by traders and the Army, the Chisholm trail ran between the Canadian River (in present Oklahoma) and Wichita. As the trail was expanded from different Texas points of origin to the central Kansas towns of Abilene, Ellsworth and Newton in addition to Wichita, the trail kept Chisholm's name.

The evolution of the Kansas cowtowns was constant. As the railroad extended further west, different towns enjoyed a boom period and then the next town down the line built stockyards and flourished until another town was developed.

As more settlers populated the Abilene area, resistance grew strong to the thundering herds from Texas who trampled crops and fences and anything else in their pathway.

Because the railroad tracks linking Kansas with the Eastern beef markets were continually being extended, and due to the rising opposition of new settlers, after 1871 Abilene was not the sole cattle center. It shared the Texas trade with other towns. As Abilene's domination was diminished, the Chisholm trail brought herds into Ellsworth, Newton and Wichita also.

The long trail from Texas took between a month and several months; kicking up huge clouds of dust, the cattle's hooves thunderously pounding, horns clicking, the herds were usually about 2,000 head, stringing out for a mile or two, they traveled 10-15 miles a day. Once begun, the herd was moved along quickly to limit damage and discourage strays. Known for their strength and stamina, they were hard to stop once underway and took expert skill to lead and keep in line. Such a powerful and massive movement obviously had the potential for great destruction, especially if the skitterish cattle were frightened into a stampede.

The cowboys cracked their whips over the backs of the leaders of the stampede and forced the group into a smaller and smaller circle. If the stampede began due to sounds in the nighttime, the cowboys leaped into the saddle and used the same method to contain.

Once the cattle were settled, the cowboys sang soft songs and chants to lull the cattle to sleep. The songs really did quiet the cattle.

As the herd reached its destination, they were pastured on the prairie close to town to fatten before final sale. Some cowboys were retained to watch the grazing herd, but most were dismissed with their wages of between $25 to $40 a month.

While some of the cattle drovers shipped their livestock East themselves, most were sold at the railhead and the buyer shipped them. Some were bought by Kansas buyers as stock for their own ranches.

By the mid-1880's, the railroad had finally been extended into Texas and the quarantine line in Kansas had been extended, too. In addition, the Kansas settlers were building towns, and fences so the boundless prairie was no longer so open for trailing and grazing and the trail drives came to a close.

The Chisholm Trail had a key role in developing the economy. Everett Dick, Western historian, summarized the trial drives and their importance in history as follows:

"The long trail was not a mere cow trail; it was a step in the course of empire. It played a part in that unfolding process which developed the great Plains and made of the Mississippi Valley the bread basket of the world.

The long drive became majestic, not only because of its physical proportions, but also on account of its social and political effect.

"The cowboy was a pioneer in every sense of the word. What the backwoodsman was to the timbered country of the East, what the forty-niner was to California, the cowboy was to the prairies."

Ruts of the Chisholm Trail can be seen near Goessel with depressions several feet deep and a block wide.

Kansas
State Historical Society
Kirke Mechem, Secretary
Topeka
March 15, 1941

Mr. Leland R. Smith
Indiana State Library
Indianapolis, Indiana

My dear Mr. Smith:

I regret to say that we have no biographical material on Albert S. Crane. I find this mention in the History of Kansas, published in Chicago by Andreas, 1883, page 1226:

Durham Park

Nearly in the geographical center of Durham Park Township is located the great cattle ranch of the State owned by Mr. Albert Crane, of Chicago, the proprietor of Durham Park, and the owner of the best families of thoroughbred bulls, and of Airdrie Dutchess third, and of Airdrie Dutchess second, the cost of both $44,600. The present Postmaster at Durham Park is William Hallowell.

and in the History of Kansas Newspapers, a publication of the Historical Society, page 234:

"DURHAM — Population (1915), 283; elevation, 1378 feet; originally Moore's Ranch; established, 1859 by A. A. Moore, and a noted trading post and tavern on the Santa Fe Trail; later on the land came into the possession of Albert Crane, of Chicago, who in the later 70's called it Durham Park Ranch; eventually a settlement grew around the post office, becoming known as Durham about 1887; telephones; is on the Rock Island railway."

I am enclosing a copy of a letter which we have in our manuscript department which may be of interest to Mr. Day, although it has little information in it. I presume the only way to find material would be through the file of a Marion county paper and it probably would take many days of research. We have files of papers covering the late 70's in our newspaper division and if Mr. Day wants research made in these papers we will try to find someone with whom he can make arrangements for such work.

Very truly yours,
Lenen M. McFarland
Librarian

HMMcF:eh

The Railroad Comes to Durham

The water tower for the railroad caught fire from sparks from a train and the tower burned down to the water line.

Durham got its railroad the same year it became a town, back in 1887. The line, then called the Chicago, Kansas and Nebraska Railroad, laid track through Durham in July of that year, setting the stage for the town to become an important stop on what later became the Rock Island Line.

A book could be written just on the railroading industry as it pertained to Durham, for there was a lot of traffic, and its importance to the town's agricultural and commercial enterprises was vital, bringing and taking away the products of exchange.

According to official records, Marion County's settlement was credited largely to the railroad's coming through. Many of the Mennonite immigrants from Russia and Germany had come to the area in the early 1870's. This was during the time that the Santa Fe Trail overland shipping and travel era was coming to an end.

Although progress had been made during the 1860's in building railroad lines in eastern Kansas, it wasn't until the 1870's that it came to Marion County, and not until the late 1880's that Durham got the main line later called the Rock Island.

But when it did, the town "took off", and it is reported that by 1900, the population of Durham stood at 350 persons, much of the development owed to the railroad, making the town not only accessable, but practical.

Durham remained a principal station between the towns of Hutchinson and Herington, and countless carlots of wheat and cattle were shipped from Durham.

The stockyards at Durham became important for local ranching and farming interests. Some huge shipments of cattle came in to local ranchers for stock purposes. Rhodes Ranch reports receiving 1100 head of Brahma cattle one day in 1929, while the Christiansens' also received large numbers of cattle.

Durham farmers regularly shipped cattle to the markets in Kansas City from the stockyards adjoining the tracks, and of course the constant usage of grain cars to ship locally grown wheat and other crops kept the railroad and the farmers dependent on each other for years.

The Rock Island depot was built in the early years, and remained a landmark, until it was remodeled, reduced in size, and finally, removed and replaced by a smaller building.

Whereas some 25 trains per day used to dash through Durham on their way west, and back again, now the train passage is slower, and limited in numbers. But the railroad remains not only a monument to the past role it played in Durham's history (including even serving as a Sunday School meeting room in its earliest days) to the symbol of our westward expansion.

"The Rock Island Line"

Growing Up On The Rock Island's Main Line
An interview with Ben Goertz

"Just like kids before me, and after me, here and everywhere else trains run, I put pennies on the tracks just to see the huge wheels squash them flat, obliterating the markings and making large ovals of the coins."

But Ben Goertz had an unusual opportunity to enjoy trains without leaving Durham when, as a young child, he was invited onto the "local" which came through daily to deliver goods and groceries to Ben's father and other Durham merchants. Ben got to play on the train.

"I was just a little tyke, about 3 years old or so, when I started accompanying my dad to the depot to meet the train and pick up goods," Ben remembers. "When the train came in, the trainmen would let me play on the train while they were making the switch to another track. I'd run up and down the aisles and look out the windows, just havin' fun. I'd pretend this was a big trip I was takin. Then when the switch was made, they'd say, 'you'd better get off now, sonny, or we'll take you with us!' Boy, I'd scamper off right away."

The Durham depot on the Rock Island Line.

Being on the main line of the Rock Island with its many freights and passenger trains coming through daily and with his dad's implement store just a half a block from the depot, Ben Goertz, as a youngster, knew first-hand the joys of being associated with railroading even if only in a vicarious way when he pretended he was a mascot of the train crews.

Part of his memories include another adventure on the local. "It would come from Herington to Hutchinson 6 days a week. It would stop and bring the freight for the grocery stores and hardware stores, and while unloading they would switch the grain cars to the elevator, picking up the loaded ones, and leaving off the others." Ben says. "I'd sneak away from my dad and even though I was pretty little for riding in a train engine, I did it. I also remember the thrill of when they'd let me blow the whistle."

The lore of trains began when the Rock Island laid the first tracks through Durham in 1887, creating the town of Durham, and giving it a link with the world.

Ben recalls that trains used to start many grass fires in the Scully pastures west of town. He remembers as many as 20 fire calls a winter and spending all night working with the volunteer fire department, too.

There were many derailments, some in and out of town, too. One derailment of a freight train was nearly 44 cars long, a half a mile of cars, just north of Durham.

"Yes, the railroad bridge over the Cottonwood had been battered and beat up by all these wrecks, (and floods) but it came through them all."

"One thing I remember, too," Ben adds, "is I was sure impressed, when my dad went to the World Fair in 1933 in Chicago on an old steam passenger train, he was able to leave right from his own home town."

Railroad Lore

The Rock Island and the Missouri Pacific lines greatly increased Kansas railroad mileage in the 1880's.

The Rock Island Line was legendary. Within less than three years, they were operating more than 1100 miles of line in Kansas, a fantastic record, according to Robert Richmond's book, Kansas, a Land of Contrasts.

There are many stories connected to Durham's involvement with the railroad. The crews who originally laid the track and who later staffed the maintenance or 'work' crews were a foreign element in the town, but not unwelcome. Special railroad cars on sidings, and on lots in town were where those people lived while maintaining the track.

One good story about trains concerns a runaway cattle car. Back in 1907, as the story goes, during the time when Waldeck stockyards were being utilized for cattle shipment, an empty cattle car was standing on a siding at Waldeck. A nighttime thunderstorm came up, and the strong winds blew the empty car onto the main line. It began rolling easterly, faster and faster, finally going through the switches at Durham and heading toward Tampa. The Durham agent, a Mr. Baker, saw it whiz past the depot and immediately wired ahead to Tampa to alert the Westbound Train number 55. Owing to the grade of the track east of Durham, and the diminishing winds, the runaway car had slowed down, and the cautiously proceeding Westbound train was able to bring it to a safe stop without damage, and push it back to Durham.

Had Train No. 55 been on time, a wreck would no doubt have occured, because they say the runaway car "beat the schedule (velocity) of the California Limited by several miles per hour."

Another feature of this event was that a fishing party of three women and a child, caught out in the rainstorm, had just crossed the railroad bridge walking back into town, when the silently hurtling empty car. . . dashing along without lights or whistle. . . came through. A few moments' difference and those people would certainly have been trapped and struck on the bridge.

The importance of the Rock Island to the new community of Durham and the enthusiasm which greeted the arrival of the tracks cannot be underestimated. The Rock Island enjoyed many decades of usefulness before operations were cut back in 1939 for financial reasons.

The Rock Island's "Golden State" pictured at a depot.

Hope Gray - Female Depot Agent

Hope Gray was one of the few female depot agents at Durham, (or anywhere) in the mid-1940's. During the war effort, when more than one train per hour carried troops through Durham, it was necessary to have depot agents on duty around-the-clock, because of the shortage of qualified men, (who were in the service) Hope got the chance to work.

She had come to the area in about 1943 from her girlhood home near Naravisa, New Mexico. Financial hardship due to the Dust Bowl days was still severe there, and Hope found a great opportunity in Durham with a well-paying job as the night-shift agent at the depot.

Since things worked out so well for her, she persuaded her two sisters, Zane and Helen, to come to Durham, too.

Durham was a busy farming community and also green and lovely. When Helen (later Mrs. LeeRoy Hein), saw the elm trees on Main Street arching over the road, touching each other and creating a canopy, she said it was the "most beautiful town" she'd ever seen.

R.W. Powers Drug Store in Durham was well-stocked, as shown in this photo supplied by his daughter, Mrs. Enid Powers Pope.

G. Meschke and Company, in early days in Durham.

The Dew Drop Cafe. Is the clerk Lillie or Madge?

Promotional Pamphlet from 1903

This account was taken from a little pamphlet that was published
by the Morris County Printing Co. , Council Grove, Kansas in 1903.

Durham, one of the most flourishing towns in Marion County

Marion County is about the geographical center of the eastern half of Kansas, and the center of the populated portion of the state.

Durham, one of the most flourishing towns in Marion County miles southwest of Kansas City, 100 miles from Topeka, the capital of the state, and 20 miles northwest of Marion, the county seat.

The land around Durham is all valley, of black sandy loam and very productive. The elevation is 85 feet lower than Tampa, the first town east of us, and 125 feet lower than Waldeck, the first station west, consequently the rainfall is greater and the summer showers more frequent.

The farmers generally are in a prosperous condition, and are surrounded with all the comforts of home life. Their farms are well improved and stocked with a high grade of horses, cattle and hogs.

The shipping facilities here are the best. Durham is located on the great Rock Island main line which spans the country from Chicago to California and over which pass the through California limited passenger trains, said to be the first passenger train service in the United States. Kansas City, St. Joe, Denver and Topeka markets, and the principal markets of Texas are reached over this great railway system.

In point of health the climate here is not surpassed anywhere. We are located geographically between the two extreme sections of heat and cold. We do not have the cold deadly blizzards of Nebraska or Dakota to retard business during the winter months, nor deep snows to hinder the farmer in hauling feed for his cattle.

During the summer season we have very few uncomfortable days, and even then we are blessed with cool and invigorating nights.

The best of wells and good water are readily obtainable anywhere, and stock water is pure as well as abundant.

This is a good country for fruit. The older residents who have attended to it have orchards, also plenty of small fruits. The McNicol orchard and nursery in this county has 220 acres in nursery and fruit. In good seasons he picks from 500 to 600 bushels of cherries, 150 bushels of apricots, 600 to 700 bushels of peaches, 6,000 to 10,000 bushels of apples, 100 crates of strawberries, gooseberries, guinces, pears, plums, nectarines, and other fruit in like proportion.

Corn and livestock are the two principal industries for fast money making. Quite a large quantity of wheat and broom corn is raised here every year. Potatoes and all vegetables do well.

Bank Wanted

This is a splendid location for a bank, and the businessmen and farmers would give one good support. The deposits and other business would be heavier than at many towns where banks are doing reasonably well. Come to Durham if you are looking for an opening.

Borton and Lasure

L. E. Borton and A. Lasure, do general blacksmithing, wheelright work, horseshoeing and general repair work. Their plant is equipped with steam power and the latest appliances for doing all kinds of work in the best manner and on short notice. They have an established business, and not only enjoy the confidence and good will of the people but their trade as well. Besides their shop work they handle agricultural implements, gasoline engines, feed grinders, corn shellers, threshing machines, buggies, wagons and furnish all kinds of repairs. Mr. Borton is also a Notary Public and Real Estate Agent. He has some choice pieces of property for sale, including the following:

South half, southwest quarter, 29, 17, 1.

Northwest quarter, 36, 18, 1, 25 acres of pasture, good two story house and bearing orchard.

South half, southeast quarter, 30, 17, 2.

North half, southeast quarter, 30, 17, 2.

Northwest quarter, 15, 18, 2.

One hundred town lots ranging in price from $15 to $75 each.

W.D. Oldfield

This gentleman lately came here from Canton, this county, and bought out the interest of Oldfield Bros; in the butcher business. He has a neat shop and keeps on hand at all times all kinds of fresh and salt meats. Also pays the highest cash price for hides. He expects to move his family here in the spring and become a permanent resident of the town. A good butcher shop is a great convenience to any town, and the people here appreciate it by giving it their patronage.

J.M. Clubine

Is a dealer and shipper of all kinds of grain. He has been a resident of Marion County for more than twenty-five years, but only recently became interested in buying grain in Durham. He is highly pleased with the business here, and expects to make this his permanent home. It will give the reader some idea of business he is handling when we say he recently bought and shipped 28 cars of corn in seventeen days. He expects to ship 150, 000 bushels of corn and 20, 000 bushels of oats this season. As a side line Mr. Clubine also handles a real estate and has quite a list of farms which he can sell at reasonable figures.

Secret Orders

We have two secret orders, the Pyramids and Woodmen. Both have a good membership composed of the representative citizens of the community.

Valley Hotel

Next in importance to a local bank or creamery is a good hotel. Last fall Mr. W. D. Armstrong completed a handsome two-story building, planned and designed expressly for a first-class two dollar house. Mr. Armstrong is "the right man in the right place. " He is very attentive and courteous to his guests and a good entertainer. The house is well lighted, well ventilated, the beds are clean, and no country hotel on the road serves better meals or affords better accommodations in every particular. Try the Valley Hotel and you will get your money's worth. Mr. Armstrong erected a large livery barn opposite the hotel, where the public can be accommodated at any time with a good rig at a reasonable price.

G.W. Thompson

Mr. Thompson has been in the drug store business here since the year 1893. Few country drug stores carry a better stock, or have a neater appearance. He also keeps a well assorted stock of stationery and school supplies. Mr. Thompson is always found in the lead in any measure calculated to advance the business or social interests of Durham.

T.J. Parry

Mr. Parry succeeded G. Meschke as postmaster here. He has had the office nearly two years. He is a gentleman of pleasing manners, and very courteous and attentive to patrons of the office. Under his administration the affairs of the office are well kept, and the business shows a very satisfactory increase.

G. Meschke & Co.

The members of this popular mercantile establishment are G. Meschke and Henry Geis. Mr. Meschke is the manager. He is a careful, prudent, energetic, young business man, and during his four years business career has built up a business that any young man might be proud of. Every year from the start the trade of this store has increased, and the year just closed was a record breaker, showing a most satisfactory increase over any of the preceding years. Henry Geis, the other member of the firm, is Mr. Meschke's father-in-law, who owns a highly improved farm seven miles northwest of Durham, well stocked, commodious house, where he lives in comfort and ease. The firm G. Meschke & Co. is a solid one, and the store is one of the permanent fixtures of Durham. They handle everything in the general merchandise line and pay the highest market price for all kinds of country produce.

D.P. Herald

The above named gentleman runs a restaurant and short order lunch stand, where the hungry farmer or traveler can get a meal or lunch at any hour of the day. He also keeps the best brands of cigars and tobacco, candies, nuts, and other confections. All kinds of cold drinks in season. Fresh bakers bread received every other day. When in town call on Mr. Herald for anything you want in his line.

Fred W. Potter

Mr. Fred W. Potter, of the firm of Potter & Baker, feeders and shippers of cattle and hogs, resides at Peabody but makes his headquarters here the greater part of the time looking after the interests of the firm at this end of the line. At the present time they are full feeding about 1, 000 head of cattle, which affords a steady market for much of the corn and rough feed, and for which they pay the farmers a good price. They make a specialty of handling a good grade of stock and are on the market several times a year with choice beef cattle. The money they pay out here annually for feed, help, and supplies of various kinds is fully appreciated by the farmers and businessmen.

Churches

Durham is represented by four church denominations, Methodist, Lutheran, Adventist and German Baptist.

H.C. Funk

The Durham Creamery is one of the substantial industries of this community. The value of such an enterprise cannot be over-estimated. Mr. Funk makes a specialty of the manufacture of pure separator butter, and garantees satisfaction in every instance. He owns his own plant, which is one of the best equipped in the state. When we say that Mr. Funk pays out about $20, 000 a year for butter fat, the reader can form some idea of the importance of such an enterprise to the farmer and businessman of a community. During the month of last June, 20, 000 pounds of butter was shipped from this creamery, all of which found ready market. Mr. Funk is shipping most of the products of the creamery now to Houston and Galveston, Texas. Take good care of the cows and they will take care of you.

L.A. Jones

Mr. Jones arrived in Marion County from Kentucky, thirty-four years ago, and needs no introduction to the people through this medium. He was at one time at the head of the Jones Bros. ranch, one of the largest in the county at that time, being enclosed with thirty seven miles of wire fence. Of late years, he has been in the general merchandise business, where he keeps in stock the best of everything. He buys for cash, gets the benefit of cash discount, which enables him to sell goods as low as the lowest. He makes a specialty of high grade flour, and has built up quite a trade in this line by handling for years the Canton Mills "Golden Sheaf" flour which his customers think is the best grade of flour on the market.

Rock Island Railway

Mr. H. H. Ingalls, a nephew of the late J. J Ingalls, is the agent at this point, having been in the service of the company here since June, 1893. The businessmen and stock and grain shippers all speak in the highest terms of Mr. Ingalls as an agent, and one possessing all the qualities of a real gentleman. The Rock Island is doing an immense business at this point, not only by car lots but by train loads. Sam Smith is the night operator. This is the principal station between Herington and Hutchinson for train orders, so Sam has plenty to occupy his attention during the night. He is a nephew of the late Robert Williams who owned at the time of his death 3, 700 acres of land a few miles east of Tampa, and of which 400 acres is in apple trees just coming into bearing.

Schultz Mercantile Co.

W. F. and S. Schultz are the members of this firm. Fifteen years ago they started in business here in a room 25 by 50 feet. Little by little, and step by step they increased their business and building until they now occupy two rooms 70 feet in length, with basement and a large warehouse for storage purposes. They don't keep anything; they sell everything. Handle all kinds of general merchandise. Their rooms are well lighted and their goods placed where they show off to the best advantage. The proprietors and clerks are attentive to customers and wide awake to the business interests of the establishment. Besides general merchandise the firm handles binders, mowers, buggies and farm implements.

J.E. Wire

There has been quite a noticeable change in the improvement of horses in this community of late years. One reason for this is the call on the market for heavier and better horses. Mr. Wire has been instrumental in bringing about this change. As a breeder of high grade colts, he had gained for himself quite a reputation. This year as usual he will advertise his Gray Norman, a pedigreed horse whose weight is 1800 pounds. Also his Hambletonian driving horse. Both these horses are well known and admired as beauties of the draft and driving kind. There promises to be a good market for several years for good horses at good prices, and the up-to-date farmer will figure on helping to supply this demand. See Mr. Wire in regard to this matter.

Schools

The school facilities here are excellent. The district owns a handsome two-story building of four rooms, and employs three competent teachers. Mr. G. L. Noce is principal, Miss Maud Rice, and Miss Mabel Moulton assistants. The school has an average attendance of about 100 and the pupuls are making very satisfactory advancements.

Badger Lumber Company

J. A. Stephenson is the manager of the Badger Lumber Co. 's interests here. Mr. Stephenson has been with the company since the yard was first started eight years ago. He is a very pleasant gentleman to trade with and is held in popular favor by everybody. The business of the yard has increased from year to year, and the year 1902 closed with a larger volume of business than any of the preceding years. The Badger yard handles everything in the line of building material, including a full stock of heavy and shelf hardware, glass, putty, paints, etc. They also handle coal, brick, sand, cement, etc. Call at the Badger Yard for anything in the way of building material.

N.A. Jones

Mr. Jones came to Marion County thirty-four years ago. He has a neat and well kept barber shop, where you can get a smooth shave or stylish hair cut. He also conducts a land, loan, and insurance business. Loans money on improved farms at low rate of interest. Represents the Aetna and Springfield Insurance Companies, two of the oldest and most popular companies doing business in this country. If you need anything in this line he will gladly give you any information desired.

Public Hall

J. A. Stephenson, one of the public spirited men of the town, last year erected a two-story building, the upper story being finished for public gatherings, and the lower room for store purposes. The building is in keeping with the town.

Durham Hotel

J. F. Eggleston, a big hearted and good natured fellow, is proprietor and manager of this hostlery. The Durham Hotel is located near the depot, and handy to the business portion of the town. Rates are $1 per day and reasonable price to those who want board by the week. He has in connection with his hotel a good livery barn, where the best of service can be had. Eggleston knows every foot of road in every direction and if you want to "get there" or anywhere else get yourself behind one of his teams.

A.C. Davis & Co.

The grain elevator at Durham is owned by A. C. Davis & Co. of Kansas City with Mr. Curtis Bartells as present local manager. The elevator has a capacity of 10,000 bushels of grain and is located near the Rock Island depot. It has been established here since the year 1891 and stands in popular favor with the farmers. They pay the highest cash price for all kinds of grain.

S.H. Smith

Mr. Smith is a harness maker by trade, but at the present time is running a general repair shop. He is somewhat of a genius at anything he turns his hand to and can mend most anything but a broken character. He makes a specialty of harness and shoe repairing, but can repair bicycles, sewing machines, guns, etc., just as well. Call on Smith for your repair work.

Thus ends the story of Durham as it was in 1903 which was written for the purpose of bringing many good people together in their march forward and onward in making Durham a better and bigger town.

Early Settlers

Cameron and Amelia Smith, longtime area residents, on their farm near Durham

Markings of the Santa Fe Trail on building...(see related story).

Early Residents

Cameron and Amelia Smith were long-time residents of the Durham community, living on a farm 1½ miles west of Durham. They saw Durham go from a saloon, dancing, wild Western town to a much quieter and peaceful one.

Cameron had lived in Marion County since 1882, but with the Smith family moved to the Durham farm in 1897. It was still a part of the Crane Ranch. He was very proud of the fact that the house (still standing) was built in Lincoln's era. He had a unique memory and a penchant for story-telling that is still a legend. His outdoor pleasure was hunting coyotes.

Amelia joined him on the farm in 1905 and they continued living there. He passed away in 1964 but Amelia remained on the farm keeping busy with gardening, milking and raising chickens.

She was on the farm until 1982, at that time still going up and down stairs to sleep in a bed that was a feather bed which she refused to give up for a modern mattress.

Amelia had lived long enough in the area to be known as "Grandma Smith" and "the person who would always have for you plenty to eat."

She lived until she celebrated her 100th birthday, passing away in late 1986.

The Jones family in front of their home, about 1911.

Supposedly the first car in Durham, driven by George and Gertrude Thompson.

This scene is on the Cottonwood River, right behind the Valley Hotel, Bill Armstrong and family, 1903.

Immigrants Settled Durham

Many are the Durham residents and descendents whose family roots began in Europe. In fact, some claim that Durham was settled in part, by people whose passage had been guaranteed by German farmers, and were originally residents of the Russian-German border areas of Europe.

While it is not possible to include every family story from Durham's 100 years in this compilation, the following accounts are presented as examples, and a representation of the immigrant settlers who came to this area, and the farm life they led, with work and productivity expected, as well as being a necessity.

Haas

The Jacob Haas family history began when Jacob was born in Stuttgardt (or Saxony, Wittberg) Germany, (sources differ) on December 12, 1859. He came to America at the age of seven, along with an older brother and a younger sister, and their widowed mother. They came to relatives in Iowa in 1867. The mother and sister worked for a farmer; the two boys were "bound out" to another farmer.

According to family recollections, it is said that Jacob worked until he was 16 years old for food, clothing, lodging and schooling. He was clothed poorly, although the man could well afford more, and Jacob suffered much abuse and ridicule for being a "poor boy" in raggedy clothes. He vowed never to be poor again, and this motivated his whole life from then on.

Jacob married Emma Farber, a full-blooded Sioux Indian, in Shelby, Iowa, and went West with gold pieces he had earned, a wagon and some stock. He filed on a quarter of a section, and built a sod house into the bluff forty miles from a town, in the area of Healy, Kansas. Seven children were born at Healy, including Fred, Benjamin, Lewis, Christopher, Lee, Herman and Josephine.

In 1900, Jacob and family came to Durham and settled on a farm one-half mile south and one-half mile east of town. Later the house was moved one-half mile north, next to the railroad track on the southeast edge of the Durham city limits, where he lived with his family until he died. It was there the last child, Walter (Red) was born.

When Jacob came to Kansas he began raising cattle, mostly, and marketed them by driving them to the nearest railroad center. He pastured them on buffalo grass, herded by horseback. Only German was spoken in the home. Among their diet items were rabbits,

Lee and Selma Haas, 1936.

quail and currants, as well as farm produce.

All the children attended school and helped their parents. In Durham, the children went to a Lutheran school, still speaking only German. Jacob then switched them to an English-speaking school, when Chris was about 11 years old, according to recollections.

Jacob was a successful farmer, a man who always found plenty to do on his farm and for anyone else who came around to see him. Leonard (Buster), a grandson, says that he remembers that his grandfather's first greeting when one showed up at his door was, "I've just thought of something you can do for me! Come with me and we'll chop the cockle burrs out of the cornfield." His average rate of pay was 25¢ per day. The family was so weed-conscious that Lewis, a son, trained his dog, Pooch, to pull weeds.

Lee told how his father always kept his sons busy on the farm. Lee said, "One real windy day when us boys were positive that, that day, Dad would be at a loss for something for us to do, we decided to sleep late. But no sooner did we get settled back in bed when we heard Dad call up the stairs, 'come on boys get up. To-day we are going to clean the cistern.'"

Jacob was one who provided well for his entire family and even remembered them after they married and had families of their own. It was nothing for Jacob to butcher seven hogs at one time and give each son and his family a whole hog to put up for the winter meat supply. He also made his own beer and wine.

At one time he owned eight farms, so his wish to avoid poverty was realized. His wife Emma died January 20, 1928 and Jacob died August 2, 1938, leaving a legacy of determination, faith and work.

Kaiser

Charley Kaiser, son of Peter and Katie Kaiser, was born in Neumesser Russia, April 8, 1889. At the age of 16 he settled near Durham, Kansas with his family in 1905.

He married Mary Knaak on March 30, 1913 and to this union six children were born: Martha Gugler, Arthur, Leland, Clinton, Darlene Ehmke, Arlene Armstrong.

Mary Kaiser passed away October 19, 1946. In 1951 he married Rosa Hiebert.

Charley farmed 46 years northwest of Durham and was very active in the community. He retired and moved to Hillsboro until his death, September 23, 1976. Eighty-seven years, five months and fourteen days, a long and fruitful life.

Christiansen

Henry Christiansen was born in 1881 at East Uslea, Denmark. At the age of eight he came to Saline County, Kansas. Soon after he worked at Moore's Ranch. In 1908 Henry married Mattie Grant Garrett and made their home on a quarter of ground purchased from Moore's Ranch.

Their seven children were born at Valley View Farm west of Durham.

After the death of Mattie in 1942, he married Rasina Sandberg in 1945. They moved to Wichita in 1948 and Henry maintained interest in family and livestock.

Irwin Christiansen was born in 1915, attended Pleasant Valley School and Durham High. In 1940, he married Muriel West and they are parents of five children. He has farmed, handled livestock and associated with auction barns since 1945.

Brothers Irwin and Merrill purchased Elm Springs Pasture. The Chisholm Trail passes through this pasture. Scenes from the movie "34th Star" were filmed in this vicinity.

Mr. and Mrs. Henry Christiansen, a Danish influence in Durham.

Dirks

A brief history of the immediate Isaac Dirks family. Grandfather Tobias and Elizebeth Dirks, parents of Isaac Dirks left their ancestrial home in Pawnee Rock, Kansas in the spring of about 1889 for a three day journey to rural Durham along the old Santa Fe wagon trail in a covered wagon with their meager possessions, and a reliable yoke of oxen following to help pull them through the mirey places.

They established their homestead and endured the pioneer days, even the fearful leaping prarie fires which appeared like the World On Fire! But Grandfather Tobias and sons saved their homestead buildings by plowing a few furrows around it. As pioneers, they broke the prairie sod with a wooden beam sulky plow and harvested their first wheat with a scythe and a threshing flail and became well established in a few years.

In about the year of 1902, Isaac, the eldest son, was united in marriage to Rachel Koehn and to this union five sons and five daughters were born: Jake, Hanna, Irvin, Tobias, Mary, Leona, Gust, Irene, Martha and Melvin.

They were all nurtured in the old time religion of Grace, loving care and disciplined living and all became self sufficient law-abiding citizens. Jake, Irvin, Tobias and Gust are graduates of our former high school in Durham. Jake was a skilled mechanic, working for Beech Air Craft, in Wichita. He designed a precision instrument for the moon modular which played its part in landing the men on the moon. Irvin is a skillful, well-manered carpenter, well known in Durham and community. Tobias became a custom worker, merchant man and manufacturer of the Hen Dandy Brand Poultry feeds which are still being sold in Durham. Gust served in the US Army and also worked at Beech Craft in Wichita and Melvin became an accomplished electrician in the Hesston Manufacturing Corp.

The Isaac Dirks daughters; Hannah, Mary, Leona, Irene and Martha all became devoted Christian mothers, keepers of home and family.

The married names of Isaac Dirks daughters are: Hannah – Mrs. Dan Koehn, Mary – Mrs Joe Unruh (deceased 1986), Leona – Mrs. William Koehn, Irene – Mrs. Dale Rhodes, Martha – Mrs. Dayton Unruh.

And now, the entire Isaac Dirks family is at large; has fond memories of Durham, its colorful history, its enduring kindly character and we cherish our great country; America.

"Long may our land be bright with freedom's holy light; Protect us by thy might, Great God, our King!

Isaac and Rachel Dirks.

Frick Family

Jacob Frick, born May 7, 1844 in Huck, Russia, immigrated to America in July 1876 with his wife Elizabeth (Zitterkopf) and six children.

They arrived at Peabody, Kansas and were taken to their destination by old settlers, behind a span of oxen. Jacob and his family settled five miles southwest of Hillsboro, paying $2. 50 an acre for land. From here he walked to Woodbine where he worked and earned enough money to buy a milk cow.

In 1883, Jacob purchased 260 acres of land east of Durham from Henry and Mary Geis for $800. Later his son, Ben, farmed this land and it is now being farmed by Ben's son, Melvin, and grandson, Curtis.

The house in which Melvin and Geraldine (Christiansen) Frick live was built in 1897. According to Melvin's father, Ben, the house was built when Ben was eight years old. Many stories have been told of happenings that occurred at that home.

Jacob and Elizabeth Frick had 15 children. Three children died in infancy. With eight sons; John, George (Phillip), Conrad, Jacob, Alex, Abe, Karl (Charles), and Ben, and four daughters; Katremage (Katherine), Anna, Sadie, and Mollie, there were numerous tales told that would be most interesting. There were memories of the hardships, privations and happiness that accompany the raising of a large family in these pioneering days, but Jacob and Elizabeth being true Christians, left a legacy of courage, cheerfulness, patience, hard work and prosperity to their many descendants.

The Frick descendants living in the Durham area are: Melvin and Geraldine Frick, son of Ben and Anna (Socolofsky) Frick. They have two sons, one daughter and seven grandchildren. Clinton and Josephine Frick, son of Abe and Hanna (Socolofsky) Frick have four daughters and six grandchildren. Monroe and Alice Frick, son of Abe and Hannah (Socolofsky) Frick, one son, one daughter and five grandchildren. Earl and Margaret Frick, son of Conrad and Sophie (Steinle) Frick and Linel Frick, son of Alex and Lula (Schlehuber) Frick.

Ben Frick with his team at Frick farm.

Zimmerman

Eva And Her Magic Basket

Mrs. Adam (Eva) Zimmerman was a mid-wife, in early Durham. She was called to help the neighborhood ladies when their babies were born.

For this she was highly respected, and, having been trained to help, she was in great demand in the area without doctors readily available.

She often stayed a few days to help care for the new baby, mother, and the other members of the family after the birth. She always took her "special" or "magic" basket with her to help, if the newborn baby had any problems.

This "special" basket came to America with her family, the Garretts, when they immigrated to the United States in the late 1800's.

Eva's grandfather was a basket weaver and made the basket she used, woven from twigs from trees in their home area of Germany.

It was thought that a sick baby placed in this basket would get well faster and have less chance of having convulsions.

Mrs. Zimmerman had calls from neighbors and friends to bring the basket when their small children were sick. With her nursing skills and the "magic basket," many babies recovered.

Mrs. Zimmerman was also known throughout the community for her butter. The butter she made was sold at the Becker Mercantile in Durham and was said to be the best butter around. "If you wanted to buy Zimmerman butter you had to get to Becker's early Saturday morning before they sold out," folks said.

Adam and Eva had 10 children, all raised in the Durham community They were: Mary, Lydia, Mollie (Keller), Sam, Anna (Helfley) Julia (Geisler), Jake, Adam, Martha and Dave.

The magic basket has been passed on to Eva's granddaughter, Morene (Mrs. R. K.) Miller of McPherson.

The basket.

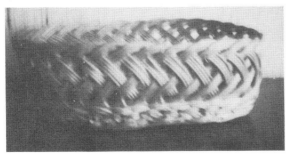

Mr. and Mrs. Adam Zimmerman, Sr., immigrant settlers in the Durham area. Mrs. Eva Zimmerman, a midwife, brought her "magic basket", woven by her family in the old country, with her when doing midwife work, to help soothe colicky babies. It was thought that the basket helped foster recovery of sick little ones.

George and Elizabeth Hein.

Emanuel and Katie Hein.

Hein

Unlike many of the families that came to the Durham area directly from Europe, George Hein, having originally come from Russia, brought his family to Durham by way of Sutton, Nebraska.

Apparently attracted by land opportunities, George arrived in the Durham area sometime in the late 1800's with his wife and four sons. He started farming east of Durham. After the passing of his first wife, George helped to bring the Schafer family to Durham when he sent for and married a widow from Russia by the name of Schafer. She came with her three children, Jacob, Katie, and Phillip Schafer. Family lore holds that upon arrival in New York, one of the children became sick and required hospitalization. The little group ran out of money due to the child's medical needs. It was apparently necessary to forward more funds to the travelers so they could complete the trip to Durham. One can imagine the feelings of these immigrants upon arrival, having experienced such a struggle to reach Durham.

One of George's sons, Emanuel, married Katie Schafer Hein, one of the widow Schafer's children. He built a large farm home three miles east of Durham and had six sons and two daughters. Of those eight children, only Paul is still living.

To those six sons, only four sons were born to carry on the family name. They are: Eugene; Kenneth; LeeRoy and Robert. LeeRoy still lives in Durham, and has operated an auto repair business there since 1951. His two sons also live in Durham. Dave is a partner in both the repair shop and the family farm, which has been passed down from LeeRoy's father, Jake. Jim is a teacher and has two children, Eric and Andrea.

The Emanuel Hein home, built in 1906, east of Durham.

Jones-Bartells

By Frances May (Jones) West

Perhaps very few people in our county today have a richer store of early day history of our county, town, and township than I.

Not only is my mother, Mrs. Laura Bartells Jones, an early pioneer of Durham, but my father, the late Charles W. Jones, an early pioneer of Marion County.

My father was born October 1, 1861 in Carroll County, Kentucky, near a little town by the name of Ghent. He was one of the youngest of eight brothers and one sister.

In the spring of the year 1869, he with his father, mother, brothers and sister, started from Ghent, Kentucky, to Kansas City, Missouri, on a steam boat. They had first class passage which cost their father one hundred nineteen dollars for the fare, including board and room for the entire family.

It took three weeks in those days to make the trip. They came down the Ohio River to the Mississippi, then up the Missouri River to Kansas City.

From Kansas City to Junction City, Kansas was by the way of the Union Pacific Railroad, a new railroad which only extended to Abilene, Kansas, at that time.

They arrived in Junction City, Kansas, March 1st, 1869. Their father rented a house in Junction City for the family to live in while he went to look for a place for them to make a home.

He had planned before leaving Kentucky to settle in the Solomon Valley of Kansas but upon reaching Junction City learned from the settlers there that only three weeks before the entire white settlement of the valley had been massacred by the Indians. It was then he knew he must find a different place in which to make his new home in Kansas. With his son, he started off on foot. In one month he came back in wagons to move them to a little log cabin with a dirt roof which stood on a 160 acre railroad claim two and one half miles northeast of Marion. Here they lived about two years.

Uncle Jimmy Jones, my father's brother told about their home.

"When we first came to Kansas there were only two stores and one hotel in Marion Centre. Dr. J. N. Rogers owned the drug store and he called it "The Everything Store." This store was also the post office. All merchandise was hauled from Junction City. We went to mill at Council Grove or Cedar Point and had our wheat or corn ground. Father made his own sorghum. Our principal meat was wild game and buffalo.

My brothers and a neighbor would go out west where Hutchinson is now and kill enough young buffalo to supply us with meat for a year. They would take a double box wagon out there and fill it with the hindquarters after they were thoroughly cooled with the hides on. There was not a bridge in the county and no fences. ''

In the meantime, the Santa Fe railroad secured a land grant from the government which took every other section of land along its route; thus their land was taken through the grant, so their father took a homestead on Mud Creek eleven miles northwest of Marion

Here, on the farm on Mud Creek, the family lived until their father and youngest brother, Joe, was taken by death; old age forced their mother to leave the farm to a renter and spend her few remaining years among the children, but making her permanent stay with her son, Jimmy and family, near Durham where she died.

Soon after my father and my maternal grandfather, Dr. Bartells, met in Funk City, my father came to Durham to make his home.

He, with his three brothers, Al, Jim and Joe and a neighbor, John Galreau fenced a thirty seven mile cattle ranch with a three wire barbwire fence. All the post holes were dug by hand. This ranch was one of the largest in the county at that time. The beginning of this ranch was about one mile southwest of Durham and extended as far west as Waldeck. These pastures were filled each summer with cattle from not only Marion County but Dickinson and Morris Counties as well. The ranch was known as the Jones Brothers Ranch of which my father was owner and manager.

Later he sold this ranch and went into the general merchandise business, this was of short duration however for when the Cherokee strip opened in Oklahoma, he went near Lamont Oklahoma and took up a claim.

After living there for five years he returned to Durham where he married my mother, Laura Bartells Jones, and both went back to Oklahoma to live.

They stayed there only one year and returned to Durham where my father once more went into the merchandise business. This trade he followed for over forty-five years and it was only when his health failed that he was forced to give up the trade he loved so well.

I have often heard him remark, "I encountered flood after flood and one fire that completely broke me but nothing could ever keep me from going back until I could no longer get there. ''

He spent over seventy-six years in Marion County before he died. Over fifty-five years were spent in the Durham vicinity.

During the eight and one half years of his invalidism, he looked forward with joy for the next day to come which would bring new hope, more friends, and visiting. This is where I grew to enjoy the stories and history of the past – this was an education in itself. I have always longed to know as many in Marion County as he did but alas, as he said shortly before his passing, "I am getting so I know few people of the county anymore all I know have their names written on the headstones in the cemetery. '' – So it is with each generation very few know those of the past until finally we are a complete stranger once more even though we spend a lifetime in one vicinity.

Willie Popp held by his mother.

Four generations of Durham residents from left, Conrad Popp, 1848 to 1926, Ralph Popp, 1922 to present, Edward N. Popp, 1892 to 1947, and William H. Popp, 1870 to 1950.

Emil and Gertie Schwemmer.

Solomon and Lottie Geis.

Sunday school pupils about 1924.

A 1916 photo of the Fricks, Mr. and Mrs. C.D. Frick, Millie, Viola Earlean and Earl.

Selma Fritch and Ed Becker.

Mrs. Savage at home on her porch. The mother of Maude Savage, the lady was known for her fondness of pipe smoking on her porch.

First Newspaper

The first newspaper ever to be published in Durham, was The Durham Journal. Volume I, Number I was published Thursday, September 13, 1906. Editor and Publisher, J. F. Hillman. Subscription price $1 per annum in advance. (Issued Weekly)

The editor of the Canton Pilot wrote, quote:

"The editor spent Monday in that thriving little town of Durham 18 miles north-east of Canton. J. F. Hillman, of Alden, Kansas will soon launch the Durham Journal. The citizens are now after a flour mill and prospects are good for them to get a hundred barrel mill this fall. The businessmen of Durham realized the value of a newspaper so they gave Mr. Hillman a $100 bonus and contracted for $600 worth of advertising the first year, and many of the citizens subscribed for five or ten copies of the new paper to send to friends and relatives. If the paper is not a success it will be the editor's fault."

Phillip Warren and C. W. Jones were the first butchers in town.

In the early summer of 1888, the first Sunday School was organized, and was held in the Rock Island depot until the school house was completed. The first superintendent was Birch Bowyer.

The Samuel Schultz Mercantile Co. was established in 1890 and is in business at this writing.

The Badger Lumber Co. was established in 1892 with J. A. Stephenson as manager, and is still doing business in that capacity.

C. W. Jones opened a general store in 1892 and is doing business at the present time.

H. C. Funk owned and operated the first creamery with no change in the management up to the present time.

In 1898 N. A. Jones opened up the first barber shop and had been running the business ever since.

D. B. Kraus and Adam Huenergardt opened a general store in 1897 and in 1900 G. Meschke & Co. purchased the stock and are doing business at this writing.

G. W. Thompson built and conducted a drug store and sold out a few years later and the business is now conducted by R. W. Powers.

In the summer of 1889 the Durham Park Cemetery was surveyed and platted.

Borton and Lasure purchased the blacksmith shop of M. L. Doberstein in 1898 and are now engaged in that business.

Dr. Chas. Kaiser opened an office in 1900 and later sold to Dr. Hayward.

J. M. Clubine & Co. established an implement and grain business in 1902 and are conducting the same at this writing.

In 1903 T. J. Parry opened a confectionery and cigar store.

In October, 1903, Rural Poute No. 1 was established with Nicholas A. Jones as carrier and Walter Armstroing, substitute.

Mrs. C. R. Shaner opened a millinery store in 1904.

W. D. Armstrong erected a two-story hotel and a livery barn in 1902, the latter being burned to the ground in March, 1906, but was rebuilt at once.

On May 28, 1903 all records were broken for high water from the Cottonwood River. The water came up to the alley of lot 13, block 14.

In April 1904 the cornerstone of the First M. E. Church (North) was laid and the following November the church was dedicated, with J. F. Severance as pastor. In the same year the Severance Chapter of the Epwoth League was organized.

In 1904 the Durham State Bank was chartered.

The State Elevator was erected in 1904.

In 1905 Ole Comstock operated the first bakery.

Andrew Lasure erected the first building in town of cement blocks. The blocks were manufactured by Marion Smith.

An account from the Durham Journal September 20, 1906

Incorporation Move

Last Monday evening at 8:00, about 25 citizens of Durham met at John Clubine's hall to consider the question of incorporation our enterprising town.

The meeting was called to order by T. B. Armstrong, after which they elected J. A. Stephenson Chairman and George Hildreth secretary. After the Chairman stated the purpose of the meeting a motion was made by T. B. Armstrong that we petition for incorporation. This was followed by a short discussion and then the voting which resulted in 19 votes for and one against. It was moved and seconded that the Chairman appoint a committee of two to circulate petition, and T. B. Armstrong and O. Comstock were appointed. Moved and seconded that a committee of three be appointed to frame a petition. The motion carried and they elected George Hildreth, W. D. Armstrong and R. W. Powers. Moved and seconded that the meeting adjourn, carried.

George Hildreth
Secretary

Incorporation Notice

September 20, 1906
(To the Honorable Board of County Commissioners)

We, the citizens and electors of the town of Durham, Marion County, Kansas, believing that we have the required population, and that it is to the best interest of this town and surrounding country, pray for articles of incorporation into a city of the Third Class with the following boundaries; to wit:

Beginning 230 feet east of the northeast corner the school grounds of district number 57, in Durham at section line, thence running west along north boundary of said school grounds 610 feet, thence south 215 feet to center of Eighth street, west 380 feet, thence south 430 feet thence west 1040 feet; thence south 2190 feet, thence east 2030 feet parallel with south line of Second street to section line, thence north 2835 feet along section line to point of beginning.

R. W. Powers
W. D. Armstrong
Geo. Hildreth
Committee

Durham Incorporated

First published in the Durham Journal, October 11, 1906

Now on this, the 6th day of October, 1906, at the regular October session of the Board of County Commissioners of Marion County, Kansas, for said year, the matter of the petition of R. W. Powers et al came regularly on to be heard by the Board, praying for the incorporation of the town of Durham, Marion County, Kansas, as a city of the Third Class and the Board after hearing the evidence in support of said petition and after consideration thereof, finds that said petition is duly signed by a majority of the electors of said town of Durham, and also finds that said petition was duly published in the Durham Journal, a weekly newspaper published and printed in said town of Durham, once a week, for three consecutive weeks, the first publication being on the 20th day of September 1906, and the last publication thereof on the 4th day of October, 1906, and the Board further finds and is satisfied from the evidence that the majority of taxable inhabitants of said town of Durham is in favor of the incorporation of said town, and that the prayer of said petitions for such incorporation of said town is reasonable and also find that the inhabitants of said town is not more than 2, 000.

Whereupon it is ordered, considered adjudged and declared by the Board that the prayer of said petitioners be and is hereby granted and it is further considered ordered, adjudged and declared by said Board that said town of Durham be and is hereby incorporated as a city of Third Class by and under the name and style of the City of Durham and that the metes and bounds thereof are hereby designated as follows to wit:

Beginning 230 feet east of the north-east corner of the school grounds of school District No. 57, in Durham, Marion County, Kansas, and at the section line at said point, thence running west along the north boundary of said school grounds 610 feet, thence south 215 feet to the center of Eighth Street, thence west 380 feet, thence south 430 feet, thence west 1040 feet, then south 2190 feet, thence east 2030 feet parallel with the south line of Second Street, in the town of Durham to the east line of Section 17, Township 18, Range Two in said Marion County, Kansas, thence north on said section line 2835 feet to place of beginning.

It is further ordered by the Board that an election be held in said City of Durham at the Township building therein, on the 23rd day of October, 1906, for the purpose of electing in said City the following City officers to wit: Mayor, Police Judge, and five Councilmen, and it is further ordered that W. D. Armstrong, Gus Meschke and John Stephenson, three qualified electors of said City be and are hereby appointed to act as Judges of said election, and that N. A. Jones and

T. B. Armstrong, two electors of said City be and are hereby appointed to act as Clerks of said election, and that J. M. . Clubine, C. R. Shaner, and G. W. Thompson, three electors of said City be and are hereby appointed to act as a Board of Canvassers to Canvas the returns of said election and it is further ordered that the proceedings concerning the incorporation of said City of Durham and the ordering of said election for the election of City officers be published in the Durham Journal, a newspaper printed and published in said City of Durham, Marion County, Kansas, and that said publication be made at least one week before the date of the election hereby ordered.

State of Kansas, ss
County of Marion,

I, D. D. McIntosh, County Clerk in and for Marion County, Kansas do hereby certify that the above is a true, complete and correct transcript of the findings and orders made by the County Commissioners of Marion County, Kansas, incorporating the City of Durham, Marion County, Kansas.

In witness whereof, I have hereunto subscribed my name attested by my seal this 9th day of October, 1906.

D. D. McIntosh,
County Clerk

PUBLICATION NOTICE

[First published in The Durham Journal November 22, 1906]

At a meeting of the City Council of the City of Durham, Kansas, held at the township building in the City of Durham, Marion County, Kansas, November 13th, 1906, the following ordiances were passed by said Council and ordered published:

Be it ordained by the Mayor and Councilmen of the City of Durham:

That the grade of Douglas Avenue shall be sixteen (16) inches above the corner stone placed in the corner of intersection of Sixth Street and Douglas Avenue; thence a decline of two (2) inches north, to intersections of Seventh Street and Douglas Avenue; thence commencing at corner stone at intersection of Sixth Street and Douglas Avenue, a decline of eight (8) inches south to center of in-

tersection of Fifth Street and Douglas Avenue; thence a decline of eleven (11) inches south, from center of intersection of Fifth Street and Douglas Avenue to the Railroad right-of-way; thence a gradual incline from this point to the main track of railroad.

C. R. Shaner,
City Clerk

At a meeting of said Council, of said City, held November 20, 1906, the following ordinance was passed and ordered published:

Be it ordained by the Mayor and Councilmen of the City of Durham:

That the sidewalks on both sides of Douglas Avenue from depot platform to intersection of Sixth Street and Douglas Avenue shall be eight (8) feet wide, including the curbing, which shall be three (3) inches thick, and extending below surface of earth three (3) inches; and said sidewalk shall be made of concrete, consisting of one (1) part of crushed rock or gravel, and shall be three (3) inches thick with a coat consisting of one (1) part cement and three (3) parts of sand, one half (½) inch thich. Said sidewalks shall extend five (5) feet beyond intersections of Fourth, Fifth, and Sixth Streets and Douglas Avenue at all corners. Said sidewalk shall be completed by October 1st, 1907.

From "The Durham Journal, May 30, 1907
There was another record breaking freeze on the night of the 26th.

Special No. 3
For Friday and Saturday
May 31 and June 1, 1907
By G. Meschke & Co. , Durham, Kansas

500 yards Colored Lawns
Worth 12¢ and 15¢ per yard . . . . Special price – 9¢
200 yards Fancy Dress Ginghams,
Worth 10¢ and 12¢ . . . . Special price – 7½¢
3 dozen Towels with colored border
Worth 18¢ and 20¢ . . . . Special price – 12½¢
One lot of Embroidery
Ranging from 7¢ to 10¢ per yard . . . . Special price – 5¢
3 lbs can Sugar Beets
. . . . Special price – 11¢
1 lb can Standard Corn
. . . . Special price – 6¢

Follow the crowd and you will find the place
PS Don't forget to ask for coupons on our
Standard Talking Machine

Another interesting advertisment from "The Durham Journal, May 30, 1907.

The following well known farmers and stock feeders have purchased and fed "The Iowa Hog and Cattle Powder. "

Emil Smith, Jacob Guhr, Charles Hoffman, J. J. Friessen, J. A. Schiffuer, I. B. Garrett, John Frants, George David, John Frick, W. M. Schlehuber, W. E. Carter, Henry Krom, Hugh Fritch, Tobias Dirks, B. P. Jantz, Jacob Miller, James Unruh, C. P. Unruh, John F. Balse, D. D. Wadel, John Holcom and Issac Dirks.

The Durham Tribune

The Durham Tribune was established Sept. 2, 1915 by the Tribune Publishing Co. , R. H. Mc Affe publisher. The press was brought from Florence to Durham by A. E. Updike. It continued to be published by different editors until it was moved to Tampa, November 25, 1920, under the name of The Tampa Times. , R. E. Campbell was the publisher.

Volume 1, Number 1 September 1915

Wadel Brothers new building is nearing completion and will be one of the finest in this part of the country. The lower floor will be occupied as a garage and machine shop and the second floor as a hall and some business offices.

N. A. Jones will erect a cement block building on his lot on the east side of Main Street about 25 x 40. It will join Wadel Brothers new building.

From Durham Tribune May 4, 1916

[Durham owned their own electric light plant at this time. The machinery was in Wadel's garage. The power plant was not turned on until almost dark and only run until midnight.]

Here are the following electric lights and prices:
Residence, 60 watt lames, minimum charge $1, not to exceed 2 lamps; 3 lamps $1. 25, 5 lamps $1. 50, 7 lamps $2. Each additional one or two lamps, 50 cents.

Residence, 40 watt lamps, minimum charge $1, not to exceed 3 lamps, 4 or 5 lamps $1. 25, 6 or 7 lamps $1. 50, 8 or 9 lamps $2 and each additional one or two lamp at 25 cents.

Business, minimum charge $2 per month, 400 watts allowed; 500 watts $2. 50, 600 wats $2. 75, 800 watts $3. 25, 900 watts $3. 50, 1000 wats $3. 75.

Main Street of Durham, about 1916.

Durham had a Fourth of July celebration and so many lights were strung up on various booths etc. that when a side show turned on their lights in their tent that it was 'too much' for the engine, breaking it down. The entire town was thrown into darkness bringing the celebration to a speedy end.

4th of July Celebrations ... Unity among people, devotion to national goals and respect for the flag.

Adolf Ingram Frantz, who attended Durham grade school and called himself a former plowboy, relates in his book, *Water From The Well*, the Fourth of July celebrations in Durham.

It would begin at sunrise when the blacksmith, Gustave Moritz, detonated a series of torpedoes on his anvil. Daytime activities were picnics, baseball games, bicycle and sack races, merry-go-round and the medicine man with his cure-alls. The main event was the mid-morning rally at the open end of Badger Lumber Company. There was a band concert featuring "Stars and Stripes Forever," introduction of celebraties and out of town guests including once governor Edward Hoch. Crowds cheered long and loud. As darkness fell many firecrackers were set off.

This poem was published in the Durham Tribune newspaper, September 2, 1915. This was Volume I, first edition, of this little newspaper, which served Durham a short time before going out of business. The poem's author is unknown.

Our Own Little Town

There are fancier towns than our little old town,
There are towns that are bigger than this;
And the people who live in the tinier town
All the city contentment may miss.
There are things you can see in the wealthier town
That you can't in a town that is small —
And yet, up or down,
There is no other town
Like your own little town after all.
It may be that the street through the heart of the town
Isn't long, isn't wide, isn't straight;
But the neighbors you know in your own little town
With a welcome your coming await.
On the glittering streets of the glittering town,
By the palace and pavement and wall,
In the midst of the throng,
You will long, you will long,
For your own little town, after all.
It was here by the stile in your own little town
Father courted your mother, a maid;
It was hear in the vale in your own little town
That he builded a home in the shade.
It was here on the hill in your own little town
That the school and the book you recall —
Every step of the way,
So your memories say,
It's your own little town, after all.
For it isn't by money your measure a town,
Or the miles that its border extends,
For the best things you gather, whatever the town
Are contentment, enjoyment and friends.
If you live and you work and you trade in your town
In spite of the fact it is small,
You'll find that the town
That your own little town
Is the best little town after all.

Memories of the 1930's

"Durham has always been home," says Leon Fast, 1940 Durham High School grad, now of Lake Charles, Louisiana. That's why he's coming back to Durham for the Centennial celebration and why he was the first person to mail in his order for the Centennial book.

Now retired from Owen Chemical, Leon fondly recalls his growing up years in Durham. His father and mother, William C., a Rock Island employee and Laura Fast, moved their family to Durham in the late 1920's when Leon was five.

Leon recalls a favorite pasttime of his pals was to go out to Marble Rock on a sunny weekend. Located 1½-2 miles west of town, and ¼ mile out in a pasture, it was a natural formation of rocks that looked like an eisenglas shelf. "We kids liked to sit under this shelf and watch the minnows in the stream. We also hunted for arrowheads and wanted to dig up the jewelry that was fabled to be buried under the Santa Fe Trail monument at Lost Springs," he said.

"Durham has always been full of friendly people," Leon said. He recalls one of his best friends was Lupe Rosas, the son of a section hand on the Rock Island. The two friends went through school together from 5th grade on and they even entered the Air Force at the same time. Both of these families were part of the railroad people of Durham and lived south of the tracks in special housing made from railroad cars.

Leon's father's job was to maintain the pump at the Cottonwood River to supply water and to keep the railroad's water tower filled. Leon remembers going with his father many times and recalls the huge task of keeping the water tower filled.

"It was a steam-driven suction operation," Fast said, of the pump. "The pump was close to the water and you'd have to build up a good head of steam in the boiler to run the pump and suck the water right up to the tower. There was a guage on the outside showing the water level. In the summertime, we'd sometimes have to fill it two times a day. It usually took between 3 and 5 hours to fill, depending on the train traffic."

When cinders later caught the tower on fire, about four or five feet were burned off the top and, "we just used what we had left," he said. Later, diesel engines made the water tower obsolete.

Leon remembers the difficult times of the 1930's. "When the Depression came, it chopped people's wages in half or even down to a third. In the summertime, a bunch of us young guys would help the farmers shock wheat or pull tractors. We earned 50¢ a day and were glad for it. In the winter, I'd hunt rabbit, too. I'd get 3¢ each. I could make a little money that way and it was also food for the table. We never went hungry, but things were sure sparse."

With two sisters still living in Herington, Leon gets the chance to go through Durham and catch up on things every once in a while. He often stops to see Earl Frick and they reminisce about those early days.

When Leon was just in grade school and Earl was a little older, Earl would let Leon drive his horse and buggy down to the Leon's house, south of the track.

"I'd wear a cowhide robe and when it was snowing, I'd make like I was having a big trip. Earl reminded me of the time the buggy got away, though," Leon says with a laugh. "Earl would wait for me at my house and when I'd show up, he'd take his buggy and go on home. This particular time, though, the horse went on home by himself. I guess he knew where to go. Earl had to walk home, and his horse and buggy were there waiting for him."

One of Leon's most vivid memories is of the 1929 flood. The Fasts' were sleeping in a section house.

"The depot agent came down to our place to warn us, and when we opened the door, I still recall he had a red light in his hand, and you could see cakes of foam floating by on the water. He took us up to the depot.

"I still remember watching out the door of the depot and seeing a rat float by on a grain door. He didn't know what was happening. And there were lots of animals lost then, too. I saw a pig in trouble down by the bridge, but no one could rescue the pig."

"Lots of people made it up to higher ground at the depot. At daylight, they had a big truck come through, and hauled us all up the hill and they spread us all out to stay at different places. People just took us in. I stayed with the Roy Davis family up on the hill. The water was up quite awhile, then it took a long time to clean it all up afterwards."

The family had come to Canada, and lived in Hugoton and Bucklin before moving to Herington from Durham in the 1940's.

His parents passed away in 1967 and 1972, and are buried in Herington.

"When I get back, I always go visit a big old Cottonwood tree my dad and I planted after the 1929 flood. It was only about 1 inch in diameter then, now it's about 3 feet in diameter. We planted it south of the tracks, about 25-30 feet. I call it 'Dad's and My Cottonwood.' I really like seeing it. And that's what it is about Durham, too. It's nice memories. It's my roots."

The Faith

Churches in Durham Area

Trinity Lutheran Church, Durham, Kansas, present day.

The churches of Durham came along right with the start of the town, and remain as centers for local faith, and worship, many of them nearly ready to celebrate their own centennials.

Although the congregations are not large, they are important and significant memberships, and very dedicated to their own denominations.

While the Baptist Church lays claim to being "first" in the area, the Methodists were close behind. It was apparently the Methodists who organized an early-day Sunday School.

In the early summer of 1888, the first Sunday School was organized and held in the Rock Island depot waiting room until the school house was completed. The Methodist minister from Canton, Kansas, would come each Sunday to deliver his sermon, returning to his home in the evening by a 5:00 train. The Sunday school superintendent was Birch Bowyer.

The First Church of God was established in 1897, with meetings held in a school until the church was completed in 1911. (See separate story).

The First Methodist Episcopal Church, the third church in the Durham community, was dedicated in November, 1904. (See program on separate page). The Methodist Church was later disbanded and the building taken for another use.

In 1913, the Seventh-Day Adventists established a church in Durham, although they had been meeting in a rural location for several years prior to that time. Their group was numbered at about 100 at the time of the church's establishment.

The Seventh Day Adventist Church, located across from the old Red Brick School, was torn down about three years ago and those members joined with the Hillsboro congregation.

The Trinity Lutheran Church was the last organized in Durham in 1920. This was a German Lutheran congregation that used the German language in services, finally compromising to alternate Sundays in German and English during the 1940's, and eventually changing to all English, as the German-speaking elderly membership had passed away, and new members' needs had to be met. A windstorm blew the steeple and bell down in the 1960's, after which the practice of tolling of the bell at the death of a member, ceased. The Trinity Lutheran Church has been remodeled and updated in recent years.

The Lutheran Church dedication.

DEDICATION OF THE FIRST METHODIST EPISCOPAL CHURCH
DURHAM, KANSAS
SUNDAY, NOVEMBER 13, 1904
F.G. Severance - Pastor
J.A. Davis - Presiding Elder

(The following was taken from one of the programs used at that dedication).

Morning Service at 10:30
Doxology - Invocation
Scripture - Psalm 84 - Hymn 862
Prayer - Scripture - Anthem
Sermon - Rev. J. A. Davis
Hymn 865 - Benediction

Afternoon Service 2:00
Voluntary - Hymn 871

Prayer - Anthem - Report of Trustees
Address by J. A. Davis

Finance - Dedication Service
Hymn 248 - Benediction

Evening Service 7:30
Song Service - Prof. George Hildreth
Sermon - Conservation Service

Taken before 1933, the Methodist Church, before it was sold to C.W. Savage to build a house.

Church Of God Congregation.

As all things have a beginning, so the Church of God at Durham had its beginnig. This beginning was brought about by Reverend Ferdinand Schweiger. Rev. Schweiger received a call from Hillsboro, Kansas in May 1897, where he held a few meetings in a private home and in a country schoolhouse. From there George Hein took him to Durham where he met the Fricks, Jacob and Con. From Durham they went to the Sokolousky Schoolhouse near Tampa, Kansas, where services were conducted from June 10 to 20 in 1897. The German Bible Class were born out of services held in the Merry-Go-Round Schoolhouse until 1911. Fourteen years after its start, this small group built the church building in 1911.

The members of this class were the following: Mr. Grentz, Sr. , Mr. and Mrs. Jacob Frick, Mr. and Mrs. R. S. Frick, Mr. and Mrs. George Hein, Mr. and Mrs. Eberhardt, George Hass, Mr. and Mrs. Henry Grentz, Mr. and Mrs. Henry Fisher, Mr. and Mrs. Con Frick and Mrs. Jake Frick. These faithful members graduated from the schoolhouse because of lack of space and built a house of worship in Durham, Kansas.

Those on the picture of the church being built in 1911 are the men from this German class. Mr. Jacob Miller is also on the picture. He is the sixth one standing in line and his son, Adam Miller, the 11 year old boy at the end of the line. Jacob Miller is the father of Adam, Sam, Dan and John Miller and Christina, Sarah, Rachel, Elma, Hannah and Lillian Miller and grandfather of LaVern and Floyd Miller. George Hein is great-grandfather of LaVern Miller. Children and grandchildren are still worshipping and holding services in 1987 in this building. (W. H. Popp also was a founding member)

Church of God after being moved to Durham. See related story.

The First Baptist Church, in its country location

The Baptist Ladies Aid, Durham, Kansas. Do you know the year and the faces?

BAPTIST CHURCH

The Durham Baptist Church can lay claim to being the first organized religious group in the Durham area, having gathered a handful of the faithful to services in the Geis school, northwest of Durham, in 1888.

According to a history of the First Baptist Church of Durham, (which this congregation later grew to be) carried in the 70th anniversary bulletin of the church in October 1966, this earliest group were called "The Cottonwood Brethren", and were a station of the German Baptist Church of Hillsboro.

Some of the families attending were: several different Geis families, the parents of Solomon and Ed Geis, the parents of Jack and Art Geis, and the Peter Geis family, also the parents of Isaac Lorenz. The Weber, Unruh, Betz, Dumler, Penner and Wahl families were among those first attending.

In 1893, a hard blow came to this group, as that was the year Oklahoma was "opened up to settlers" and quite a number left to make the "run for new land", although a loss to the church's beginning, it was the means to start a number of Baptist churches in Oklahoma.

The mother church of this group, the Hillsboro Baptist Church, kept watch over it, and a trip by horse and buggy to meet with the Hillsboro people for business reasons was "no small task". So an attempt was made in 1896 to form a separate unit.

On November 15, 1896, the church was officially recorded by the state association, and for the first three years was served by Brother John Kohrs, followed by Brother Dalke and Brother John Pankratz, among others.

By the time Reverend F. W. Socolofsky arrived, there was a need to build a special house of worship, and in 1910, plans were made to build a new church and was completed the next year.

Until 1914, there was no full time pastor, until the call went to Reverend Geissler, and he helped organize the Ladies Mission Society, and give more sustenance.

During early 1920's, the congregation considered and then begam the task of moving the church and parsonage to the city of Durham. Work started in the fall of 1924, and was completed and dedicated the next May, in 1925.

According to records, "the Depression hit hard, but during those hard times, records show a remarkable increase in membership."

In 1942, Reverend H. L. Smith began his ministry, and by now the congregation had begun to slowly change over from the use of the German language to English. The name of the church was also changed, from German Baptist, to The First Baptist Church of Durham, during that time.

Reverend Henry Baerg of Tabor College accepted a call in 1947 and served until May 1953.

New additions were added during this time, and remodeling took place. At the time of the 1966 celebration, the membership stood at 152.

The Friedenstahl Mennonite Church is another early-day congregation which has seen an update of its facilities, with the abandonment of the old frame structure, and the purchase of the former Grand Central school building, which was converted to be a new house of worship. Renamed the Central Heights Mennonite, the church is also located north of Durham. The old church building still stands.

Friedenstahl-Central Heights

In August 1899, a group of brethren got together to form a church, and in Sept. 1899, a constitution was drawn up with 33 members. In 1901 the group was named the North Lehigh Church, but in 1902 the name was changed to Friedenstahl Church.

A building was completed and dedicated in 1907, and used until 1972, undergoing remodeling in 1944.

In 1972, the church group purchased the unused Grand Central School and remodeled it for a new church, named "Central Heights."

This congregation has sent out four missionaries.

The present Central Heights Church houses the previous Friedenstal Mennonite congregation in the old Grand Central Country School building. This change was made in 1972.

The Morning Star Church, north of Durham.

The Morning Star Church, a member of the Church of God in Christ Mennonite Conference, is probably the oldest congregation in the area, having been established by some early families during the 1880's, when their people immigrated from Europe. At times, ministers from various other affiliated churches served the pastorate including Lone Tree, Inman, and Hillsboro.

The beautiful brick sturcture, built in 1966, seats 400, and the location is located seven miles northwest of Durham near the original church. Ransom Wiebe, Claude Unruh, and Bruce Dirks are pastors.

This congregation also supports it's own private school, Cottonwood Grove Christian School which has a new facility just northwest of Durham, near the famed Cottonwood Crossing.

The Gentle People

The gentle faith of the "Holderman" Mennonite people has been a large, important and positive part of Durham's community life and development since its earliest years.

The followers of a spiritual leader from the Old Country include leading lives of gentleness, courtesy, honesty, simplicity, and loving kindness to others, in the practice of their faith.

Known for their peace-loving and non-violent commitment, they have lived in rural Durham in harmony with many kinds of people, carrying out business relationships without compromising their strong religious heritage.

Among the leaders of this group, the Morning Star Congregation (formerly Logan Mennonite Church) are their pastors, Claude Unruh and Ransom Wiebe. Both are widely known and respected as leaders of this flock of believers.

"Claude Unruh is one of the most respected men in this whole area," one Durham resident noted. "He's just a gentleman, and you don't see that much anymore."

Mr. Unruh is always willing to share information about the Santa Fe Trail with visitors from near and far.

Durham Church Takes New Name
On Dedication Sunday
(From the Mennonite Weekly, May 1966.)

The 80-member congregation of the Church of God in Christ Mennonites seven miles northwest of here (Durham) chose a new name at the forenoon services last Sunday and in the afternoon dedicated its new house of worship.

Formerly called Logan Church, it will henceforth be known as Morning Star Church.

Crowds estimated at 700 to 800, attended the all-day meetings.

Harry Wenger, Hesston, preached the dedicatory sermon, with his father, F. H. Wenger, Moundridge, also giving a message. Claude Unruh, one of the ministers of the congregation, led in the dedicatory prayer. The Abe Jantz family, Livingston, Calif., sang and C. C. Wedel gave an appreciation talk.

According to the historical report given by Unruh, the first building with seating capacity of about 200 was erected in 1904, at a cost of $2,050. The last regular service was held there March 13, 1966. Cost of the new brick and block structure, placed on the same location, was $44,000, with much of the labor furnished by members of the congregation. Seating capacity, with overflow space, is about 500.

The present ministers are Jacob N. Yost, Claude Unruh and Ransom Wiebe. Sunday School attendance averages between 90 and 100.

Tent meetings were a part of religious life in the Durham area.
This photo was an M.B. song festival at Lehigh, summer, 1917.

When the roll is called up yonder
And our time on earth is done...
When the roll is called up yonder,
I'll be there...

A farm pond baptism; cattle on the horizon.   Expressions of
faith.

Cemeteries are a place for remembering...

Cemeteries

Cemeteries in the Durham area include the Durham Park Township Cemetery, located a mile south of town on Highway 15, several church cemeteries, including the Baptist Cemetery and Morning Star Cemetery, both west of town at the sites of the respective original churches, and other country cemeteries of Central Heights and Elm Springs. In addition there are the family plots of the Frick, Pankratz, Kaiser and Beltz families.

The list of burials for the Durham Park, Baptist and Frick cemeteries has been made available for this publication, including only the date of death. Birthdates were not available in most cases.

Anyone interested in pursuing a genealogical search for ancestors is invited to contact any of the Centennial Committee, to be directed to the caretaker of the respective cemeteries for further information.

Cemeteries are as follows:
Durham Park Township Cemetery
Baptist Cemetery
Morning Star Cemetery
Frick Cemetery
Kaiser Cemetery
Beltz Cemetery
Pankratz Cemetery
Central Heights Cemetery
Elm Springs Cemetery

In addition, one other burial of note is that of Edgar Miller, aged 18 years, last person killed by Indians in this area, who was murdered and scalped by the Cheyennes while carrying a message, riding horseback along the Santa Fe Trail, back in 1864. The story of the Miller episode is carried elsewhere in this book.

Local Servicemen Killed in Action

Two area men were lost during WWII. They were:

Private Johnathan Jantz who was killed in combat duty in France on February 22, 1945.

Lieutenant Burtis E. Weible who died while on duty in Guam, May 20, 1948.

Durham Park Township Cemetery

NAME	DATE OF DEATH
Mrs. L. E. Borton (Sara A)	June 21, 1899
Harry Sealock	December 5, 1900
John Kraft	No Date
William Henry	—1899
C. T. Branton	No Date
Charity White	October 18, 1900
Infant Peter Funk	No Date
Infant Dave Herbel	No Date
Infant Fred Hinter	No Date
John Harsh	No Date
Mrs. John Harsh	No Date
C. C. Walker	—1927
Mrs. W. H. Eggleston (Emma L)	May 18, 1906
R. Smith	No Date
Archie Booth	December 4, 1906

T. B. Branton	No Date	Laura E. Bartel	August 13, 1921
Fred Helms	No Date	Katie Moolong	October 30, 1921
Infant Elmer Schwemmer	—1909	Julia T. Parry	August 17, 1922
Mrs. Andrew (Katherina)	1868 to 1909	John Smith	August 18, 1922
Edward Barnett	March 26, 1909	Amelia H. Moritz	January, 1923
Infant D. A. Baker	No Date	Loren Gloy Becker	March 16, 1923
Infant C. F. Thompson	No Date	Walter E. Haas	May 15, 1923
Child George Kline	No Date	Jacob Miller	July 4, 1923
Will Hoffman	No Date	Wilma Ellen Schlehuber	October 19, 1923
Infant Martin Helmer	No Date	Infant Howard	October 29, 1923
Infant Miss Mosky	No Date	Katy Schneider	November 2, 1923
Child Laruma Herald	July 17, 1908	Katherine Miller	December 31, 1923
J. D. Mickay	No Date	Laura Eichenhour	April 5, 1924
Miss Clarabelle Haas	No Date	Katherine Gertrude Ellis	April 10, 1924
Infant Schneider	No Date	Adam H. Miller	April 22, 1924
Miss Schneider	No Date	Gottfrid Laubhan	July 1, 1924
Reuben Schneider	No Date	Melvin Wayne Weible	October 1, 1924
Thomas Parry	April 26, 1912	Ed Wire	No Date
John Isheim	June 24, 1913	Albert Elmer Updike	August 31, 1925
Arthur Schultz	October 14, 1913	Alice Laubhan	September 7, 1925
Ruth Elvina Miller	February 2, 1914	Florence L. Krieger	April 17, 1926
Eretta Friesen	No Date	Katherina E. Winters	July 16, 1926
Mary Elizabeth Mock	March 21, 1915	Mary Lucile Haas	August 5, 1926
Sadie Rexius	March 29, 1915	George Klein	December 13, 1926
Edward Isheim	June 8, 1915	Chas. Crittindon Walker	January 2, 1927
Selma Weitzel	November 10, 1915	Henry Krieger	March 5, 1927
Unknown	No Date	George Wu. . . (illegible)	August 27, 1927
Fred Knaak	No Date	William Howard Smith	July 28, 1927
Adam Smith	No Date	Louise Becker	September 20, 1927
Misa Malies	No Date	Emma R. Haas	January 20, 1928
William Schneider	January 27, 1916	Anna M. Doan	August 15, 1928
Walter H. Eggleston	March 30, 1916	Jacob Weinmeister	September 9, 1928
Katie Langhoover	April 29, 1916	Ben G. Haas	March 31, 1929
Alexander Hale	No Date	Ester M. Smith	October 2, 1930
Jacob Wooster	October 6, 1918	Katherine Sween	February 4, 1931
Elsie Ellis	November 5, 1918	Matilda Helms	January 26, 1932
Peter P. Schneider	November 28, 1918	Jake Huenegardt	December 26, 1932
George Alderson	December 17, 1918	Nickolas Heiser	March 26, 1933
Andy Lasure	September 22, 1919	Infant Helmer	April 15, 1933
Wilber G. Friesen	September 30, 1919	Evelyn Weibert	April 23, 1933
Edna Worster	September 27, 1920	Adam Youk	July 15, 1933
Edward Andrew Knaak	October 28, 1920	Elizabeth Hempel Schaffer	August 9, 1933
Andrew Schwemmer	December 19, 1920	Henry E. Wohlgemuth	October 10, 1933
Wm. Savage	April 5, 1921	Anna Klose Fisher	November 15, 1933

Mary Catherine Streckbein	March 3, 1935	Mrs. Barbara Lipps	August 24, 1947
Lenhard Theodore Curvey	March 4, 1935	Amelia Meier	August 25, 1947
Mary Lucy Darby	May 8, 1935	Lt. Burtis Weible	May 20, 1948
Gottlieb Weimer	November 9, 1935	Emanuel Hein	September 13, 1948
Henry Schneider	1936	Mrs. Geo. Laubhan	October 3, 1948
Kathrina Youk	October 20, 1936	Henry Dick	November 20, 1948
Mrs. Schneider	January 1937	Ted Curvey	March 8, 1949
Gotfrey Schneider	February 1, 1937	Lucy Weible	July 4, 1949
Susie Ann Schuber	April 18, 1937	Marion Smith	January 24, 1950
Mrs. C. Huenergardt	May 14, 1937	D. A. Eichenour	March 26, 1950
Elizabeth Frances Savage	June 23, 1937	Mrs. Lizzie Knaak	May 27, 1950
Josephine Branton	September 20, 1937	Janet LaVann Klein	July 28, 1950
Mrs. John Shattack	November 6, 1937	Geo H. Meier	August 16, 1950
Gerald G. Klein	February 4, 1938	Loren Douglas Klein	September 12, 1950
Fred Klose	June 24, 1938	Charlie Toman Branton	October 4, 1950
Jacob Frederich Haas	August 2, 1938	Jacob Schafer	October 4, 1950
Elizabeth Morlong Hempel	August 2, 1938	Mary Katherine Meier	October 1950
Lydia Schafer Kerbs	August 28, 1938	Rose Carter	February 27, 1951
Henry C. Funk	March 22, 1939	Christ Weible	May 21, 1951
John A. Hein	May 5, 1939	Ed Becker	July 18, 1951
Phillip Hempel	June 14, 1939	Rebekah Ann Klein	January 15, 1952
Peter Schneider	July 15, 1939	Conrad Laubhan	May 27, 1953
Fred Brunner Sr.	August 15, 1939	John D. Classen	June 17, 1953
Katie Decker Seleska	July 29, 1940	Reinhart Huber	September 27, 1953
John Adam Morlong	September 16, 1940	W. E. Carter	October 17, 1953
Herman Moritz	May, 1941	Laura Jones	November 22, 1953
Merrill Alan Klein	June 12, 1941	Denise Ann Kerbs	April 30, 1954
Sadie E. Brunner	March 22, 1942	Anna Dick	October 8, 1954
Katherine Heiser	April 7, 1942	Mary Hein	May 9, 1955
Ellen Seleska	January 20, 1943	George Dick	May 25, 1955
Jacob Brunner	September 5, 1943	Henry Lorenz	July 3, 1955
Mary Weimer	November 22, 1943	Anna Meier	May 5, 1956
Katie Hein	June 21, 1944	Jacob Winter Jr.	August 2, 1956
Phillip Schafer	September 12, 1944	Lena Brown	March 23, 1957
George Dick Sr.	March 3, 1945	Kenneth Glenn Klein	August 3, 1957
George Klein	April 25, 1945	Eva Heinitz	August 28, 1957
Charles Wesley Jones	August 26, 1945	Jacob Meier	December 21, 1957
Sam Klein	January 26, 1946	Lewis Haas	January 26, 1958
Roy Eichenour	May 24, 1946	Arthur Weiss	July 12, 1958
David Hupp	May 31, 1946	Mrs. Alex Laudner	September 14, 1958
William F. Schultz	June 16, 1946	Reuben H. Funk	January 26, 1959
Lenard C. Curvey	November 10, 1946	Solomon Schuber	February 9, 1959
Henry Meier	April 1, 1947	John Hein	April 2, 1959
Mollie Huber	May 2, 1947	Lydia Kerbs	June 16, 1959

Henrietta Louise Roberts	August 3, 1959	Dan Hein	November 1, 1967
Susanna Helmer	October 9, 1959	Hannah Nuss	December 15, 1967
Mrs. John Schneider	February 22, 1960	Katherine Elizabeth Funk	December 26, 1967
John C. Mohn	March 26, 1960	Ray Meier	December 29, 1967
Christina Schafer	May 28, 1960	Alex Becker	February 12, 1968
Julia Klein	September 9, 1960	Herman Schultz	May 9, 1968
Mrs. Sara Krieger Miller	September 9, 1960	Theodore Niederhouse	June 25, 1968
Lena Becker	October 11, 1960	Jacob Winter	June 28, 1968
Elmer Questnow	October 15, 1960	Seth Bartel	August 31, 1968
Fred H. Schneider	May 17, 1961	Henry Youk	January 7, 1969
Sherry Denise Klein	July 6, 1961	Maude E. Savage	May 22, 1969
Wm. Schuber	October, 1961	Peter Weibert	July 2, 1969
Katie Lorenz	February 21, 1962	Fred J. Sween	July 20, 1969
Sarah Klassen Shinkle	March 18, 1962	Emma Marie Youk	September 10, 1969
Jacob Brunner	June 8, 1962	Harry W. Ollenburger	September 15, 1969
Wesley L. Schultz	September 24, 1962	Bertha Hamm	November 12, 1969
Mary Catherine Zitterkopf	November 20, 1962	John Fred Kerbs	February 12, 1970
Martin Helmer	March 9, 1963	Carrie Wedel	February 26, 1970
Marie Laubhan	April 5, 1963	John Schattack	March 20, 1970
Mollie Bernhardt Wooster	June 28, 1963	Herman Weyand	June 21, 1970
Katie Brunner	July 8, 1963	Cornelius Berg	August 12, 1970
Melvin Hein	August 6, 1963	Samuel Eitel	Jaunary 22, 1971
Harry Hamm	August 20, 1963	Jake Hein	October 26, 1971
Henry Kaiser	September 6, 1963	John Oliver West	October 29, 1971
David Klein	October 17, 1963	Gottfried Klein	January 8, 1972
Mollie Weibert	March 15, 1964	Sam Laubhan	April 19, 1972
Eva Noyes	April 21, 1964	John Seleska	August 19, 1972
D. D. Bartel	April 27, 1964	Marie K. Eitel	October 2, 1972
Carl Kirschner	July 10, 1964	Jake Kerbs	November 3, 1972
Sam Klein	August 15, 1964	Katie Eitel	January 21, 1973
Cameron Smith	October 26, 1964	Mary Schneider	February 10, 1973
Jay Dean Donahue	October 26, 1964	Flora Jean Carlson	August 2, 1973
E. M. Becker	December 12, 1964	Edward Hamm	August 2, 1973
Michael Brown	March 3, 1965	Ralph R. Frick	September 8, 1973
Lee Haas	March 15, 1965	Michael Allen Monares	September 16, 1973
Sol Sween	May, 1965	George E. Meier	September 25, 1973
George Yauk	August 25, 1965	William Hamm	November 25, 1973
Jacob Zitterkopf	February 27, 1965	Amelia Hein	April 26, 1974
Alice Vogel	September 22, 1965	Esther Lorenz	June 10, 1974
Henry Unruh	February 9, 1966	Jeremy Monares	June 20, 1974
Janet Klein	August 20, 1966	Amelia Youk	July 1, 1974
Ezra Lorenz	September 3, 1966	Henry Laubhan	September 12, 1974
Ed L. Klein	November 22, 1966	David Schneider	March 14, 1975
Jonah George Huber	June 14, 1967	John Miller	July 26, 1975

Norma Winter	July 30, 1975	Fred Kaiser	December 8, 1985
Ed Berg	August 23, 1975	Richard Ball	December 10, 1985
Eddie Klein	October 19, 1975	Helen Louise Hein	January 21, 1986
Mary Hein	October 30, 1975	Julia Geissler	January 29, 1986
Carl Winter	November 27, 1975	Elizabeth Kerbs	February 7, 1986
Herman Haas	December 10, 1975	Marie Zitterkopf	February 25, 1986
Anna Klein	December 7, 1976	Albert Weible	July 3, 1986
Walter Schlehuber	March 20, 1977	Lorene Laubhan	July 7, 1986
Jerald Dean Hamm	August 18, 1977	Amelia Smith	October 22, 1986
Edward Schlehuber	January 27, 1978	Wallace Kerbs	October 22, 1986
Lydia Cross	April 12, 1978	Linda L. Shaw	November 28, 1986
Maude Haas	August 6, 1978	Mary Unruh	January 17, 1987
Ralph Unholz	September 8, 1978		
Mollie Borton	June 19, 1979		
Eva Winter	November 27, 1979		
Junior Lee Medley	December 5, 1979		

Baptist Cemetery

D. Eugene Hood	December 20, 1979	Katharina Kaiser	January 3, 1904
Rachel Hiebert	December 30, 1979	Katharine David	August 15, 1906
Mike Schafer	May 10, 1980	George David	September 11, 1909
Elizabeth Becker	March 13, 1981	Christian David	April 28, 1911
Samuel S. Beisel	June 6, 1981	Sarah Geis	1912
Mary Elizabeth Eubanks	July 22, 1981	Jacob Geis	1890
Sarah Bessel	August 19, 1981	John Geis	1899
Marie Schafer	September 14, 1981	Anna M. Geis	1891
George Schafer	October 2, 1981	Anna L. Geis	January 5, 1899
Mary Mohn	November 16, 1981	Phillpine Geis	June 18, 1917
Harry Nuss	January 14, 1982	Maria Geis	April 5, 1894
Linda Lou Hamm	June 2, 1982	George Geis	1894
Mollie Weibert	July 29, 1982	Maggie Lorenz	1894
Evo Franklin Curvey	October 8, 1982	Lydia Geis	1905
Richard D. Belton	November 7, 1982	David Geis	1901
Arthur Kaiser	November 9, 1982	Alice Beltz	March 31, 1920
Infant M. Janzen	November 13, 1982	Jonas Hefley	April, 1, 1920
Hannah Miller	November 23, 1982	Woodrow Lorenz	August 9, 1920
Reuben Hein	December 16, 1982	Philip Schwabauer	July 23, 1922
Henry Geissler	May 25, 1983	August Moeske	July 13, 1923
Anna Bartel	March 30, 1984	Anna Fromm	September 7, 1923
Harvey Mohn	June 3, 1984	Adam Zimmerman	December 19, 1923
Katie Hein	July 4, 1984	John Fromm	October 13, 1925
Alvie Rader	February 17, 1985	Frederick Schlehuber	June 7, 1927
Mollie Schafer	March 19, 1985	Maryanna Geis	June 13, 1927
Flossie Unholz	October 16, 1985	Peter Geis	July 10, 1927
John Bartel	October 18, 1985	Daniel Schideman	December 20, 1927
Alvina Pinyerd	November 5, 1985	Walter Nuss	January 24, 1928

George David	April 3, 1928
Clara Bauerle	August 12, 1928
Henry John Lipps	February 5, 1929
Infant Hamm	1930
Alwood G. Ehrlich	January 17, 1931
Marsene Geis	December 23, 1931
Henry Peter Lipps	July 25, 1933
Mildren Mae Nuss	September 20, 1933
Infant Herbel	December 21, 1933
Conrad Heinrich	April 1, 1934
Jacob Beltz	June 18, 1934
Henry Geis	May 5, 1935
Katie Geis	June 4, 1935
George Nuss	July 3, 1935
Leonard Ollenburger	July 10, 1935
Mary K. Ollenburger	May 10, 1936
Jacob E. David	August 24, 1935
Jacob J. Geis	August 2, 1936
Fred Hefley	August 1, 1937
Mrs. Lewis Ollenburger	September 2, 1937
Geo. D. Herbel	April 29, 1938
Mary Katie Lipps	July 15, 1938
Jacob Beltz	May 14, 1940
Anna Marie Geis	August 28, 1940
Lee Roy Nuss	February 9, 1941
Ruby D. Sader	July 19, 1941
John Lorenz	July 27, 1941
Maggie Heinrich	January 1942
Eugene W. Herbel	April 17, 1942
Infant of Mr. & Mrs. Edward Hamm	July 23, 1942
Darrel Loy Schlehuber	February 21, 1943
Marjorie Hamm	June 7, 1943
Alexander D. Schmidt	January 11, 1944
Betty Lee Beltz	June 9, 1947
Christine Beltz	November 15, 1947
John David	November 17, 1947
Fred Geis	August 26, 1949
Anna Herbel	July 12, 1952
George Herbel	August 31, 1952
Merna Lee Zimmerman	September 18, 1858
Anna Elizabeth Geis	August 28, 1958
Rachel Knaak	May 9, 1960
Elsie Ann Zimmerman	November 30, 1963
Anna E. Herbel	September 23, 1964

Katie Lorenz	April 3, 1965
Solomon H. Geis	January 9, 1968
Mary Nuss Kaufman	May 27, 1969
Lottie Geis	February 14, 1970
Sam Zimmerman	June 12, 1971
Peter Geis	October 29, 1972
Anna H. Beltz	November 17, 1973
Arthur Geis	March 22, 1974
Jacob Zimmerman	August 31, 1974
Leah Geis (Mrs. Ed F.)	November 15, 1975
Jacob J. Geis (Jack)	May 19, 1979
Mollie Lorenz	February 5, 1980
Edward F. Geis	July 13, 1980
Mollie David	October 18, 1980
Nannie Zimmerman	1981
Isaac Lorenz	January 27, 1982
Martha Zimmerman	May 4, 1981
David Zimmerman	March 3, 1982
Esther Geis	June 17, 1985
Leah Geis	August 8, 1985
Pauline Geis	October 1986

Frick Cemetery

Land donated by Jacob Frick

Catherine Bartel	1895
Peter Bartel	1895
Enoch Frick	1895
Mary Steinle	September 7, 1897
Samuel Frick	1902
Ester Frick	April 15, 1904
Infant Frick	December 19, 1904
Katrina Frick	May 25, 1905
Christina Frick	June 14, 1906
Willie Frick	November 29, 1906
Catharine Popp	March 3, 1912
Julia Socolofsky	1913
Elizabeth Frick	July 22, 1915
Adam Zitterkopf	August 10, 1916
Adam Bartel	1918
Caroline Ewert	January 24, 1930
Conrad Zitterkopf	February 22, 1924

Arthur L. Popp	March 13, 1931
Caroline Popp	October 29, 1931
Jacob Frick	December 30, 1932
Frederick Socolofsky	1934
Naomi Frick	February 3, 1934
Jacob L. Frick	July 31, 1935
Anna Marie Lehr	November 19, 1935
Mary Bernice Frick	July 22, 1935
Freda Popp	March 18, 1922
Wm. H. Popp	February 9, 1950
Marvin K. Frick	May 29, 1951
John Frick	April 16, 1953
Elda Irene Frick	November 13, 1956
Sophie Frick	1960
Conrad Frick	1961
Daniel D. Popp	September 11, 1963
Louise Lehr Frick	December 10, 1964
Anna L. Frick	December 9, 1967
Alex N. Frick	February 22, 1967
Lula Frick	January 15, 1967
Anna M. Bartel	1968
Frank Ewert	March 10, 1969
Abraham Frick	October 28, 1970
Hannah Frick	April 13, 1970
Elmer Frick	April 28, 197
Benjamin C. Frick	November 8, 1979
Pearl Frick	September 21, 1982
Lydia Frick	November 20, 1985

Logan Cemetery

Since the Logan cemetery roster lists most of the causes of death to read the cemetery list is to understand something of part of Durham's life, on the hardships of people's lives and of their heartaches.

Among the causes of death over the 95 year span of Logan Cemetery are: "premature births, lightning, heart attack, old age, pneumonia, cancer, head-on car accident, and heart failure while on a tractor."

These griefs and losses are of course, a part of life and living. And among the deaths are many who lived full and productive lives of work and faith, achieving old age in triumph, passing on to eternal glory, with all the rest.

Adina Unruh. . . . . Oct. 26, 1889	Henry Schmidt. . . . . May 10, 1915	Isaac Dirk. . . . . July 16, 1951
Henry D. Buller. . . . . Feb. 9, 1892	Peter Jacob Weadel. . . . . . Jan. 24, 1917	Leah Redger. . . . . Aug. 26, 1951
Katherina D. Buller. . . . . . . Feb 6, 1892	Alfred Voth. . . . . May 25, 1925	Irven B. Jantz. . . . . Dec. 23, 1952
Helena Koehn. . . . . Feb. 6, 1892	Effe Redger. . . . . May 15, 1923	Leaster Redger. . . . . Jan. 24, 1953
Henry Koehn. . . . . No Date	Anne Ratzloff. . . . . April 9, 1912	Helena Voth Unruh. . . . . . Aug. 9, 1955
John J. Jantz 1904	Paul Unruh . . . . Nov. 20, 1912	Judith Leora Dirks. . . . . Jan. 3, 1958
Lena Jantz. 1908	Martha Schmidt. . . . . . . Dec. 20, 1918	Byron Dean Unruh. . . . . . April 27, 1958
Eva Jantz. 1904	Infant Marie Voth . . . . Jan. 1, 1920	Daniel Eck. . . . . May 19, 1961
Blandia Zeiset. . . . . Feb. 6, 1904	Infant Harry Voth. . . . . . . Jan. 1, 1920	Arthur Dean Redger. . . . . . Nov. 1, 1962
Belinda Zeiset. . . . . Jan. 1, 1904	Ara Clarence Grentz. . . . March 1, 1920	Dennis Walter Osborne. . . June 23, 1963
Ernest Voth. . . . . No Date	Infant Melvin Voth. . . . . . April 3, 1920	Kevin Lee Osborne. . . . . . March 4, 1964
Glades Voth. . . . . No Date	Tobis Dirks. . . . . April 3, 1910	Gladys Redger Wiebe. . . . . May 5, 1965
Alfred Voth. . . . . No Date	Eva Koehn. . . . . Aug. 31, 1927	Della Unruh. . . . . June 3, 1965
Mrs. H. Koehn. . . . . No Date	Amos Koehn . . . . Dec. 3, 1928	Julius Redger. . . . . March 16, 1966
Benjeman Voth. . . . . No Date	Susanna Unruh. . . . . Jan. 12, 1931	Fred H. Redger. . . . . July 14, 1967
Peter Unruh. . . . . No Date	Adolf Schuetzer. . . . . Jan. 1, 1932	Sharolyn Kay Koehn. . . . . Sept 25, 1968
Anna Koehn. . . . . No Date	Elizabeth Dirks Becker. . . April 19, 1932	Gladys Carol Wiebe. . . . . . July 21, 1969
Benjaman Jantz. . . . . . March 18, 1904	Katherina C. Unruh . . . . Dec. 23, 1934	Lillie Florence Jantz. . . . . . Jan. 14, 1970
Eva Ratzleff. . . . . Dec. 1, 1904	Andrew Koehn. . . . . May 16, 1935	Ida Redger. . . . . Sept 15, 1970
Lena Lang Nightengale. . Sept. 16, 1910	David C. Unruh . . . . Feb. 24, 1937	Arlene R. Osborn. . . . . March 27, 1974
Tobis Schmidt. . . . . November	Effe Eck. . . . . Dec. 1922	Justina Isaac. . . . . July 3, 1974
Elizabeth Schuetzer. . . . . . . Dec. 1908	Lloyd Delton Weibe. . . . . . Dec. 6, 1938	Pete E. Koehn. . . . . March 14, 1977
Abraham Koehn. . . . . May 20, 1910	Luella Mae Jantz. . . . . . . Dec. 15, 1938	Ira I. Redger. . . . . Sept 21, 1977
Lena Koehn. . . . . Aug. 14, 1907	Infant Jantz. . . . . March 10, 1939	Arthur Isaac. . . . . March 21, 1978
Soloma Koehn. . . . . Jan. 2, 1910	Ben C. Eck. . . . . Dec. 14, 1939	Alfred H. Koehn. . . . . Aug. 16, 1979
Susian Koehn. . . . . Nov. 17, 1906	Lucille Fay Dirks. . . . . . . March 4, 1941	Malinda Koehn. . . . . Aug. 25, 1979
Fred Jantz. . . . . Oct. 29, 1913	Kathleen Kay Dirks. . . . . March 5, 1941	Ethel Harger. . . . . Dec. 31, 1979
Obed Dirks. . . . . June 18, 1913	Rachel Dirks. . . . . June 7, 1941	Cornelius C. Wedel. . . . . . Jan. 19, 1983
Andrew A. Becker . . . . . . June 28, 1913	Johnie Wiebe. . . . . Aug. 31, 1945	Luella Redger. . . . . July 29, 1985
Archie Unruh. . . . . Sept. 24, 1913	Josephine Eck. . . . . July 16, 1941	Helen Marie Woods. . . . . . Nov. 1, 1985
John C. Unruh . . . . Sept. 8, 1913	David Buller. . . . . July 2, 1943	Vada Joyce Wiebe. . . . . . . Aug. 31, 1986
Tobis H. Schmidt . . . . . . Nov. 12, 1913	Fred P. Unruh. . . . . March 20, 1947	Helen Wedel. . . . . Jan 19, 1987
Murtle Schmidt. . . . . Sept. 1, 1914	Vernon F. Isaac. . . . . Feb. 19, 1948	Harry Dale Rhodes. . . . . . April 8, 1987
Eli Ezra Redger. . . . . April 4, 1915		

Mayors

Alex Becker was Mayor for 35 years.

Mr. Alex Becker had the honor of serving as mayor for 35 years and Mr. Ben Goertz has been mayor since 1973.

Following are Durham ordinances that regulated the lives of its people.

The roster of mayors who served Durham from the time of its incorporation in 1906 until now is as follows.

Mayors and Their Terms

J. A. Stephenson	1906
A. H. Miller	1907
John Smith	1911
C. W. Jones	1913
G. W. Thompson	1915
Adam Youk	1919
R. W. Powers	1921
H. E. Wohlgemuth	1923
Glenn Wilson	1925
R. L. Knybel	1927
Alex Becker	1930
Ben Goertz	1967
Wendell Dirks	1971
Ben Goertz	1973
	to present

Ordinance No. 121

March 2, 1943

An ordinance providing compensation for the Mayor and Councilmen for their services.

Be it ordained by the Mayor and Council of the City of Durham, Kansas:

Section 1

That on and after the fourth (4th) day of May, 1943 the governing body of the City be paid for attending regular monthly meetings as follow;

Mayor one (1) dollar

Councilmen one (1) dollar

Section 2

This ordinance shall take effect and be in force from and after its publication according to law.

Chas A Borton   Alex Recker

Clerk   Mayor

Ordinances

Ordinance Number 3
Durham, Kansas November 20, 1906

Be it ordained by the mayor and the councilmen of the City of Durham, Kansas:

That it shall be unlawful for any one to use profane or vulgar language within the corporate limites of the City of Durham, Kansas.

Any violation of the same shall be punishable by a fine of not less than one (1) dollar or more than five (5) dollars.

C. R. Shaner,   J. A. Stephenson
city Clerk   Mayor

Ordinance Number 6
Durham, Kansas December 18, 1906

Be it ordained by the Mayor and the Councilmen of the City of Durham, Kansas:

That an occupation tax shall be levied as herein listed payable on or before the 1st day of January 1907.

Creameries	5. 00
Cream Stations	5. 00
Banks	3. 00
Express Companies	3. 00
Elevators	3. 00
General STores	3. 00
Lumber Yards	3. 00
Implement Dealers	2. 00
Meat Markets	2. 00
Drug Stores	2. 00
Groceries	1. 50
Manufacturers	1. 50
Repair Shop	1. 00
Contractors	1. 00
Hotels	1. 00
Blacksmiths	1. 00
Confectioners	1. 00
Furniture	1. 00
Coal Dealer	1. 00
Milliners	1. 00
Livery Stables	1. 00
Stable Horses	1. 00
Jewelers	1. 00
Doctors	1. 00
Barbers	1. 00
Telegraph Co.	1. 00
Hardward	1. 00
Printing Shops	1. 00

C. R. Shaner   J. A. Stephenson
City Clerk   Mayor

Ordinance Number 7
Durham, Kansas February 5, 1907

Be it ordained by the Mayor and the Councilmen of the City of Durham, Kansas:

That peddlers on foot shall pay a daily license tax of one (1) dollar for each days work or fraction thereof. Peddlers with wagons, two (2) dollars per day or fraction thereof. Auctioneers, fifty cents (. 50) per day or fraction thereof. Shooting galleries, one (1) dollar per day. Pleasure devices of all kinds shall be on a bisis of 10% of the gross receipts per day. Shows shall be on a basis of 10% of the gross receipts per day or fraction thereof.

C. R. Shaner   J. A. Stephenson
City Clerk   Mayor

Ordinance Number 9
Durham, Kansas April 9, 1907

Be it ordained by the Mayor and the Councilmen of the City of Durham, Kansas:

That the voting place of the City of Durham shall be at the Durham Park Township building or at a place designated by the council.

L. E. Borton   J. A. Stephenson
Clerk   Mayor

Ordinance Number 14
Durham, Kansas June 25, 1907

Be it ordained by the Mayor and the Councilmen of the City of Durham, Kansas:

That it shall be unlawful to ride a bicycle on the sidewalks in the corporate limits of the City of Durham, Kansas. Any one violation this ordinance will be subject to a fine of not less than one (1) dollar or more than twenty five (25) dollars.

D. A. Eichenour   A. H. Miller
Clerk   Mayor

Ordinance Number 15
Published July 4, 1907

Be it ordained by the Mayor and the Councilmen of the City of Durham, Kansas:

That the levy for the fiscal year of 1907 shall be 10 mills on the dollar.

D. A. Eichenour
Clerk

A. H. Miller
Mayor

ORDINANCE VACATING STREETS
July 11, 1907

Be, and it is hereby ordained by the Council of the City of Durham, the Mayor concuring, that Abilene Avenue shall be vacated, a 70 foot street, from 4th Street north to C. R. I. & Prailroad right-of-way, and a street 60 feet wide, known as Railroad Street, south of railroad right-of-way, from Abilene Avenue southwest, parallel to said railway right-of-way, to Lawrence Avenue.

First reading July 10, 1907. Notice is hereby given that the above ordinance will be passed July 23, 1907, unless there are some legal objections to same.

A. H. Miller, Mayor
D. A. Eichenour, City Clerk

Ordinance Number 17
Durham, Kansas July 30, 1907

An ordinance relating to the levy and assessment of taxes

Be it ordained by the Mayor and Councilmen of the City of Durham, Kansas:

Section 1

That there be and is hereby levied upon all real and personal property within the corporate limits of the above named City a tax of 10 mills on the dollar for general purposes.

Section 2

All ordinances and parts of ordinances in conflict with this ordinance is hereby repealed.

Section 3

This ordinance shall be in full force and effect from and after its publication in the Durham Journal.

D. A. Eichenour
City Clerk

A. H. Miller
Mayor

Ordinance Number 24
June 3, 1908

Be it ordained by the Mayor and the Councilmen of the City of Durham, Kansas:

Section 1

That it shall be unlawful for any one to get on or off any moving train within the corporate limits of the City of Durham, Kansas.

Section 2

This ordinance shall not construe to mean those regularly employed by the railroad company.

Section 3

Any violation of this ordinance shall be subject to a fine of not less than five (5) dollars nor more than ten (10) dollars.

D. A. Eichenour
City Clerk

A. H. Miller
Mayor

Ordinance Number 32
November 7, 1941

An ordinance regulating the speed of automobiles and motor vehicles, and for the sounding of alarms and displaying of lights on same, within the City limits of the City of Durham, Marion County, Kansas, and fixing penalties for violation thereof.

Be it ordained by the Mayor and the Councilmen of the City of Durham, Kansas:

Section 1

That it shall be unlawful for any person driving or in charge of any automobile or motor vehicle to drive or operate the same on any of the streets within the corporate limits of said City at a speed exceeding ten miles an hour.

Section 2

It shall be unlawful for any person or individual to dirve or operate any automobile or motor vehicle upon any of the streets within the limits of said City during a period from one (1) hour after sunset to one (1) hour before sunrise without displaying on said automobile or motor vehicle two good white in front and one red light in the rear of said automobile or motor vehicle.

Section 3

All persons driving or in charge of any automobile or motor vehicle, running the same within the limits of said City shall sound an alarm of sufficient volume to be heard at least two hundred (200) feet on their approach to intersections of all public highways.

Section 4

Any person who shall violate any of the provisions of this ordinance shall upon conviction thereof be fined in any sum not to exceed fifty (50) dollars and the costs of prosecution.

Section 5

This ordinance shall be in effect after its publication as required by law.

L. E. Borton
Clerk

John Smith
Mayor

Ordinance Number 35
November 7, 1911

An ordinance to prevent minors under the age of sixteen years from loitering in, playing upon or frequenting the streets, alleys, or other public places in the City of Durham, Marion County, Kansas, after certain hours during the night-time unless accompanied by parent, guardian, or other legal custodian.

Be it ordained by the Mayor and the Councilmen of the City of Durham, Marion County, Kansas:

Section 1

That it shall be unlawful for any minor under the age of sixteen years to loiter on or play upon or frequent the streets or alley or other public places in the City of Durham during the night time after nine o'clock in the evening from the first day of March to the first day of October and after eight o'clock in the evening from the first day of October to the first day of MArch in each hereafter unless such minor shall be accompanined by parent, guardian or other person having the legal custody of such minor or in the performance of an errand or duty directed by such parent, guardian or other legal custodian or where a duty or employment makes it necessary for such minor to be on the streets or in other public places during the night time and after the hours herein named.

Section 2

It shall be unlawful for any parent, guardian or other person having the legal custody or care of any such minor under the age of sixteen years to allow or permit such minor to loiter in or play upon or frequent the streets or alleys or other public places in the City of Durham during the time prohibited in the preceeding section.

Section 3

Any person violationg any of the provisions of this ordinance shall upon conviction thereof be fined not less than one (1) dollar nor more than ten (10) dollars.

Section 4

This ordinance passed November 7th, 1911.

L. E. Borton   John Smith
Clerk   Mayor

Ordinance Number 39

An ordinance to protect public health

Be it ordained by the Mayor and the Councilmen of the City of Durham, Marion County, Kansas:

Section 1

That it shall be unlawful for any person, firm or corporation to create or place upon their premises whether owned or leased by them or to place on any street, alley or common any one or more of the following to wit.

1) Animal manure in any quantity which is not securely protected from flies.
2) Privies, vaults, cess-pools, pits or like places which is not securely protected from flies.
3) Garbage in any quantity which is not securely protected from flies.
4) Trash, litter, rags or anything whatsoever in which flies may breed or multiply.

Provided that between the first day of April and the first day of November of each year, where manure or garbage is not securely protected from flies, such manure or garbage is required to be removed at least once every ten days and destroyed by burning, burying or scattering over a field for fertilizer.

Section 2

It shall be the duty of the Chief of Police, Marshall and Health Officer, upon learning in any way whatsoever of the existence of some or more of the unlawful conditions described in Section 1 of this ordinance, to notify the offender in writing upon blanks provided by the city clerk to remove or alleviate said unlawful condition, stating the shortest reasonable time for such removal or abatement, in the event of the refusal or neglect on the part of the notified offender to abay such order, the Chief of Police, Marshall or Health Officer shall file complaint with the proper city authorities for the enforcement of the law and collection of the penalties prescribed by Section 3.

Section 3

Any person, firm or corporation found guilty of having created or placed on premises, either owned or leased by them, or upon any public or private property, any one or more of the unlawful conditions named in Section 1 of this ordinance, shall be punished by a fine of not less than one (1) dollar or more than fifty (50) dollars.

Section 4

All ordinances or part of ordinances in conflict with this ordinance are hereby repealed. This ordinance shall be in effect after its posting.

D. A. Eichenour   John Smith
City Clerk   Mayor

Ordinance Number 40
May 7, 1912

An ordinance relating to transient merchants

Be it ordained by the Mayor and the Councilmen of the City of Durham, Marion County, Kansas:

Section 1

That all transient merchants coming into the City of Durham, to sell general merchandise in competition with our regular merchants, shall pay an occupation tax of five (5) dollars per day for each and every day doing business in the city.

Section 2

The ordinance will be in force and effect from date of posting.

D. A. Eichenour   John Smith
City Clerk   Mayor

Ordinance Number 46

An ordinance prohibiting the use of sidewalks for coasting, and etc.

Be it ordained by the Mayor and the Councilmen of the City of Durham, Marion County, Kansas:

Section 1

It shall be unlawful for any person or persons riding tricycles, wagons or other vehicles coasting, transfering or carrying goods or articles of any kind on the sidewalks of the City of Durham, Kansas at a greater speed than a person would walk in a usual way.

Section 2

That the riding of horseback on the sidewalks in the City of Durham, Kansas, other than at regular crossing is prohibited.

Section 3

Any person or persons, violating any of the provisions of Sections 1 and 2 of this ordinance shall be subject to a fine of not less than one (1) dollar or more than five (5) dollars.

D. A. Eichenour   C. W. Jones(?(
City Clerk   Mayor

Ordinance Number 89
February 6, 1923

February 6, 1928

An ordinance regulating and licensing pool halls and bowling alleys

Be it ordained by the Governing Body of the City of Durham:

Section 1

That a pool hall is herein defined to be any place where a pool table or pool tables are kept for the purpose of hire and profit.

Section 2

That a bowling alley is herein defined to be any place where a bowling alley is kept for the purpose of hire and profit.

Section 3

That it shall be unlawful for the owner or proprietor or any agent or employee of any pool hall or bowling alley to permit, allow or suffer any minor under the age of eighteen (18) years to play any game of pool or any other game on any pool table or to bowl in the pool hall or bowling alley or loiter in the place.

Section 4

It shall be unlawful for any pool hall or bowling alley to remain open later than twelve o'clock, midnight, Saturday, or to open on the first day of the week, commonly called Sunday.

Section 5

A license fee of fifteen (15) dollars per year for the first pool table and five (5) dollars per year for each and every additional pool table, and ten (10) for each bowling alley shall be paid by any person, firm or corporation operating a pool hall or bowling alley. Such license fee shall be paid on or before the first day of May of each year, and it shall be unlawful to operate a pool hall or bowling alley without the license herein provided, and each ten (10) days violation shall constitute a separate offense.

Section 6

Any person, firm or corporation violating any of the provisions of this ordinance shall be deemed guilty of a misdemeanor and upon conviction shall be punished by a fine of not less than five (5) dollars or more than twenty five (25) dollars for each offense.

Section 7

This ordinance shall take effect and be in force from and after its publication according to law.

Chas A. Borton   R. L. Knybel
City Clerk   Acting Mayor

Town Pasture

In August 1923, an ordinance was passed by the town council stating that "pigs and other livestock could not be kept within the city limits". . . a step towards civilizing the town and improving the atmosphere, it seems.

The purpose of this ordinance appears to have to do with feeding and fattening the animals, rather than keeping them for use as a supply of milk, but at any rate, for many years, Durham had its own city pasture, outside the town limits, and this pasture, in the first section north of town on Highway 15, was made available to anyone who wished to pasture an animal, at a going rate charged by the actual owner of the pasture.

Many a town youngster remembers going out to the pasture in the evening, to milk the family's cow, or to accompany a friend on a similar mission.

Some remember that one of the townspeople used to make the job more pleasurable by becoming inebriated, and singing to his cows while doing the milking. The songs were lusty and melodious, and neither the animals nor the other patrons of the pasture seemed to mind.

"We're All Equal" was Durham's ideal

To the casual observer, Durham is not just like any other small town, even at first glance. As stated in the "Visitor's Viewpoint, " Durham has the feel and aura of a Western town.   It has a boardwalk and some false storefronts reminiscent of another era.

How many other towns have visible reminders of their place of importance in history, such as the Santa Fe Trail ruts outside of town?

There is a definite pride and active interest in Durham's part in history that is shared by Durhamites today.   Jim Hein, whose ancestors have been in the Durham area since the late 1800's, says with enthusiasm, "I really wish I had been around in the 1930's and 40's. . . there's a real romance to that era.   I guess Durham was in its heyday then.   The elm trees shaded Main Street, arching over the street to touch each other. During World War II, the troop trains gave a reminder to of the ongoing fight for the same freedoms for which the pioneers had come to this area. "

Hearing stories of growing up years in Durham, some aspects of the town become clear. The school was really like a big family and there was no such thing as a clique.

Everybody tried to get along and like each other. You could hardly walk down the halls and not speak to someone you met.   There was an acceptance of one another and a lack of concern with "coolness" of today's kids.

"Silliness" or "shenanigans" was more prevalent than "snobbery", and lacked the inherent put-down of snooty behavior. As a result, fun times were had at no-one-in-particular's expense.

Instead, like a family, tolerance, forebearance and respect especially for elders were the essence of relationships in Durham.   Confidence and self-esteem flourished in that atmosphere.

Centennial Logo Designer

Durham resident, Leila "Lin" Boucher, is the designer of Durham's Centennial logo which is featured on various articles, including belt buckles, hats and license plates, as well as the book cover.

The design incorporates various features of Durham's fascinating history.

In the distance is a scene of a covered wagon pulled by oxen past a large Cottonwood Tree, symbolizing the Santa Fe Trail and the important role the Cottonwood Crossing played in its development.

Just northwest of town, the Cottonwood Crossing was where travelers forded the river and traded at Moore's inn and trading post in the 1860's.

The Durham Bull, prominently featured, represents the Crane Ranch, located on the same spot as the Moore Ranch, and the development of the milking shorthorn breed by cross-breeding Texas longhorns with purebread Scottish cattle, notably the Durham breed. The ranch was named "Durham Park" for the imported cattle on the ranch.

On the bull's side is depicted a map of North America with a star pinpointing Durham's location.

Toward the bottom of the scene is a railroad track, symoblizing the important position Durham held on the main line of the Rock Island and its connection to the rest of the world at-large.

At the far left is a shaft of wheat denoting the agricultural focus of Durham.

Mrs. Boucher is an artist who accepted the challenge to help capture the Centennial mood in Durham.

Places and Faces

Over the meadow and through the woods, or, around the pasture and past the barn. This old photo is from the Funk family album, 1915.

Bathing beauties ... Irene Smith, Emma Borton, Mildred Powers, Bernita Voth, Martha Smith and Ona Smith. The fashions can help you guess the year this was taken.

Some members of the Baptist Church Ladies Aid, Durham

Dignified group of students...

Marion Smith's filling station on K-15.   Marion and Cameron Smith, pictured.

Longtime telephone operator Martha Zimmerman, at left, with Anna Frick, in front of the Frick home which also served as the phone company, with a room built on the side for the office.

This photo was taken about 1918 when the Yauk Grain Elevator was being built in Durham. Boys are George Weitzel, Harvey Yauk (middle of three in back) Clinton Yauk holding the reins, and Alex Weitzel. The other three are boys from Herrington.

Alma Clubine Armstrong and Walter Armstrong, taken by William Armstrong in 1906.

Mr. and Mrs. Pete Ratzlaff, Badger Lumber company manager, and daughter, 1916.

Mrs. Emil Ratzlaff, Mrs. Peter Ratzlaff and Mrs. Ben Ratzlaff, all fashionable yet serious young women.

Fred and Polly Kaiser.

The cellar beside the railroad tracks on Highway 15 in Durham was used by the Smith family as potato storage for many years. It included a pulley system on an overhead track to move merchandise inside.

The Wichita Eagle carried this photo of Durham's old fire bell, with the following caption on Thursday, June 23, 1966. "The Relic. Durham, Kansas, 10 miles north of Hillsboro, may be the only town in Kansas still able to boast a working fire alarm bell. Residents say the bell works fine and see no need for an expensive siren." (This bell has now been placed on a low mounting in front of the new fire house on Durham's Main Street.)

To School On Horseback

Willie Popp rode a horse to school in Durham from his family farm northeast of town for all 12 years of schooling in Durham. He remembers
that many other students also rode horses. The school had a red barn
north of the school to stable the horses and when the gym was built the
barn was moved. The barn often housed 15 - 20 horses a day, plus
some buggies and wagons.

"Grandfather" Oblander, with the livery stable, 1916.

John Borton of Durham joined in partnership with Clinton Chalmers in 1926 in Kansas City. The firm grew to be the nation's largest builder of grain elevators.

Jean Oblander submitted this photo of her father, George Peters, center, playing cowboy with friends.

Emanuel Becker, a local merchant, banker, and supporter of the town.

Durham's 75th anniversary gathering included festivities in front of the present post office building, then a cafe.

In 1977, Durham had a celebration to mark the town's ninetieth anniversary. Mrs. Amelia Smith, 90, eldest resident of the town, received a corsage. Other activities were turtle races, balloon races and frog races for the kids, and picnic and visiting for the grown-ups.

Hannah, Jake, Irwin, Tobias, Mary and Leona Dirks as children. Part of the Isaac Dirks family.

A few quilters in Feb., 1960. Standing, Mrs. Oblander, Elizabeth Kerbs, Tena Jacobs, Seated, Emelia Youk, Maude Haas, Emma Stammeyer, Gertie Schwemmer, Katie Becker.

Morene Zimmerman and her uncle, Jake Zimmerman, custodian of the school, doing summer cleaning.

The Funk family, in front of the home place, 1937, Edna, Arch, Grandma, Grandpa, R.H. and Adolph.

Grandma Garrett

The Garrett home, rural Durham with Edwin, Lillie, Grandma Garrett, and Great-Grandmother Ellis out front.

Celebration of 1947, Melvin and Geraldine Frick and children, Janet and Galen.

Marion Smith's bridges were uniquely designed with an arch and
bannister and a round knob on top.

Bridges by Pavey Smith

Beautifully scupltured bridges around Marion County were the handiwork of Marion ("Pavey") Smith, of Durham, who developed his own "trademark" (as bridge builders did) and built a great many early bridges in the area, some of which still remain.

Bridges, spanning creeks and rivers, and connecting two separate areas, seem to represent a transcendent quality for many folks, and provide a special link. They were vital to the development of area roads, and so, bridge builders were much in demand and respected for their skills.

It is interesting to note that then county commissioner John Smith recorded that in 1919 Marion Smith was paid $318 for nine bridges, among which were two Lehigh bridges, the J. P. Moore bridge and the Jacob Becker bridge. The labor was recorded at about $53 for all nine.

"Pavey" is shown with some of his family members in one of these scenes.

Bridges

Another bridge being built by Marion Smith...also known as Pavey.

Durham Buildings

Does this look like a movie theater? Those "in the know" remember June 5, 1950. Around 1950, Durham merchants, led by Alex Becker, sponsored Monday night outdoor movies free to the community. The "screen" was a large white canvas placed near the rear of the cafe, and an itinerant projectionist showed movies, mainly westerns and general fare. The entertainment attracted large crowds who sat on blankets or folding chairs in front, while packed cars jammed the streets nearby. A colorful page in the town's life: and an example of the creative endeavor of merchants.

Durham Oil Company, 1920, owner H.W. Schultz.

Valley Hotel livery barn, in early days.

Nina M. Youk was prioprietor of the Valley Hotel in the 1920's and early 30's. Her daughter-in-law, Dorothy, wife of Dennis Youk who tends the Santa Fe Trail ruts near Durham, remembers Nina's description of the hotel's main floor plan. Just inside the front door and to the left was the lobby and behind it were the living quarters for the Youk family. The guests stayed upstairs. It was a very gracious and pretty place to stay. Later the Dave Rhode family occupied the hotel as a home.

Durham Jail was a local landmark for half a century

A sketch of Durham's jail, a 10-by-12 foot building of cement blocks, with a double door, (one wood, one steel), and a barred window.

It had one window, barred, and a steel door, and was demolished sometime during the 1960's. Although efforts have been made to obtain a photo of it, none seem to exist, and so the Durham Jail, like many other faces, names, activities, traditions, and landmarks, in this book, will be held cherished in the memories of those who knew them.

April 2, 1912

Ordinance No. 38

An ordinance providing for the construction of a City Jail to be erected within the City of Durham, Kansas.

Be it ordained by the mayor and the councilmen of the City of Durham, Marion County, Kansas.

Section 1

That a cement block building shall be erected within the corporate limits of the City of Durham, for the use as a city jail.

Section 2

That said building shall be built in the southwest corner of block K of said City and such building shall be 10' wide and 12' long outside measurement and not less than 8' high from the inside. Said building shall have a cement foundation, floor and arch roof. The wall upon this foundation shall be made of 9" cement blocks to extend with this thickness up to the beginning of the arch and 5¼" cement block the rest of the way up. Two ventilators shall be provided on the roof and one door on the south with a small window, 9" x 12" above it and one small window 9" x 12" on the north end.

Section 3

That the City shall purchase the ground from Marion Smith upon which the said building is to be erected, commencing 2' north of the northwest corner of the building of block K then direct east to the south line of block K then along south line of block K to the south west corner.

Section 4

That when said building is completed upon the described lot, the city shall receive a deed for the ground from Marion Smith and said party shall agree to deed over the ground to the City furnish the material except the door for the jail and construct the building for the amount of $175. 00 to be paid to Marion Smith out of the General Fund.

D. A. Eichenour   John Smith
City Clerk   Mayor

The Becker family has been in business in Durham for a long time. Dorman Becker, grandson of Jacob Becker, is president of the Durham State Bank. The Becker building, later operated as a mercantile by Alex and Immanuel, is presently in use as the town's community building, and Senior Citizen Center.

Badger Lumber yard.

Photo taken during the 1930's shows Rice Grain Co. elevator, and was part of Durham. Oblander service station shows at left of elevator.

Ted Oblander's service station, as shown on their Christman card one year.

RECOLLECTIONS OF SATURDAY NIGHT IN DURHAM
IN THE MID-1940s

"Saturday night,
"Saturday night,
"Ain't you glad we got Saturday night!"

If ever there was a built-in reason for entertainment and socializing, it was Saturday nights in a small town, and Durham was no exception.

"You could not get a parking place anywere on Main Street," remembers Anna Mae Goertz. "The town was always crowded, the stores were all open, and the farmers had come to town to do their shopping and trading. It was a lively, and fun evening and you could plan on seeing everyone you knew."

Anna Mae was a young student at Durham High School during the mid-1940s. Her sister, Martha, was married to Mr. Eldo Frantz, who operated Frantz Grocery, one of three grocery stores in the town at that time, and Anna Mae remembers clerking in the store after school, and also on Saturdays, which were something extra special.

"Saturday was a very busy night in the grocery store, starting around 6 or 7 p.m. Farmers hurried through supper and chores, then headed for 'town.' We were busy exchanging cream and eggs for credit on groceries, writing up and packing the orders. In those days, the lunch meat was in long tubes, and we sliced it up on the slicing machine to order. And cookies and potatoes were bulk items that had to be weighed up according to each customer's needs."

The other two grocery stores were Becker's, which also had a dry goods store and meat market, and Temples Grocery, run by an older couple. Beckers had a creamery adjoining it, and was on the west side in the north block. Frantz Grocery was on the corner, diagonally across from the bank, in the building later occupied by Mac's Grocery (or Dick and Mac's) while Temple's was located south of the bank. (After Temples closed down, Frantz later had his grocery store in that location).

"As I said, there wasn't a parking place to be found, with all the farmers' cars in town, and there was quite a lot of traffic, as the young men drove their dad's cars around and around. The girls, junior high age and up, had a tradition of walking around the business district, circling the area and looking for friends. And there were the bench sitters, too... the merchants provided ben-ches in front of their places of business, and the old-timers, 'men who were wishing they were still young', would sit there watching the activities."

There wasn't a lot to see, but Durham was 'the place to see and be seen' on Saturday nights.

Since this was before the advent of television, and since Durham never had a movie theater, all entertainment was confined to inter-personal relationships... a fact which suited the young folks just fine.

There were two cafes at that time – Riffel's Cafe, and Dick's Cafe. Each had a lot of business on Saturday night. Hank Dick's place was known for its 5 and 10 cent hamburgers, and Riffels, (known as Jenny and Abie's Place) had a juke box that played all the hit parade favorites... five songs for a quarter.

"The young people would get together and crowd into booths at the two cafes. That's the way a lot of romances started. Boys and girls would crowd in, order something, sit and tell jokes, flirt, or giggle, or listen to the jukebox," Anna Mae said.

There were some domino and punchboard activities for the older folks. It was a friendly atmosphere.

While the grocery stores were doing a brisk business, and the streets and cafes were jammed with patrons, one of the biggest-selling items over at the hardware and implement store was Aladdin Lamp chimneys and mantles. Because of the absence of electricity in rural areas, kerosene lanterns were an essential part of farm life. Also selling well were bb shells. Rifle shells did a brisk business too, because at that time, rabbits were fair game, and their pelts could be sold in town for extra money. (The hardware store was one of the last to remain open on Saturday nights).

Christmastime in Durham featured Christmas lights of all colors, cross-crossing above the streets for the holiday mood.

After the formation of the Durham Lions Club 29 years ago, the Lions Club took on the project of bringing Santa Clause to town to visit with the children and hand out free candy and peanuts. His visit was timed for Saturdays, even though by the 1960s, with changing times, Durham no longer "stayed open" for business on Saturday nights.

"But back in those days, this town was a sight to see on Satur-days," Anna Mae Goertz concluded. "Oftentimes we didn't close the store until 11:30 or midnight, whenever we got all the customers taken care of. Those are nice memories."

A scene of early-day Durham includes the post office, Funk's Grocery, Dick's Cafe, Laubhan Shoe Shop and Creamery, and Charlie Jones General Store.

"A Visitor's View of Durham"

"My hobby is the Model T Ford, " says Larry Buller of Goessel, a shop teacher at Marion Schools. "I've learned to appreciate used and unrestored items regardless of condition. "

"There were 15 million Model T's built, and many of these still exist. But historical sites are one of a kind, and their existence is precarious.

"Durham, Kansas, has quite a number of original, unrestored sites, to be seen before they disappear or are restored. In fact, I believe the downtown area gives the impression of an inhabited town of the late 1800's. "

One of Buller's earliest impressions of Durham was on opening day of pheasant season, when all the pheasant hunters came for the Pancake Feed, sponsored by the Lions Club.

"I noticed the western atmosphere of the town, the square false storefronts and the boardwalk underneath the overhang by the cafe, that definitely gives it a western appearance. "

Buller said he was also intrigued by the old hotel, because it hasn't been restored and the hitching rail (in front of G and R Implement). . . all reminders of Durham's proud and noble past.

Buller is hoping to put together a Model T Car Club Tour of this area, probably in 1988.

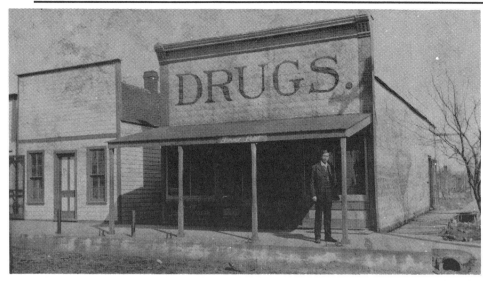

Power's Drug Store, with Walter Powers in front.
The R.W. Powers Drug Store preceeded Newall Drug Store.

Main Street of Durham in 1939 taken from the railroad track, looking north. The second hotel in town, The Blue Goose or Durham Hotel, had burned down by this time, but had been located in near right of photo.

The Durham State Bank before its remodeling in 1975.

THE TRACKS

Durham's two railroad crossings, one on Highway 15 and the other at the south end of Main Street, saw a lot of rail traffic over the years. Eventually the highway crossing had a guard and signals put up, but to this day, Main Street crossing is unguarded. Given the fact that there were up to 25 trains a day through town during the height of the railroad period, and during WWII, troop trains passed about every 40 minutes, day and night, east and west bound, and the fact that the town was intersected by the track, one would think the inevitable would have taken lives, yet few fatal accidents involving trains occured.

Main Street of Durham today...looking north from the railroad tracks. Ben Goertz crossing street.

60th ANNIVERSARY OF DURHAM
1887-1947
Wednesday, Thursday, May 28-29

A Word of Appreciation

The executive committee of the Durham Chamber of Commerce wishes to take this opportunity to express its sincere appreciation of the whole-hearted generosity and cooperation of the many persons whose efforts have made this show possible. Thank you, folks – hope you all enjoy the celebration.

Rules and Regulations

The show, being of a mutual and cooperative nature, will not be responsible for any accident that may occur to any horse, person or property, or damage to any vehicle at the show, or loss of any property.

Wednesday, May 28, 1947

1. 11:00 a. m. Parade
   A. Bands
   B. Old Settlers
   C. Bearded Men
   D. Floats (As Durham Was)
   E. Floats (Durham of Today)
   F. New Automobiles, Machinery
   G. Bicycles, Ponies, Pets
   H. Livestock

2. 12:00 noon Stunt flying
   12:30 - 1:00 p. m. Platform Appearance and Introduction of Old Settlers.

3. 1:30 Horse Show
   Grand Entry
   Canton Drill Team
   Melvin Christner, Trick and fancy roping
   Marion Drill Team
   Klinkermans, Trick and fancy roping
   Virginia Reel (Marion Club)
   Melvin Christner, Trick roping
   Bundle Race (Open)
   Potato Race (Open, young men)
   Potato Race (Open, old men)

Potato Race (Open, women and kids)
Chair Race (Open)
Stock Horse Race (Open)

(Admission: 50¢ and 25¢)

4. Children's Contests on Streets
5. 7:00 p. m. Ball Game, Durham vs. Canada

(Admission, Free)

6. 8:30 p. m. Ark Valley Boys (at Gymnasium)

(Admission: 50¢ and 25¢)

7. 10:00 p. m. Dance and Street Program
8. Bearded Men Contest

THURSDAY, MAY 29, 1947

1. 11:00 a. m. Parade
   A. Marion County Veterans
   B. Peabody Rodeo Personnel and Equipment
   C. Cottonwood Valley Saddle Horse Ass'n. and other horse entries.
   D. School Bands
2. 12:00 noon Stunt Flying
   (A) Horse shoe Pitching
3. 1:00 p. m. Military March and Drill
4. 1:30 p. m. Peabody Rodeo
   1. Grand Entry
   2. Calf Roping
   3. Bundle Race
   4. Potato Race
   5. Chair Race
   6. Clowning

Jerry Hindricks and Jerry, of Nickerson, Kansas with his trained mules will be an outstanding feature of the rodeo. Jerry has clowned some of the largest rodeos in the middle west in the past 5 years.

(Admission: 50¢ and 25¢)

6. 7:00 p. m. Ball Game, Tampa vs. Durham

(Admission Free)

7. 8:30 p. m. Amateur Program
   Selected numbers who excell in their art.

(Admission: 50¢ and 25¢)

8. 9:00 p. m. Lottery Drawing
9. 10:00 p. m. Platform Dance
   (1) Street Program

(A unit from the Rockwell Shows will be on the street both days).

60th Anniversary Celebration

A Time
To Remember

MARION RECORD
Your County Newspaper
Marion, Marion County, Kansas

Thursday, May, 8, 1947
Around Durham They're Really Itchin' For The Big Celebration
May 28, 29 1947

Durham Makes Big Plans For City's 60th Birthday
* * * * * * * * * * * *

Two Days Event May 28 and 29 To Be Complete With Parades, Games, Stage Shows, Horseshow And Exhibitions.

Plans are nearly complete at Durham for an elaborate celebration May 28 and 29 to commemorate the 60th Anniversary of the incorporation of Durham as a city.

Anyone visiting the vicinity is immediately aware something is brewing, for the men of the town are sporting mustaches, beards, and side burns of some weeks' growth for the occasion. One event the first day will be a parade of bearded men with a prize to be awarded for the best beard exhibited.

The tentative program for May 28 includes a parade of floats, including floats of old settlers that are, or formerly were, around Durham.

The morning will also include a commercial parade and a farmers stock parade. A three hour horse show will be featured in the afternoon. At 7 p. m. the Durham ball team will meet Canada and at 8:30 p. m. the Ark Valley Boys of KFH Wichita will stage their program at the high school auditorium.

May 29 plans are laid for a military parade headed by a bugle corps in which all the veterans of Marion county are invited to join.

A rodeo and other contests presented by a Peabody group, and a parade by the Cottonwood Valley Horse Association will be featured in the afternoon. A ball game between Durham and Tampa to be followed by an Uncle Ezra program at the high school auditorium will wind up events in the evening.

School bands will take part in the parade. An added feature each noon will be stunt flying by Ed Stenzel, an accomplished acrobatic pilot.

Shorty Klein, with "Emma S. and Berniece L." along Main Street. Bustles and uniforms seen at the event.

Men's Celebration Beards Link Modern Durham With Days Of Yore

FRONT ROW LEFT TO RIGHT:
Ralph Steiner, Dave Laubhan, Gotfrey Klein, Henry Plett, H. H. Kaiser, Roy Jantz, Clinton Frick, Alex Becker-Mayor, Irwin Geis, Pete Frick, Henry Dick, Irwin Dick, Carrol Rhodes, Cocky Frick, Virgil Bryan.

SECOND ROW LEFT TO RIGHT:
G. E. Weins, Cameron Smith, Alfred Steiner, Louie Stammeyer, Georgie Klein, Chas. McDowell, Dave Dick, Preston Rhodes, Willie Popp, Donald Duke, Cecil Medley, Dale Rhodes, Ben Jantz, LeRoy Hein, Jack Rhodes.

THIRD ROW LEFT TO RIGHT:
Martin Helmer, John Lais, John Bessel, Harry Garrett, Melvin Meier, Merle Dick, Frank Ewert, Clinton Haas, Merrel Christiansen, Johnnie Petker, Ernest Petker, Lou Steiner, Gaylord Hamm, Junior Medley, Ruben Funk, Henry Goertz.

FOURTH ROW LEFT TO RIGHT:
Wm. Dobbs, Wayne Belton, Harvey Mohn, Earl Frick, Francis Steiner, Reinholdt Winter, Carl Winter, Ed Klein, Dan Goertz, Carrol Christiansen, Sam Laubhan, Edwin Winter, Bob Rhodes.

LAST ROW LEFT TO RIGHT:
Fred Schneider, Clif. Negley, Wesley T. David, Eddie Klein, Jake Hein, Lawrence Klein, Roland Kerbs, Geo. Peters, Chas. Borton, Ben Frick, Dave Klein, Harry Laubhan, Howard Schultz, Ralph Unholz, Emanuel Becker, and Emil Schwemmer.

HISTORY OF DURHAM

DURHAM TODAY AND AS IT WAS
By
W. T. David

Durham is essentially a part of and a product of its surrounding communities. In view of this it is felt that any summary of this city that does not include this territory would leave much lacking. Also it is felt that a mere arrangement in chronological order of the events leading to the founding of Durham and its development and of the surrounding area that did not include our present potentialities, advantages, way of life, and a bit of our philosophy would be highly incomplete. Therefore, the above are included not only in the hope that it may prove of interest to the visitor to whom it is our pleasure to extend our hospitality on this occasion, but also to us who are residents of this city or one of its communities in order that it may give us pause, to consider our heritage, and perhaps ponder the many natural advantages a far-seeing Providence has seen fit to bestow on this region.

This commercial segment of our business and professional men is composed mainly of those who have been long-time residents of Durham or its surrounding area. Due to their vast experience and ours from carpet tacks and groceries to the most modern power equipment they aren't prepared to furnish or service. Further you will find their code requires they personally stand behind every transaction, and service. Their interest in the service they have rendered, transaction they have made and in you individually doesn't end when you close the door. In a nation where it often seem a man's personal worth is gauged by the size of the check he can write, it is indeed refreshing to find that priceless small city and rural virtue wherein a man's personal integrity and character count far more than his worldly goods.

Durham and its surrounding communities can perhaps best be described as being typical of the predominately rural areas of the middle west. The human frailties and virtues, sorrows and joys, to which the flesh is heir, though perhaps more dramatized in other places, also have their counterpart in our lives. If the charge sometimes leveled at us by our big city cousins, that we are vocally overly interested in the private affairs of our neighbors has foundation in fact, we take comfort in feeling that the recording angel will find, we also care for them when they are sick. Our educational requirements are met by our local schools, our spiritual needs by our city and community churches.

This writer, after observing the moral level not only in widely separated centers of the nation but of many nations in different parts of the world for over a period of twelve years, feels the chances of going to Heaven via our spiritual institutions in Durham will in all probability be equal to that of most places, and will indeed surpass many.

Our economy is basically agricultural. You may read or hear of regions that boast as being the "land of the orange blossoms," "Where the tall corn grows," or "where cotton is king," without ever realizing that we too have a just claim to fame, that can surpass that of most. This is the region of diversified agriculture. To amplify this we can state that most of the leading grain crops thrive here. The yields and quality are both good. Our wheat is among the best. The native bluestem patures are the equal of any in the nation. The production, raising, and feeding for market of quality beef herds on locally grown feeds has been one of our earliest industries. The dairy industry has thrived and is rapidly growing on the same basis. The commercial raising of poultry and its allied products is practiced to a greater or lesser extent almost without exception on every farm. The raising of both swine and sheep is successfully practiced here, and almost entirely on locally grown products. The above list is far from complete, but it should show why we lay claim to fame, as the home of diversified agriculture, and by the same token it should show the marked superiority in economic soundness over regions whose economy is based on one or two leading crops or industries.

In this occasion we are commemorating the 60th anniversary of the founding of Durham. You have no doubt noticed our attempt to bring back a bit of the color of frontier days, and perhaps wondered what we have to offer in our past association with history making days. An investigation revealed an astonishing amount of material in connection with the settlement and development of Durham, and its outlying territory. Unfortunately it is beyond the scope of this narrative to cover it except in a general manner. To cover the names of all persons prominent in our early history, the events worthy of recording and the establishment of the various enterprises in an impartial manner and with the detail of which they are worthy would easily fill a small volume.

To anyone with a sincere interest in the history of this region it can be said that a good part of it is still a living page. There are still a few of the old timers remaining, men who can recall when the site of what is now Durham was a meadow from which they cut hay. They can recall the time during which the Rock Island built the railroad through here, and the day, July 9th, 1887, when the first train ran on the new rails through what is now Durham, and the gradual establishment of the places of business and residences of what is now our city.

Located one-half mile west and about one north of town stands a marker showing where the old Santa Fe Trail ran. This trail was opened in 1822 to establish trade with Santa Fe, New Mexico, then a part of Old Mexico and a colonial possession of Spain. The fame of the Santa Fe Trail is well known. Books have been written on it, and screen versions of some of the publications shown. This nevertheless seems an appropriate occasion to remind us that a short distance west of Durham ran a trail famous in the history of the nation and our state. Men who became historically famous figures in the frontier west, such as Kit Carson, Jim Bridger, and a host of others passed here. Over it went troops on their way to the Indian Wars, and soldiers on the march during the Civil War, and last but far from least those pioneers whose dauntless courage opened the Southwest. More than one traveler on this trail found our part of the Cottonwood Valley a fair land, and when circumstances permitted, a number again returned and made their homes here, several of these early settlers later becoming prominent public figures in the county and state. The color of the old western frontier long lingered here, in the form of the immigrant trains and overland freight outfits. Their outfits would have as many as sixty or eighty wagons pulled with eight or ten yoke of oxen. A thousand head of working cattle to pull the caravan for one outfit was no unusually large number. Some of the wagons held as much as one-half a carload of freight. In addition they usually carried from one hundred to a hundred and fifty passengers. A trip required from six to eight months. West of town on the Santa Fe Trail in what is now known as McDonald's pasture in 1865 occurred one of those grim tragedies often attended to travel in the west at that time. Two immigrants wagons were found here, with four adults and three children killed and scalped by Indians. They were found by soldiers returning from the Civil War, at least one of whom settled in this community very shortly thereafter. From this it becomes evident that those epics of courage, endurance and high hopes that marked those stirring days found full expression here. Men living in this community attended the ceremony when the Santa Fe Trail marker northwest of Durham was erected in 1906. They can well recall the principal speakers of the day, and what is a note of more than passing interest, also well remember seeing a program of the day with the names of the principal speakers and their texts, along with a copy

of the newspaper, "The Marion Record", and a penny being placed in a copper box, sealed, put in the stone marker and cemented in place.

Located on the Santa Fe Trail a short distance north of "The Cottonwood Crossing" about a mile and a half northwest of Durham was a stage coach station, a trading post and later a post office and bank. Also a company of soldiers from Fort Leavenworth were stationed here for a time to hold the Indians in check. Legend has it that this company of soldiers at one time hotly pursued by Indians, spiked and dumped a cannon in the Cottonwood River at a point later known as "Cannon Hole". Although efforts have been made in the past to locate the lost cannon it has never been found as far as is now known.

The above named establishments also marked the location of the headquarters of a ranch, a famous showplace in its day and from which the name of our city was derived. This ranch was purchased by Albert S. Crane in 1872 and consisted of 4160 acres. It was started with an initial capital of three million dollars. Although this ranch was best known by the name of "Crane's Ranch" the name "Durham Park" was the one bestowed on it by its owner. The name Durham was taken from the large herd of fine Durham cattle, imported from Scotland. The owner tried to lay out his domain in the general plan of a park, hence the name Durham Park. The post office on the ranch was known as the Durham Park Post Office, and when in 1888 it was moved to the present site of our city, the name went with it. Since this township also has the same name derived from the same source it is at once evident why our city was called Durham, a shortened version of Durham Park, and why the nationally known figure of a "Durham Bull" is our official letterhead.

Some of the features that distinguished "Crane's Ranch" were the large three hundred square foot cattle sheds strung out over a distance of ten miles. These sheds had hay barns in the center with a capacity of three hundred ton of hay. Most of the time an average of one hundred and eighty head of cattle were haltered and stalled in these sheds. An additional five hundred head of stock cattle were cared for. There were seven tenant farms on this ranch. The balance was farm and meadow land. The entire unit was enclosed by twenty-two miles of four board fence. The main ranch residence, built by the owner, was a large house best known as the "White House," since it was the only building of that color on the ranch. The local wits however also referred to it as the "House of Lords" since it was often remarked it seemed no one was allowed to enter it except English Lords. It was in fact first managed by an English Lord, T.A. Reed, nicknamed "Porcupine." Charles W. Jones related in a letter written in 1940 that the largest of the Durham cattle weighed as much as three thousand pounds, and ranged in price from five hundred to thirty thousand dollars.

Also he saw two hogs weighing thirty-two hundred pounds.

It was during the time the Durham Park Post Office was located here that the mail carrier driving a mail cart from Hillsboro to Abilene and delivering mail here enroute was drowned fording the Cottonwood west of Durham. As can be readily seen a complete history covering the life of the ranch, its operation and management would fill a long chapter in itself.

The above are but a few of the many tales that could be told in linking this territory with a past that has its full share or more of frontier, historical lore. It has been wisely said, we see the things we look for. We hope, we have supplied that want at least partially in this narrative of "DURHAM TO-DAY AND AS IT WAS."

We wish to acknowledge our debt and gratitude to the following named persons whose information and hearty cooperation made this work possible: Marion Smith, Cameron Smith, Miss Frances Jones, Mrs. Laura Jones, and Wm. Carter.

The following is a listing of names, places, events, and a few news items directly connected with the founding of Durham, as supplied by Miss Frances Jones. We include them not only because of their historical value and because they serve to establish our "local landmarks," but also to pay tribute to the memory of those named who are no longer with us, and for the sake of "Auld Lang Syne" and those memories and sentiments of days gone by, so dear to the hearts of the "old timers" of this community.

In February, 1887, the town of Durham was platted by the Golden Belt Town Co., and the following June the Chicago, Rock Island and Pacific Railroad was built through the town. Early in the same year Funk City was started on the land adjoining Durham on the east, south of the railroad, (the farm which is now owned by Lewis Haas) and a number of business houses and dwellings were erected.

J.A. Stephenson was appointed town agent.

The first dwelling erected in Durham was by Fred Auschivitz, on February 21, block 8, south of the railroad. J.A. Stephenson built the first dwelling north of the railroad. T.A. Wardrop built the first blacksmith shop.

In June, 1888, J.A. Stephenson was appointed post master, Minnie Holmes, assistant, and the post office was moved from the White House (Crane's Ranch) one and one-half miles northwest of Durham.

During the spring, population began to increase rapidly, and Frank Peaslee, of Glen Elder, Kansas, opened the first dry goods and grocery store, and Theodore Smith, the first lumber yard.

Geo. Crawford erected a dwelling on the corner of Sixth Street and Lawrence Avenue (the present home of Wm. Carter) and opened a hardware store on Main Street. Richard Ross and David Ehman erected the first carpenter shop.

In 1888 the school district voted to change the location of the school from Crane's Ranch to Durham, and build a two story, four room building. The proposition carried, and the building was constructed and completed by Theodore Smith on the northeast corner and Lawrnece Avenue (the present home of Wm. Carter) and the teacher employed was Mrs. J.P. Gardenire, who taught three terms in succession.

Dr. P.H. Bartell thinking Durham would be a more prosperous town than Salina contracted with Ross and Ehman for the construction of a two story dwelling (now the home of E.M. Becker) on the southeast corner of Sixth Street and Lawrence Avenue.

During this time David Whiteman, John Heidel, Henry Weident, Herman Luck and Fred Reising all built dwellings south of the railroad. While on the north side of the railroad Frank Baker, Richard Ross, Thomas Bell, Ella McArthur, Conrad Shaffer and others rivaled in the town boom.

By this time J.C. Dyck, who had a large building and stock of dry goods and groceries in Funk City saw that Durham was the great metropolis so decided to move him improvements and stock of goods to Durham (Mr. Tobias Dirks has his feed mill in the building at the present time). Others seeing this fine move that Mr. Dyck had made, moved their buildings from Funk City to Durham, thus leaving Funk City in ruins.

Conrad Stebbins started the first livery stable and hotel in town.

Phillip Warren and C.W. Jones were the first butchers.

In the early summer of 1888, the first Sunday School was organized and held in the Rock Island Depot waiting room until the school house was completed. The Methodist minister from Canton, Kansas would come each Sunday to deliver his sermon, returning to his home in the evening by a five o'clock train. The Sunday School superintendent was Birch Bowyer.

The Samuel Schultz Mercantile Co., was established in 1890.

The Badger Lumber Co., was established in 1892 with J.A. Stephenson as manager.

C.W. Jones opened a general store in 1892.

H.C. Funk owned and operated the first creamery which was later destroyed by fire.

In 1898, N.A. Jones opened up the first barber shop.

D.B. Kraus and Adam Huenergardt opened a general store in 1897 and in 1900 G. Meschke and Co. purchased his stock.

In 1890 Joe Pickerel established the first drug store.

In the summer of 1889 the Durham Park Cemetery was surveyed and platted.

Herbert Thorpe of Marion opened the first bank in Durham.

Some of the early blacksmiths were T.L. Wardrop, M.L. Doberstein, T.L. Bauslin, L.E. Borton, Andy Lasure, Herman Moretz and Frank Neil.

J.M. Clubine and Co. established an implement and grain business in 1902.

The year 1903 found J.T. Parry in a confectionary and cigar store.

October, 1903, Rural Route No. 1 was established with Nicholas A. Jones as carrier and Walter Armstrong as substitute.

Mrs. C.R. Shaner opened the first millinery store.

W.D. Armstrong erected a two story hotel and livery barn in 1902, the latter being burned to the ground in March, 1906 but was rebuilt at once.

In April, 1904, the cornerstone of the first M.E. Church was laid out the following November the church was dedicated, with J.F. Severance as pastor. In the same year the Severance Chapter of the Epworth League was organized.

In 1905, Ole Comstock owned and operated the first bakery.

Andrew Lasure built the first building in town of cement blocks. The blocks were manufactured by Marion Smith.

The following are some to the first teachers and pupils that can be recalled by Mrs. Laura Jones:

Mrs. J. P. Gardenier	Mr. Will Dodge
Miss Eva Boyce	Miss May Wood
Mr. E. M. Rider	Miss Jenny Corby
Miss Eva Dickerson	Mr. R. W. Powers
Mr. C. B. Wolf	Mr. George Orr
Mr. I. C. Meyers	Miss Daisy Graham

PUPILS 1888-1890

Will Armstrong	Phillip Lauback	Henry Peaster
Curtis Bartells	Frank Stephenson	Alice Thompson
Tom Armstrong	May Kniffin	Mary Kniffin
Uriah Warren	Dan Smith	Cory Smith
Minnie Holmes	Eugene Keefer	Edith Branton
Horace Phillips	Jim Keefer	Katie Schaffer
Rosa Phillips	Ben Frantz	Edith Holmes
Laura Bartells	Peter Frantz	con Frick
Alta Bartells	Edward Frantz	Anna Frick
Harley Stephenson	Emil Frantz	Phillip Frick
Arthur Stephenson	Eva Unruh	Sadie Frick
Floyd Stephenson	Henry Unruh	Alex Frick
Clint Bowyer	Minnie Unruh	Charlie Bowyer
Henry Whiteman	Monel Baker	Mittie Bowyer
Lydia Schaffer	Libbie Peaster	Maud Ross

Eddie Walker	Grace Heatwol	Henia Schaffer
John Crawford	Leah Bowyer	Lizzie Zitterkoph
Mary Thompson	Leota Bowyer	Anna Peaster
Katie Meng	Edna Rupp	

PUPILS OF 1894

Anna Herald	Harry Swift	Amanda Clark
Yates Herald	Emma Clark	Maude Swift
Blanche Herald	Hollis Smith	Dess Smith
Nora Swift	Marion Clark	Amelia Wymer

Durham people are partial in the use of nicknames. We doubt if any town in this part of the state has as many according to its size as Durham and here they are:

Beckham	Coon	Post Crugier
Sheenie	Badger	Tiriff
Spider	Cummie	Schnook
Spoke-Wheel	The Peaches	Sijach
Schemer	Scully	Mike
Brick	Tim	Sliver
Boots	Rastus	Honey
Smoke	Joshua	Peanut
Nicholas Allison	Lizzie	Doc
Dummy	Winter	Steel
Doley	Padukie	Castings
Rabbit	Old Dad	Dutch
Happy	Old Honesty	Germany
Bean Pole	Vag	Deannie
Wart-on-a-log	Gates	Bryan
Raincoat	Tub	Ezekiel
Ex-convict	Digie	Spot
Cheese	Bill	Kalsie
Dude	Lolla	Tar Heel
Hockum	Dingie	Picat
Bunker	Pavey	Chink
Cub	Hoogans	

How many of these can you old-timers identify?

In conclusion the executive committee would like to add a few remarks. First of all we wish to express our thanks to "Wesley T. David" for the splendid job he did in writing up this history of Durham.

Durham as it is today, is progressing very successfully under the leadership of Alex Becker, Mayor, who has served this City in that official capacity very faithfully for more than twenty-seven years. Our schools are directed by our board of education, namely Mr. D.D. Regier, Superintendent; Mr. Henry P. Goertz, Director; Irwin Geis, Clerk; and Mr. R.R. Frick, Treasurer.

Business establishments which are in operation in this city at this time are the respective business men whose advertisements you see in this program.

This celebration is sponsored by the Durham Chamber of Commerce under the leadership of H.P. Goertz, President, D.D. Regier, Vice-President, Irwin Geis, Clerk and Emil Schwemmer, Treasurer.

LIST OF DONORS

Dr. L. G. Jaeger, Hillsboro, Kans.
H. D. Houlton, Abilene, Kans__
Lloyd Morrison, Salina, Kans.
R. R. Melton, M. D. , Marion, Ks.
Stock Yards National Bank, Kansas City, Mo.
Riddle Quarries, Inc. , Marion, Ks.
Case & Son Insurance, Marion, Ks.
Kansas Power & Light, Topeka
Maxwell & Furnish Comm. Co. ,
K. C. , Mo.
Sheeley Baking Co. , Emporia, Ks.
Lee Hardware Co. , Salina, Ks.
H. N. Goertz, Hillsboro, Ks.
McPherson Concrete Products,
McPherson
Nesbitt's Bottling Co. ,
McPherson, Ks.
Theo. Poehler Merc. Co. , McPherson
Dr. P. R. Hoeppner, Hillsboro
Jake Groening Motor Co. ,
Hillsboro, Ks.
Rollins Meat Products, Wichita, Ks.
Sutorius Bread Co. , Newton, Ks.
Wolf Creamery Co. , Marion, Ks.
Kansas Egg & Poultry Co. ,
Hillsboro, Ks.
Buller Manuf. Co. , Hillsboro, Ks.
C. S. Klassen, Hillsboro, Ks.
W. L. Schultz, Hillsboro, Ks.
Dr. Herbert C. Eitzen, Hillsboro, Ks.

H. F. Jansen, M. D. , Hillsboro, Ks.
Robert Jost, Hillsboro, Ks.
Harlan Tatge, Ramona, Ks.
Klassen Cleaners, Hillsboro, Ks.
Groening Impl. Co. , Hillsboro, Ks.
Otto Schroeder, Hillsboro, Ks.
D. Loewen, Hillsboro, Ks.
Schultz Grocery, Hillsboro, Ks.
Cornelson Motor Co. , Hillsboro, Ks.
Herb's Auto Service, Hillsboro, Ks.
J. V. Friesen, Hillsboro, Ks.
Schaeffler Mercantile Co. ,
Hillsboro, Ks.

SPECIAL PREMIUM DONORS
The ribbons have been contributed by the Shepler's Saddlery Company, Wichita, Kansas.

Oh, the 60th anniversary of Durham was a time to remember. It seemed that almost the whole town got involved to make it a great celebration. As you'll see from the following advertisers, a lot hasn't changed from then to now. Except maybe the product name or the current manager/owner. Oh yes, one thing has certainly changed – phone numbers! From a 1-2 digit (and maybe a letter) to a current 7 digit number, providing you're calling locally. Do they really call this progress?!?

Norris Grain Company
The Place To sell Your Wheat
Chas. A. Borton, Mgr.
Phone 44A   Durham, Kansas

DURHAM HARDWARE
H. P. Goertz, Owner
Minneapolis-Moline and Oliver
Farm Implements
Perfection Stoves
De Laval Cream Separators and
Hardware
Phone 5-A   Durham, Kansas

DICK AND MAC'S GROCERY
We have a Full Line of Fresh
FRUITS and VEGETABLES
Also Up-to-date Line of Groceries
We buy EGGS, POULTRY and CREAM
Phone 38   Durham, Kansas

RIFFEL'S CAFE
Cold Drinks – Ice Cream – Cigarettes
Beer – Meals
Durham, Kansas

DURHAM STATE BANK
Prompt Courteous Service
Member of Federal Deposit Insurance Corporation
A HOME OWNED INSTITUTION
Durham, Kansas

DICK'S CAFE
Sandwiches – Beer
Short Orders – Pop – Chili
Regular Meals
Durham, Kansas

For Your Locak Livestock and
Grain Hauling
CALL
DURHAM TRUCK LINE
Phone 55-Y   Adam Jantz, Tampa, Ks.

- or -
Phone 1042   Donald Ewert, Durham, KS.
DURHAM, KANSAS

WOLF MOTOR CO.
Ford Sales and Service
"FIRESTONE"
The Mark of Quality and Symbol of Service
NORGE APPLIANCES
See Norge Before You Buy – A Borg-Warner Industry
Phone 27   Durham, Kansas

JOHN J. BESSEL
Sinclair Products
Auto Parts and Auto Repair
Phone 8   Durham, Kansas

B & R TRUCK LINE
Pick Up and Full Load
Call Victor 9030, Kansas City
747X, Herington, Kans.   1531, Durham, Kans.

BECKER MERCANTILE
General Merchandise
MEAT MARKET
Phone 18   Durham, Kansas

FRANTZ GROCERY & MARKET
Headquarters for Fresh Fruits and Vegetables
WE BUY POULTRY AND EGGS
Phone 13   Durham, Kansas

MARION COUNTY CO-OP. ASS'N
Gasoline – Oil – Grease – Tires – Tubes
and Radios
8-ft. Home Locker Units, Immediate Delivery
VIRGIL R. BRYAN   Durham, Kansas
EARL CRANDALL   Tampa, Kansas
ED J. UNRUH   Hillsboro, Kansas

DUKE'S SERVICE STATION
Derby Products Lubrication
SERVICE IS OUR BUSINESS
Phone 42-A   Durham, Kansas

Irwin Geis in the 60th anniversary parade.

Among the riders on this 60th anniversary float were Mesdames Yauk, Zimmerman, Hamm, Dick, Medley, Peters and Rhodes.

Geis School was represented by this Hudson Terraplane in the parades and fairs.

Durham's celebration, May 30, 1947, Pow-wow.

George and Molly Schafer

Marie Schneider and friend.

Charlie and Molly Borton with Ruby Yauk
and daughter, Muriel,

D. D. Regier is credited with doing a "tremendous job in organizing the 60th anniversary celebration. . . He was the ramrod of the whole celebration," it is reported. Mr. Regier also made a movie of the 60th celebration, which can be viewed on videotape during the Centennial.

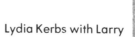
Lydia Kerbs with Larry

Jake and Hannah Hein

From left, Joyce Medley, Mary Katherine Rhode, Helen Hein, Mrs. Fred Schneider, and Mrs. Margaret Miller

The 60th celebration included a parade of horses.

From left, Anna Kaiser, Martha Lais and Marie Wiens.

Sports

Durham Bulls

Little Lucille Schwemmer, holds the ball for the Durham City Basketball Team, "Champs" in 1939. Back row; Shorty Holderman, Melvin Frick, Clinton Haas, Irwin Christiansen, Ralph Frick and Gilman Smith, with Emil Schwemmer. Front row, Lloyd Hein, Carl Buehler, Carroll Christiansen, Burtis Weible, Raymond Ratzlaff and Leonard Haas.

By Dean Nelson

For over a period of sixty school years, the community of Durham spent many hours of entertainment through the schools' and community's involvement in baseball, basketball, softball, track and football.

During its early days, baseball was a pastime for local men that formed a Durham Baseball Team. Al Jones, a local barber, was their manager and they traveled, by train or cars, to surrounding towns to play Saturday afternoon games.

An early-day baseball field was southeast of the Rock Island tracks, directly across from the present Co-op gas station.

Baseball was also played in a pasture, one-fourth mile north of town on the west side of Highway 15. Later, a baseball diamond was built on the site of the last Durham High School building, and all baseball and softball games were held on that diamond for many years.

Upon construction of this last High School building, in 1955, additional acres were purchased to construct the present ball diamond and local volunteers moved light poles and constructed backstops and fences, bleachers and a concession stand; these still stand but are not in use in the Durham Centennial year, 1987.

Durham's High School baseball and softball players enjoyed enthusiastic and loyal support, and these teams won many trophies through the years, and at various times had outstanding baseball and softball talent.

In 1933, Durham men organized a town baseball team. They were called the Durham Possums. They played up until 1940. Their games were mostly played with town teams from the North Marion County League, and were usually played on Sunday afternoons.

The Possums also played in various tournaments in the area. Their manager was Vic Riffel. Following is the roster of players and their positions: Hank Dick, pitcher; Dave Dick, catcher and second base; Melvin Frick, first base; Buster Haas, catcher and second base; Carl Bieler, shortstop and pitcher; Irwin Geis, third base; Emil Schwemmer, third base; Harvey Dick, outfield; Harvey Yauk, outfield; Pete Frick; second base and pitcher; John Belton, outfield; and Corky Erion.

An early-day ball team includes the following people: Standing, Jake Riffel, N.A. Jones, Alex Weimer; Second row, Cornelius Knaak, Red Redelgheifer and Menno Buehler; Third row, Frank Stephenson, Jake May, Bill (Cat) Lasure, Harley Stephenson, and mascot Arthur Funk. Taken in 1909.

A girl's basketball team at Durham School in 1923.

In the 1940's, a City Softball Team was organized which Willie Popp managed, and they played into the 60's on a regular basis. Fred Schneider was the umpire for the City softball team and also some of the High School teams.

The high school provided a steady supply of softball players, and many of these boys played at various times over a period of years. (See photo of those on the 1951 team).

Durham's City softball teams had good support from the community and tournaments were held with teams from Tampa, Lost Springs, Romona, Lincolnville, Burdick, Lehigh, Hope, Herington and others.

Some of the pitchers who pitched for the town's softball team during the 40's and 50's, included Marvin Kaiser, Loren Burch, Don Ewert, Delmer Klein, Kenny Klein, Dennis Klein, Bobby Hein and Larry Klein.

Cars would fill the parking lot behind the playing field and up the third and first base lines. And if a player could hit a pitch into the elm trees in left field, or to the gym wall in center field, it was surely a home run, and likewise for a line drive hit down the hill in right field.

In 1950, Dwight Nelson organized a boys baseball team, for ages 10 to 15 years, and managed them for two years. Fred Schneider also managed them later, and both managers had good win records. Local businesses provided uniforms for this team, and donations paid for equipment and balls. They played baseball and fast pitch softball.

Some of the youthful players on the kids' team included LaVern Dick, Ralph Vogel, Calvin Mohn, Dennis Kelin, Kenny Klein, Larry Klein, Tommy Belton, Jerry Bryan, Richard Klassen, Bobby Hein, Marvin Hamm, Soren Medley, LaVern Laubhan, Gary Kaiser and Dean Nelson.

The boys uniforms included the name of the donation company inscribed on the back, and a large 'D' on the front of the shirt.

Durham Red Brick High School was completed in 1910 and a gym was added in 1925, but prior to that, basketball was played in a room upstairs over the Ed Becker garage, and due to the low ceiling and support posts, this could make the playing of basketball really interesting. This building is directly north of the present post office.

1913 ball team, kneeling, Carl Riffel, Roy Walker, B.F. Belton, Dr. Harry Davis, E.M. Becker, Chris Haas, Henry Schletthauer; sitting, Ed Becker, Dave Riffel, Arthur Schultz, Henry Yauk and George Riffel.

Basketball continued into the 1930's and track was also a school sport. Girls' basketball was in, and their games were played prior to the boys' games.

Just to show how much Durham loved to play basketball, this story is told. A tournament was being held in Tampa in the 1930's, and because of snow, roads were closed, so the team was to go to Tampa by train. Buzzy Smith, one of the players, arrived late, missing the train, so what to do? He then decided to walk down the Rock Island tracks to Tampa, about seven miles, and made it in time to play ball.

During the years 1936 to 1938, Durham High had a good basketball team. They were called the Blue Jays, and colors were blue and white. Later, the school teams were known as the Durham Hornets, and their colors were green and white.

A local sports fan, wearing

the Durham Possums uniform.

City of Durham Softball Team, 1951
Left to right, back row, Oliver Mohn, Donald Ewert, Don Klein, Lewis Steiner, Lloyd Hein, Loren Burch, Melvin Frick, Marvin Kaiser, Harvey Martens, Lawrence Klein. Front row, Bill Medley, Merle Dick, Dorman Becker, Tommy Belton, Fred Schneider, Umpire, Willie Popp, Mgr. Alfred Steiner.

Dean Nelson, LaVern Dick and Ralph Vogel...summer of 1951.

The D.G.S. team includes, (from left, front) Jim Donahue, Loren (Fuzzy) Nuss, Keith Mueller and Randall Popp, and (back row) Eugene Steiner, Donald Schlehuber, and Emil Schwemmer, the volunteer coach. Cheering are Lucille Schwemmer and Janet Rhode.

About 1939, Durham had a good town basketball team, called the Durham Bulls. Their picture and the trophy they won appear with this book.

Tampa-Durham games were always competitive, and the gym was usually packed, including the stage and balcony. To keep score, a mechanical scoreboard stood on the stage and a small, square time clock hung on the east gym wall, to keep track of the games time.

A brake drum was bolted on the scorekeeper's table to signal time out or time in, when struck with a hammer. A 22-caliber revolver using blanks was fired at half-time, and to signal the end of the game time. Melvin Frick was usually timekeeper for games.

The year 1951 proved to be a good year for Durham High School Basketball. This team, coached by Loren Burch, won their District tourney at Canton, their Regional tourney at Juction City, which qualified them for a trip to the State Tournament at the Convention Hall in Hutchinson, Durham's first trip to a state tournament. However, they were defeated in the first round by Sylvia. Their record was 20 wins, 6 losses, and they provided many thrills in close tournament games, with several won by 1 or 2 points, coming from behind in the last quarter. Their photo also appears.

For the 1950 and '51 basketball season, a new time and score clock was purchased for the gym, and it was a real improvement. It had a large round time clock that glowed green and then turned red with one minute of time left to play. Score was kept on this clock, and it also showed the quarters. When the clock was acquired, an "unveiling" was held. It was hung on the wall, covered by a cloth, and before the game started that night, the clock was dedicated and unveiled before its first use.

During the middle 1960's, a second modern basketball scoreboard and clock was installed in the gym.

In 1954, Durham High's Basketball team had a record of 17 wins and 6 losses. However, they lost in the league and district tournament semi-finals, both times by one point. These boys also did well in softball and baseball. The coach was Harold Hauch.

The following year, 1955, the basketball team's record was 16 wins and 7 losses. Winning the league tournament second in league play they then took first place in the district at Lehigh. Going to the regional, they lost in the first round. Their coach was Chuck Brehm.

Up until the 1960's, Durham played in the NMCL, (North Marion County League). This consisted of Durham, Tampa, Ramona, Lost Springs, Lincolnville, Lehigh, and Goessel. Due to schools' consolidating, Durham was now competing in the "D-M league," the Dickinson and Marion county league which included Durham, Goessel, Solomon, Hope, Lehigh, and Tampa.

In 1961, Durham High School won all of the softball games which included the league tournament. In baseball, they won the league, and the league tournament, and also went to the regional and state tournaments, losing the first (state) game to Chetopa. Coach was Myron Goering.

The 1951 Durham High School basketball squad, from left, with Coach Loren Burch, includes players Dwaine Klassen, Jim Donahue, Ronald Unruh, Delmer Klein, Junior Unruh, Gus Hamm, Harold Nely, Harlon Unruh, Donald Schlehuber, Glenn Boelke, Donald Garrett, Daggmer Schlehuber, Kenneth Klein, Gene Duke and Richard Klassen. Twenty wins and six losses was the season record.

The Pep Band

Back row: Mr. Brown, Eugene Steiner, Rodney Penner, Janice Frick, JoAnn Negley, Soren Medley.

Middle Row: Joyce Decker, Janet Rhode, LaDonna Schiehuber, Lucille Schwemmer, Doris Geis.

Front Row: Don Garrett, Ed Young, Joan Dirks, Judy Peters, Sharon Frick, Hanky Steiner, Donna Geis, Morene Zimmerman, Marvin Frick.

The majorette team at Durham High, left to right, Janet Frick, Loretta Schneider, Deanna White, Myrna Zimmerman, Sharon Frick, Sharon Klein.

In the early 1960's, Durham was doing well in all sports, and by 1962 had an excellent basketball team, Coach was Dennis Bruner. They won first in league play, and also the league tournament, winning from Tampa by one point.

At the district tournament in Lehigh, they took second, losing to Walton, but this qualified them for the regional at Brookville.

Winning their first two games, they played Walton again, this time defeating them, to win first place in the regional. Going on to the state tournament, they lost in their first game to Netawaka, by two points. Their record for the season was 20 wins and only four losses.

In 1963, Durham High School's basketball team came back even stronger, winning in league play, and taking the league tournament. They went to the district tournament at Lehigh undefeated, winning the district tournament over Galva in the finals. Then they went on to the regional at Rosalia, winning first over Dexter, then Hamilton, and defeating Cassoday for first place.

This put them in the state tournament for the second year in a row. At Dodge City in the state tournament, they won from Prairie View, then met Dwight in the semi-finals, and won from them. Durham then defeated Corning 56 to 39, to win the state "Double B" Basketball Championship. This ended a perfect season of 26 wins, no losses.

The coach was again Dennis Brunner, and in his two years they won forty-six games and lost four.

The winning of the state basketball championship was duly marked by a billboard placed on the north edge of town, a sign on the school property proclaiming the Durham High School team, the 1963 Kansas State Basketball Champs.

That was a year the players and fans will never forget, an accomplishment always hoped for and finally achieved!

Football became a school sport in the fall, replacing softball, around 1963. The playing field was laid out on the baseball field, and goal posts were put up. Football was played until 1968. Track and cross-country was a school sport also. In 1967, the football team had four wins and four losses, coach was Mr. Thomas. He was also track coach.

In basketball, their team won 13 games and lost 9, winning the district tournament and also the first game in regional play. Coach was Mr. Powell. Durham was now playing in the McPherson County League and fast-pitch softball and baseball were no longer school sports.

The year 1968 was Durham's last year for football. The coaches were Mr. Catherman and Mr. Thomas.

The 1968 basketball team won 16 games and lost 9. They won the district tournament over Galva, 49 to 46, and went on to regional play, winning from Dorrance 52 to 45, but then losing the next two games.

By 1970, school consolidation was about to become a fact, and in 1971 the last high school class graduated. The grade school continued for a few more years before closing. This ended the Durham School's long history of sports competition, but leaving lots of memories for those who played, and the cheerleaders, pep clubs, and pep bands who urged them on, but especially for the townful of loyal fans who supported them, win or lose.

Thanks to Willie Popp and Melvin Frick who contributed a lot of information for this article, and also those persons who lent school annuals for research and photographs.

Other Sports Activities

Among other sports activities in Durham was trapping, which was a winter activity for some young men who earned extra money trapping and selling pelts.

Hank Dick was known to be the expert on the location of all the choice fishing holes on the Cottonwood River, around the railroad bridge.

In the late 1940's, and early '50s, Durham Trap-Shooting Club was organized. A trap range was located one mile south of Durham, and about a city block east, in a pasture on the north side of the road.

Two trap houses were built, and there was also a clubhouse. Turkey shoots were held in the fall and prizes were hams, turkeys and money, for breaking the most blue rocks out of 25.

Five shooters competed at a time and in case of a tie the distance was increased and a shoot-off was fired, until the tie was broken by a miss. These turkey shoots were well-attended and it was also rumored that a little big-time gambling occurred in the clubhouse during these turkey shoots and sometimes late into the night.

Also hunting was a pastime for hunters seeking pheasants, quail, rabbits and ducks. Night coon-hunting with trail hounds was another sport. The local hunters included Marvin Kaiser, Dwight Nelson, and others.

Coyote hunting with sight dogs was popular too. Several of the Steiner brothers owned the greyhounds. Coyote roundups were also held with a large group of men with shotguns. Several sections were circled at a time and hunted. There was a bounty on coyotes of $2 each at that time.

Hunting

Dave Schlotthauer, Junior Yauk and Harvey Yauk dug up a den of 13 baby coyotes, for which bounty was paid. Taken in 1940

TRACK

1968 Track Team. Back row; Mr. Thomas, L. Winter, E. Schafer, K. Rector, R. Drake, K. Becker, Mr. Catherman. Front row; B. Oblander, D. Dirks, K. Unruh, L. Dyck, D. Christiansen, W. Winter, T. Krotz.

1967 Football Team. Standing; Mr. Powell, J. Bernhardt, T. Christiansen, S. Wedel, D. Ewert, N. Winter, E. Schafer, L Winter, K. Rector, Mr. Thomas. Kneeling; S. Unruh, K. Becker, W. Winter, R. Unruh, D. Christiansen, A. Longstreth, T. Unruh, M. Miller.

1961-62

1961-62 ball team includes, (back row) Larry Kerbs, Lauren Frantz, Gaylen Frick, Larry Wedel and Robert Unruh. Front Row, Rick Riffel, Bob Klein, Warren Wiebert, Lloyd Meier and Dwight Negley.

1963 State Basketball Champions

Durham, the Kansas State Basketball Champs, 1962-63. Coach Dennis Brunner, at left, back row, with the team: Gaylen Frick, Lauren Frantz, Larry Wedel, Larry Kerbs, Rick Riffel, Warren Wiebert, Ken Pankratz, Lloyd Meier, Bob Klein and Dwight Negley. Front row includes cheerleaders Mona Christiansen, Kathy Schwemmer, Judy Klein and Theresa Dirks.

Durham High School basketball team of 1929 included, Front Row: Larraine Meier, Herman Brunn, Dan Helmer. Back Row: Clennis Miller, Bud Geis, Morris Detter, Harvey Yauk. The team beat Hope, Kansas for the 1929 District Championship. The score was 30 to 29. Dan Helmer made the last shot to beat Hope in a close game.

1954 D.H.S. Ball Team

Back row: Mr. Hauck, Richard Klassen, Kenny Klein, Ralph Vogel, Dean Nelson, Gary Kaiser, LaVern Dick, LaVern Laubhan. Second row: Dennis Klein, Bobby Hein, Calvin Mohn, Marvin Hamm, DeWayne Dirks. First row: Richard Dirks, Dennis Zitterkopf, Tobias Dirks, Soren Medley, Wayne Ollenburger, Alvin Bergman.

1961 Softball and Baseball Team. Back row; R. Christiansen, R. Laubhan, S. Dyck, V. Frantz, L. Frantz, L. Kerbs, G. Frick, W. Winter. Second Row; D. Negley, W. Weibert, T. Kraft, L. Meier, L. Wedel, K. Goentzel, R. Riffel, K. Pankratz, R. Klein. Front Row; M. Goering - Coach, D. White, R Unruh.

Leisure-Time Activities

John Bessel, fishing at the dam south of the railroad bridge, about 1917.

Neighbors

A painting by Charles Russell, entitled "Laugh Kills Lonesome", and depicting a group of cowboys seated around a nightime campfire, their animals in the distance, says much about life on the prairie in early days.

Human companionship was at a premium and a little get-together, with some yarns told, could often help with that ever-present malady suffered by settlers. . . loneliness.

One has only to imagine early life in Durham to perceive the truth of "Laugh Kills Lonesome ", and the tremendous inter-dependence of those early settlers on one another, and the essential function of neighborliness.

Neighbors were the glue that held these people in place, geographically, socially, and emotionally.

It is difficult for modern-day folks, mobile as we are, and in touch with the entire world by television, radio, and daily newspapers, to imagine what life was like for early settlers in Durham.

The social exchanges, the availability of needed items or supplies or even intellectual stimulation were not readily available.

In most cases, one's best asset were one's neighbors. . . the people who lived close to you, and were not only accessible, but had mutual concerns.

The farm families around Durham relied heavily on neighbors, and "neighborliness", as a way of living. When the day's work was finally done, getting together with folks for a picnic or a chat gave sustenance to one's emotional and social needs.

West of Durham, these neighbor families got together regularly for outings and meals out of doors, to enjoy the natural beauty and weather. At other times, when emergency or tragedy struck, it was the neighbors who were called in first to lend aid or comfort.

This scene portrays two neighbors sharing time together near the well-known big Cottonwood tree on the river west of town.

Marney Wardlaw, Elsie Ratzlaff.

Apples, dungarees, and lazy days for kids in Durham, combined to make fun times with friends...Doris Geis, Phyllis Yauk, Donna Geis, Lucille Schwemmer.

Activities during leisure time

"It's no use, Martin,
"From bridge to bridge,
"Blotkopf has caught them all."

(Conversation overheard between Martin Helmer and Conn Laubhan, about 1947, discussing the uselessness of fishing where another avid fisherman had already been, and referring to the much-fished area between the Old Wagon Bridge, and the bridge over Highway 15.

Leisure time in Durham has almost always taken the form of sports activities such as ball games for men and boys, and sometimes girls, and this meant anything from two people throwing a basketball at a hoop, to organized sports activities. (Covered in story on Durham sports).

But there were other things to do, too. Fishing was a favorite for all ages, with the Cottonwood River, and various ponds and streams offering a selection of catfish, sun perch, carp, etc. There were some who like hunting, all the way from coyotes to raccoons, and others who preferred a quiet ride in the country on a favorite steed.

But whatever you chose, you did it at your own pace, with whoever you wanted for a companion, (or alone, if you preferred) and leisure time was truly leisurely, back in the old days in Durham.

Coon hunting was a popular pasttime...Marvin Kaiser, Hank Kaiser, and Dwight Nelson with their dogs and 22 coons taken in one night's hunt.

Abe and Hanna Frick out with their horses. The photo suggests the peaceful quality to a ride in the country.

Snook Schultz, about 1915.

On an Outing
Oct 22 1916

An outing near Durham in 1916 includes Reuben and Katie Funk,
Maude Savage, Ethel Ingalls, and other friends.

SOCIAL LIFE

As Durham evolved from a rough and tough cattle town to a more civilized community, attempts were made to dignify and organize activity. As early as 1906, there were two organizations, the Woodmen and Pyramids. As each of the churches was established, bringing with it the women's group and young people's activities. more structure and guidelines existed. Social life took on yet a new flavor with the organization of the Home Circle Club.

In recent years, the Senior Citizen's group has become very active, and it provides a hub for activities in Durham nowadays. Among its members are people who are in their 70's and 80's and who have lived all, or nearly all, of their lives in Durham.

Sweet were the pleasant days of summer, and relaxation together with friends.

Relaxing on the porch was an activity practiced by many, as well as reading books, both pleasures of Anna Nelson, here

A 1931 bridal shower for Inez Popp, bride-elect of David Krispense, drew these friends to the event hosted by Mollie Borton. Back Row, left to right, Mrs. Ben Frick, unknown, Anna Frick Shieve, unknown, Juanita Smith Popp, Mrs. Harvey Schlehuber, Mrs. Joel Geis, Mollie Schlehuber, Margaret Geis, Maude Savage, Selma Haas, Katie Becker, Edna Funk Sawatsky, Lottie Geis. Front Row, left to right, Mrs. Dan Popp, Goldie Arbeiter, Gertie Niederhouse, Inez Popp, Mollie Heinrichs, Margaret Niederhouse, Juanita Geis, Pauline Ollenburger, Alice Geis, and Mollie Borton.

The Home Circle Club is 35 Years Old

Thought to be a photo of the Home Circle Club. Lydia Klein with little daughter, Judy, and Jeane Peters Oblander, in front row with long hair. "We really had fun. Took our dinner pails, too," says the note on the back of this old photo.

The Home Circle Club

Mrs. Tom Donahue, the current Home Circle Club president, has provided the club's history, as excerpted from the introduction to The 1951 Cook Book, compiled by the Home Circle Club of Durham, Kansas.

A group of former Farm Bureau women met at the home of Mrs. Pearl Smith, Durham, Kansas, January 20, 1944, and organized a club. Mrs. Anna Bartel suggested the name, The Home Circle Club. This name was approved and adopted.

The charter members were the following:

Pearl Smith	Enid Pope
Leah Hamm	Lucy Wieble
Lillie Rhodes	Mabel Grentz
Muriel Christiansen	Anna Bartel
Ruby Yauk	Emelia Youk
Ruth Peters	Anna Frick
Geraldine Frick	Johanna Beltz
Josephine Medley	Petrona Krotz

Officers were elected as follows: President, Josephine Medley; Vice President, Lucy Wieble; Secretary-Treasurer, Emelia Youk

The Program Committee to prepare the yearbooks were: Enid Pope, Lillie Rhodes, Pearl Smith and the officers.

The organization met once a month having a lesson on some interesting topic, which was given by one or two of the members.

Our first project was to prepare a Christmas Box for a children's hospital to which the members were to contribute throughout the year. This project has continued through the years.

It has been our pleasure to give other contributions to Capper's Fund for Crippled Children, Father Flannagan's Home for Boys, The March of Dimes, Red Cross, Cancer Fund, cash donation and electric fans to a local hospital, several hundred pounds of food and chothing to the destitute Indians of New Mexico and Arizona, Christmas boxes and magazines to Veterans' hospitals, Christmas boxes to sons of the club members who are in the service, Christmas boxes of food and clothing to some local needy, cards, flowers and visits to the sick.

We also sponsored hot lunches for school and helped equip the school kitchen. A fund for a new stage curtain in the school auditorium was started and we made a substantial payment on its purchase.

No doubt you are wondering how we finance all these projects. The club dues are $1 per year.

Each month we have "Swap Shop". The President appoints two ladies to act as captains. They choose sides. One month one side brings the articles to be sold; the next month the other side takes its turn. Just anything may be brought for this sale.

The ladies each take their turn in acting as auctioneer as the President appoints her. Having the two sides works up a little friendly competition. The losing side must entertain the winning side to a party at the end of the year.

It was necessary to limit our membership to twenty-six members, due to the fact the homes were not spacious enough to accommodate a larger group. Visitors are always welcome.

We take great pride in the fact that all our women are church members. We have Catholics and seven denominations of Protestants, all working together in harmony and union. There has never been any friction whatsoever.

Our hearts were deeply saddened on July 4, 1949, when one of our most beloved members, Mrs. Lucy Wieble, was taken in death.

This organization has taught us that great things can be accomplished when working together with a definite purpose. It also has given us a better understanding and a deeper affection for each other.

Our latest achievement of which we are justly proud is the ownership of a beautiful painting, purchased from Capper's Crippled Children's Fund by a generous donation.

We are beginning our eighth year's work with renewed energy and great expectations that this year will be bigger and better and with greater achievements than we have yet known.

Members of Home Circle Club – 1951

Honorary Member: Mrs. W. J. Smith

Mrs. Clyde Ahlstrom	Mrs. William Hamm
Mrs. Dave Bartel	Mrs. Ed Klein
Mrs. Dorman Becker	Mrs. Frank Krotz
Mrs. Duane Belton	Mrs Cecil Medley
Mrs. Virgil Bryan	Mrs. Virgil Oblander
Mrs. Irvin Christiansen	Mrs. George Peters
Mrs. Merrill Christiansen	Mrs. Rueben Pope
Mrs. Ben Frick	Mrs. Steven Tajchman
Mrs. Irwin Geis	Mrs. Melvin Frick
Mrs. Henry Goertz	Mrs. Harvey Yauk
Mrs. Henry Grentz	Mrs. Henry Youk
Mrs. Dave Zimmerman	Mrs. Harvey Schlehuber
	Mrs. Lillie Rhodes

The Day They Flew the Home-Made Airplane

The American dream, complete with youthful ingenuity, creative urge, and a flair for promotion, came to fruition one day back in 1939, when an airplane, built by 2 Durham teenagers, was flown before a crowd of nearly 3,000 curious spectators in a pasture near Durham. (See accompanying reprint of newspaper article at that time.)

Teenagers Willard Goertz and Lester David had started their project in 1936, and Willard's dad, Henry, had allowed them to use space in his implement building for their inventive project.

Today we take flying for granted but looking back we know how major an accomplishment it was to even fly a plane in the 1930s. It was an even greater triumph for these two teenagers to have successfully constructed an airworthy plane.

The plane was powered by a rebuilt Ford Model A motor, which Willard had found in an auto salvage, and other materials they acquired from various sources. Working in their spare time on weekends and evenings, they completed the plane in 1939.

The two-seater plane was 18 feet in length, with a wingspan of about 29 feet. They named the plane the 'Pietenpol' after the designer, Bernie Pietenpol.

While the boys had invested about $600 in the plane, all of their costs were recouped in that first Sunday flight, as there were many willing to pay the 25 to 50 cent admission charge for the big event. Joe Brewer of Elmo was the test pilot for the thirty-minute flight.

Chet Houghton, McPherson, was in the crowd that day, when people gathered, tantalized by the question, "Will it fly?"

"It was a big crowd," Houghton recalls, "and the sponsors had a platform and speakers set up in the pasture. They had even brought in a singer from the city, and made a big event out of it. When it was time for the plane to take off, the pilot just ran it down the pasture and up it went without any problems. It was exciting to see."

It was said that there could have been a test flight prior to the so-called "maiden voyage" of the little plane, but no one will admit to it.

Willard Goertz never flew the plane, but Mr. Lester David,who

The little plane as it begins taxiing for take-off.

became a TWA flight engineer, and is now retired and living in Sunappee, New Hampshire, still owns and stores the plane. He said that before he ever had any flight training, and after the big show, he felt the need to take off and test his wings. He was taxiing around the pasture, just listening to the motor, and decided, "I just had to try it." He made a successful short spin, and he credits that experience with leading him to his career in flying.

Some of the crowd can be seen with the platform and piano, as spectators gather to see the homemade plane on its initial flight.

Article from the Marion County Record, published on June 1, 1939.
WILL THE PLANE FLY, OR WON'T IT?
Durham Youth Complete Plane and Will Hold Public Dedication
and First Flight Sunday, June 11th

W. J. Goertz who operates a machine shop at Durham, Andrew David and Lester David, Durham youths have completed a two-seater plane after a construction period of well on toward two years, and will hold a "public christening and offical test flight" Sunday afternoon, June 11th.

The flight, for which an experienced test pilot has been selected from several applicants for the task will be held in a pasture six miles west of Durham and 2½ miles south and about eight miles northeast of Lehigh.

Dr. Klassen of Hillsboro will make an address at the christening and the ship will be offically christened by pretty Paula Hunter of Salina, shown in the picture with the plane.

Asked if he had studied aerial mechanics, Mr. Goertz replied "I've read about all the books tell a person." And the machine which he and Lester David have made with financial aid of Andrew David, looks like a professional job to a layman's eye.

It is a trim little monoplane, with 29 foot wing spread, powered by a Ford Model A motor. Examination of the construction throughout shows that all the fittings, joints, braces, etc., are made with infinite care and precision.

The plane has been named "Bonita" and will be so christened at the opening ceremonies the 11th. A band will be on hand to furnish music, a flying service out of Newton will put on stunts in the air, parachute drops, etc., to thrill the crowd. A sound truck with public address system will make the events of the day heard by all the crowd.

Advertisement appears on another page.

Humor and Hi-Jinks

In a small town, there are lots of advantages, one of them being the freedom with which to engage in hijinks, practical jokes, and other pranks.

Space would not permit, and threat of identification of the guilty would not allow, the naming of names, but a general description of some of the light-hearted fun that took place in and around Durham over the years, by the high-spirited, the confirmed practical joker, and the "testy", can be divulged, and those "in the know" can enjoy a few chuckles, in recollecting those lighter moments, such as:

"Hiding the car" – When a stranger came to Durham, particularly one who was possibly visiting a local young lady, it was considered a fine trick to dispose of the intruder's car, while he was otherwise occupied. This was easily accomplished, because no one locked their cars, and a prankster could slip behind the wheel, push the gear shift into neutral, and some pals could get behind the car and give it a good shoving until it came to rest in a secret parking spot, such as someone's empty garage. When the owner went to get in his car, imagine his surprise to fine it gone! Only after a search of the nearby alleys and garages was he able to go back to his own town, and count his blessings. While no one has admitted to the same stunt, using horses, the same quite possibly applied in the earlier era of "real horse-power".

"Snipe hunting" – Long a trick played on the unsuspecting, who were given instructions as to this nighttime pursuit, and taken to a remote spot, where they were left to watch for snipes. After a long night of studying the sky and listening for the mythical snipe, the gullible one gradually came to realize that there was more to this than he'd figured, and it was going to mean a long walk back home, too.

"Screech marks of infuriation" – No names here, but there were certain young men, who drove their cars onto the narrow sidewalks in Durham business district, and would drive along to where they wanted to leave screech marks in front of a certain hapless

businessman. It is a tribute to the drivers' skill, and to the wariness of shoppers stepping out the doors of the business, as well as the patience of the persecuted businessmen, that no harm came from any of this.

"Chase the sons-of-guns out of town!" – Another sport engaged in by the young men of the community. When would-be suitors from nearby towns would cruise into Durham seeking to court a local girl, the young men were often inspired to escort the intruder hurriedly back to his own community, chasing in hot pursuit over

Humor carried people through difficult times. This photo of the 1929 flood shows this group with water all around them, adding water to the car radiator.

dirt roads, a carful of lusty hunters speeding, and even throwing items, after the one who was making his way hastily back where he'd come from, often a town to the northeast of Durham. . .

Not actually a prank, but rather an enjoyment of freedom previously mentioned was:

"Swimming in the buff, " – boys only. This was a 1930's pasttime at the Railroad Bridge when as many as 15 to 20 boys, aged 5 and up, would gather to swing out over the water, and otherwise cool off from summer's heat and dirt, in joy and and privacy, except for the passing trains and some possibly surprised passengers who caught sight of the "scenery. "

Halloween was another occasion for fun. As Durham was without its own sewer system, and toilets sat discreetly behind most homes, (Concealed by honeysuckle and other vines) this provided an excellent target for pranks. One could expect to see many overturned outhouses following the October holiday. But in most cases, this required only a righting of the little building, back onto its foundation by a few strong arms.

However, one particular fall day, following Halloween, a group of young people were playing football behind one of the churches (to say which church would perhaps identify the situation) in the open area. Boys and girls played football together in those days, with a set of rules known only to the participants. However, in the course of the game, a high-kicked ball went flying back, back, back, 'way out to the alley, and an eager boy ran to catch it. He saw the ball coming over his head and was making a last desperate reach, when he fell into the overturned privy area. At this point, he found what friends aren't for, and as they surveyed his miserable plight, they turned and deserted ship, as it were, leaving the boy's mother with the task of fishing him out and cleaning him off.

Oh, how tiresome it must have seemed, to the grocery store and cafe owners, when the youngsters, getting their first taste of impertinence, would telephone the local merchants and ask, "Do you have Prince Albert in a can?" "Yes. " "Well, then let him out!" Ha ha ha! The pranksters thought. "Oh, those kids. " No doubt thought the proprietors.

Some of the pranks got to be a bit heavy-duty, such as stuffing objects in tailpipes of the cars, or trying to get someone to run through the school-yard privet hedge at night, unaware that the janitor had placed wires through the area, to prevent just such trespassing. The faster the speed of the runner, the farther he flew when he tripped and catapulted in his nighttime trajectory.

Some events could have been tragic, yet they turned out safely, such as the time four friends got inebriated, and somehow while making a wide turn, jammed their car sideways on the railroad tracks. This inadvertently shorted the signals, and when the westbound passenger train, rounding the bend from Tampa on the main line of the Rock Island, actually came into town, the signal had turned red so that the train was proceeding at a cautious 5 mph instead of its usual 60 mph. The engineer got out, peered into the car and inquired, "What are you fellas doing?" "Oh, we're just rolling along!" responded one jolly gentleman.

Elsie, 'Pookie' and Ona, having fun.

Fall 1930, all grades

Schools

"When a School goes, something happens to a town's spirit."

Durham High School's most famous building. Built in 1910, the fine red brick structure housed both high school and grade school for many years. First principal was Ben McIntosh and first graduate was Gladys Eichenour. Originally, basketball teams practiced and played in a low-ceilinged hall over a pool room downtown, but in 1925 a fine gymnasium was added.

Durham High School, October 12, 1925.

DURHAM SCHOOL DISTRICT NO. 57

Even though the 1860 census lists only 74 people in all of Marion County, the northwest area of the county, then the Crane Ranch, had attracted enough people with families that school took form there, and children began attending grade school classes, in 1875, with about a dozen students.

Not much is known about those first few years in the official records. However, about the same time that Durham was being founded as a town, in 1887, Durham had become the site of a school, with a student body of eighty students in the first eight grades. By 1897, there were nearly 150 pupils, indicating the growth of the area, and the vitality and concern for education by its citizenry.

There are many photographs of the first school erected in Durham, it being two-story white frame with four rooms and giving way to the well-known and loved red brick school in 1910.

No high school classes were offered until about 1903, and it wasn't until over a decade later that the full four-year high school program had been in effect long enough to have achieved a graduate. She was Gladys Eichenour, who became Durham High School's first graduate in the year, 1916.

For many years, all twelve grades went to school together in the big red brick building, but in 1954 a new high school building was completed. After Durham High consolidated with Lehigh and Hillsboro in 1971, the school was used as an elementary school, until that, too, was dissolved and consolidated in 1979.

The 1910 8th and 9th grade includes, back row, 5th from left, Lee Haas; 7th from left, Ella Popp. Front row, 4th from left, Enid Powers Popp, others unidentified. Do you know them?

Our Roots – The first school house of District 57 in Durham, built in 1888, was a two-story, four-room wooden structure painted white with red trim. The first year there was one teacher; in 1892, two; in 1894, three; and then the number dropped to two again.

The teachers, mostly from Marion, taught all eight grades, regardless of the number of students or teachers. Mr. Rider and Eva Dickerson were two of the earliest teachers.

The school census – sometime exact, sometimes not – showed that of the 113 children between the ages of 5 and 21, only 56 attended school in 1892. Six years later, there were 127 of a possible 152.

The sole qualification for graudation at that time was to pass a stiff county examination. Many failed, so it was indeed an honor to graduate. First eighth grade graduate in District 57 was Will Armstrong. As the story goes, Will sat up all night with his feet in cold water to stay awake studying for his next day's exam. When he passed, it was an occasion for a big celebration led by a good friend, Laura Bartell Jones. Everybody shared in the event, as it meant prestige for a young school and a young man.

Next graduates were two young women, Laura Swift and Amelia Weimer, in 1904. This called for the first ceremonial commencement. It was held at Tampa, with surrounding districts participating that year.

Length of the school year varied – from five to six, seven or eight months. One year, however, there were only 12 weeks of school.

Each desk accommodated two pupils, but sometimes three had to sit together.

Oh yes, there was the legendary pot bellied stove in each room to provide heat. Teachers had to build the stove fires, tend them, and carry in their own kindling and fuel besides performing all the janitorial duties!

The only timepiece was the bell in the belfry. It rang at eight o'clock, nine o'clock, noon, and for all recesses. As for playground equipment, there was not even a teeter-totter. The youngsters' favorite game was "Crack the Whip." Although there was no stage or even a raised platform on which to perform, patriotic holidays were always observed with a program.

Two of the young pupils who attended that schoolhouse in the early days became Durham's oldest citizens. They were Mrs. Amelia Weimer Smith and Mr. Ben Frick.

Education begins

In 1888, the school district voted to change the location of the school from Crane's Ranch to Durham, and build a two story, four room building. The proposition carried and the building was constructed and completed by Theodore Smith. Later in 1910, this building was torn down and the brick school building was erected by Sharp Brothers from El Dorado, Kansas.

An old photo of Durham Grade School. prior to 1910.

From a program used at "The First Commencement of the Durham Schools District No. 57 - 8:00 - M. E. Church. Friday evening, April 28, 1905, Durham, Kansas.

Visitors Entertained Free
Trustees - A. H. Miller, J. L. Jones, W. D. Armstrong, G. W. Hildreth
Entertainment Committee
George Hildreth, Lillian Huenergardt, Mabel Parry, Gladys Stevenson
Music Committee
George Thompson, Mabel Moulton, Iva Parry, Maude Rice

Class Motto:
Truth is the path and thought is the motor of life.
Class colors:
Lavender and White
Class of 1905
Lillian Hunergardt
Millie Frick
Gladys Stephenson
Adelbert Stephenson
Reuben Funk

Teachers
S. W. Hildreth
Principal
E. Mabel Moulton
Intermediate
Maude Rice
Primary

Board

L. E. Borton
Director
J. L. Jones
Clerk
Marion Smith
Treasurer
Programme:
Music - Orchestra
Prayer
Rev. Severance
Music
Orchestra
Oration
"Getting the Right Start"
By Reuben Funk
Music
Oration
"No Excellence Without Labor"
By Adelbert Stephenson
Music
Orchestra
Valedictory
"Attention the Soul of Genius"
By Lillian Huenergardt
Class Address
D. D. Mc Intosh
Oration
"Riches and Poverty"
By Gladys Stephenson
Music
"Drifting With the Tide"
By Quartette
Music
Presentation of Diploma
Prof. L. M. Knowles
Music
Orchestra
Music
"Good Night" Quartette
Benediction
Rev. Severance

5th grade, 1912. This postcard school picture was taken at the entrance of the red brick school, of Miss Maude Savage's 5th grade baseball players and 6th grade boys.

An old photo of Durham Grade School, prior to 1910.

On April 25, 1904, Durham's first eighth grade graduates were Amelia Weimer and Laura Swift, pictured here with Principal George Hildreth. Their graduation ceremony was held in Tampa. The next year's class had their graduation ceremony in Durham and the program from this event is shown on the facing page.

Durham School, George Hildreth, teacher and principal, 1906. A
Miss Rice was teacher, too, a note on photo indicates.

The Durham first and second grade, 1910.
do you recognize anyone?

A group of students, about 1916.

This high school picture has been identified as to the back row, boys, as follows: Bill Crist, Ed Becker, Wesley Schultz, Adolph Funk, John Eichenour. Girls are unidentified.

History of Durham High School
* * * * * * * * * * * * * * *

The old red brick school house, "our high school" to most of us, is now a memory. It is only fitting that a brief history be given here.

Built in 1910, the fine brick structure housed both the high school and grade school for many years. First high school principal was Ben McIntosh and the first graduate was Gladys Eichenour, in 1916. An early picture taken during the 1915-16 school year, shows a high school enrollment of 16 students.

There were no graduates the next year, but in 1918, there were two. . . Flossie Smith Unholtz and Enid Powers Pope. Since then classes have graduated each year.

Orginally, basketball teams practiced and played in a low-ceilinged hall over a pool room downtown. but in 1925 a fine new gymnasium was added to the red brick building.

As years passed, the old red school house became inadequate, so a new building was constructed and the high school moved into the new one in 1956. Athletics and dramatics still continued in the old gym and strong ties remained.

Through the years Durham High School students have won many local and statewide honors in music, track, drama, baseball, and basketball. The school's 1963 basketball team won the state championship.

In 1971, the last class graduated from Durham High School as unification of school districts took place. More than 600 students graduated during the school's 61 year history.

To name all the principals and teachers who were such an important part of our high school lives; to be able to list all the successes and accomplishments of all Durham alumni would be an impossible task.

But we all remember.

And the old brick school house, gone but not forgotten, will always remain alive in our fond memories of high school days in Durham.

School Song
Oh when that D. H. S. team falls in line
We're gonna win this game another time
For the dear old school we love so well
We're gonna yell and yell, and yell
and yell and yell,
We're gonna fight, fight, fight for every score
We're gonna win this game and then some more
We're gonna roll old (Tampa) on the floor
and 'neath the floor
Fight, fight, fight.

New school, 1911, Durham Grade School enrollment.

THE GYM

[After the new school was built in 1910, there remained only the
need for a gymnasium, which was realized some 15 years later.
The following provides the details.]

Taken from the **Marion Record** newspaper

Thursday, November 12, 1925

WILL DEDICATE NEW BUILDING

Durham To Formally Open New Gymnasium Auditorium Next
Tuesday

The people of the Durham community will gather next Tuesday
evening at exercised dedicating the new addition to the educational
equipment of that place, when the new auditorium gymnasium will
be formally opened.

Sup. Paul Loveless, who has been superintendent of the schools
there for several years, has done fine things for the community in
school matters and the community has built this fine addition to better care for the school and community needs.

The addition is built for use as an auditorium and as a gymnasium. A dinner will be served Tuesday evening. After that there
will be a program given, comprising speaking and other numbers.
After the program a cake walk will be held in the big room.

The 8th grade class at Durham in 1935.

Students of Durham High School 1929-1930 school year.

Country School Memories

Geis Country school recesstime. Students are Doreen Schlehuber, LaDell Oblander, Lois Zimmeramn, and Joyce Jantzen.

COUNTRY SCHOOLS...ONLY MEMORIES REMAIN

"We used to put the teacher on the end, when we played 'crack the whip', so that her feet came right up off the gound!"

That's the way one former student of a Durham area "country school" recalls those bygone days, an era in education that yielded to the progress of school consolidation during the 1940s and '50s.

"There were between twenty-five and thirty students in grades one through eight, and the teacher taught all the classes, giving us work to do while she was busy with the other grades.

"We all had to take turns bringing in the cobs and coal, to put in the pot-bellied stove to heat the schoolroom. And we brought our lunch in dinner pails. If it was nice weather, we ate lunch outdoors; in bad weather we ate at our desks. "

Although this interview wass conducted with one person, it is intended to represent, and the recollections are consistent with, those from many of the one-room schools which were sprinkled through the countryside all around Durham. Therefore, no names are given, and no tell-tale incidents reveal from which student in which school these episodes occured. Suffice to say that going to school at a one-room country school is a memory held dear by many now in the Durham area.

In those days it was considered natural and expected that the children walk to school, sometimes two or three or more miles, from their farm homes to the schools, the locations of which are given following this article.

As this individual recalls the class work, "We all had assigned seats. The littler kids were on the right side of the room, and we progressed to the left, as we got to the higher grades. "

There was a library in the back of the room, and there were assigned times to study in the library.

No doubt the teacher had a difficult time of it, in some cases. One Roxbury country school student remembers having nine teachers during one school term, apparently due to discipline

A country schoolhouse, old Merry-Go-Round School.

problems, the final teacher being the county superintendent of schools herself. By all accounts, however, that was an unusual case; most teachers taught a year or two at country schools, and then moved on.

At any rate, teaching duties were broad and required a great deal of skills to coordinate the study of the various classes and many extracurricular jobs, such as coming early to get the fire started in the afore-mentioned pot-bellied stove. She (or he) also had to plan and coordinate the Christmas program. That event, held one evening prior to Christmas, drew all the parents of the students, and other interested persons and was a highlight for memories.

"One year, we all carried lighted candles as we marched in, and some of the kids weren't paying much attention, and one bumped another, and his candle hit a girl's hair and it caught on fire." The ever-capable teacher quickly put out the girl's hair-fire, and the program went on, according to recollecton.

Schoolyards included playground equipment, an outdoor toilet, and a coal shed.

As transportation became easier, and children could be bussed into the town school, and as the country schools had smaller enrollments and were too costly to maintain, they became impractical, outdated, and are now only a memory, most of the buildings having also been destroyed.

In no particular order, the following schools, their district numbers, and locations from Durham, are now listed.

Bell Top School was located approximately nine miles northwest of Durham. It was a doubleroom school, with two teachers and eight grades.

It was furnished with double seats and the younger ones often shared seats with the older ones. It was closed to merge with the Grand Central School. Members of several Jantz families attended.

Square Top, No. 94, 6 miles northwest of Durham, 1885-1956.

Ashcraft, No. 68, 3 miles northwest of Durham, 1884-1953.

Columbia, No. 118, 9 miles west of Tampa, 1893-1953.

Pleasant Valley, No. 84, 5 miles northwest of Durham, 1883-1950.

Geis School, No. 119, 4 miles west of Durham, founding date not known, closed 1947.

Warren, No. 87, 3 miles southeast of Durham, 1883-1958.

Merry-go-Round, No. 120, 3 miles west of Durham, 1883-1950.

Elm Springs, No. 83, 7 miles northwest of Durham, 1882-1953.

Endeavor, No. 67, 3 miles northwest of Durham, 1884-1953.

Victory, No. 125, 5 miles southeast of Durham, 1887-1957.

Private School

An exception to this trend is the school operated by the Holdeman Mennoites west of Durham, whose school, Cottonwood Grove Christian School, supported by Morning Star Mennoite Church is big and better than ever. Morning Star's new school, constructed near the Claude Unruh property near the site of the famed "Cottonwood Crossing," is a large, fine one-story building, built in 1985, and housing a good many students, all seeking to gain a good, parochial education in compliance with their religious faith.

Finally, the consolidation movement took the beloved Durham City School system, District No. 57, which had been in operation since earliest days, dating back to 1875. It is now a part of Unified District No. 410, which includes Hillsboro, Lehigh and Durham.

Incidentally, a typical 19th century one-room school from Marion County has been restored, and can be seen on the campus of Emporia's Kansas State Teachers' College, having been dismantled stone by stone, moved and rebuilt, donated by its owner, Harvey Kruse. The Dobbs School was originally located northwest of Marion, and displaced by the construction of the new, big Marion Lake and Reservior.

The new Cottonwood Grove Christian School has an enrollment of about 30 students and is located northwest of Durham.

Top row, Vernon Geisler, Gearhard Peters, Leonard Bartel, Preston Rhodes, Leland Kaiser, Gust Dirks, Wilbur Kreiger, Lloyd Hein, Willard Goertz, Harvey Hefley, Quentin Geis, Paul Weinmeister, Leland Yauk, Alvie Hefley, Melvin Fritsch, Edwin Weibert, Elmer Wasmiller. Second row, Matthew Rudolph, Andrew David, Frances Steiner, Fred Hein, Clifford Beltz, Arlo Garrett, Ethelyn Ewert, Evelyn Wohlgemuth, Louise Heffner, Eunice Geis, Ferretta Jacobs, Verna Hein, Rozella Beltz, Zella Borton, Edna Peters, Elizabeth Popp. Third row, Emily Steiner, Regina Knaak, Julia Frick, Florence Belton, Georgia Davis, Irene Belton, Elsie Mae Fast, Geraldine Christiansen, Evelyn Bessel, Willie Popp, Harvey

Weinmeister, James Davis, Cecil Bergman, Wayne Popp, Clifford Beltz. Fourth row, Genavieve Becker, Barbara Herbel, Millie Maniger, Beatrice Schlehuber, Bernettie Kreiger, Mr. Rehrig, Mr. Alhstrom, Miss Culbertson, Mr. Reimer, Miss Sellers, Louise Hatfield, Nettie Weis, LeElla Hoffman, Leona Geisler, Clinton Yauk. Fifth row, Burtis Weibel, Alfred Steiner, Willard Schlehuber, Edwin Winters, Linda Mohn, Mary Frick, Elda Frick, Elsie Peters, Delphia Frick, Orlean Geis, Marlys Wasemiller, Arnold Yauk. Sixth row, Carroll Christiansen, Clinton Haas, Steve Tajchmann, Raymond Ratzloff, Levi Seleski.

The year isn't known, but the familiar background of the old school building marks this as a Durham school photo.

Operetta cast on stage. These events were made flexible by the directors, so as to include every child, if only in the role as 'townspeople', so that all could be a part, a 'plus' of small schools ingenuity.

7th and 8th grades at Durham School, 1948.

The stage in the old gym at Durham School

Miss Frances Jones with her class.

Miss Margaret Niederhouse with her class 1947.

Scenes from the Junior-Senior Banquet, 1925, apparently featuring a Dutch theme.

From the Funk family album. Year unknown.

Cheerleaders boost the team.
The year is 1969, in the old gym.

Durham School, grades 1 through 8, about 1912.

The fifth and sixth grade classes, on the first floor of the old school-house, 1960-61, with teachers, Evelyn Schmidt, left, and Esther Klein, right.

1936 Second grade: front row from left; Loretta Steiner, Virginia Miller, Cecil Scholtthauer, Miss Martin - teacher. Second row from left - Floria Krotz, Georgia Peters, Marjorie Lorenz. Third row from left - Jean Buehler, Arthur Klassen, Dean Duke.

1935 First and Second grade: front row, left to right; Miss Martin - teacher, Georgia Peters, Carol Schlehuber, Jean Schlotthauer, Harvey Siebel, Erma Hein, Jean Buehler, Loretta Steiner, Dean Duke. Back row; left to right - Ruth Riffel, Velma Popp, LeeRoy Hein, Virgil Gooding, Vera Fast, Alice Tajachman, Leslie Wohlgemuth.

Built in 1956, the last of Durham's three schoolhouses saw over 200 students through high school.

The first superintendent was C. J. (Clyde) Ahlstrom, of whom the first graduating class wrote, "... his enthusiastic interest in all our activities has added much to our achievements."

Achieve they did. Through the years Durham High School students won numerous local and statewide honors in music, track, drama, baseball, and basketball.

And in 1963, the school's basketball team won a state championship.

This remarkable achievement was a far cry from earlier days when Durham basketball teams practiced and played in a low-ceilinged hall over a downtown pool room. In 1925, a gymnasium was added to the red brick schoolhouse and used in conjunction with the third school's facilities until 1971 when the school district was reunified.

The last senior class to graduate was one short of the 16-student class that graduated in 1956. And of all the 200 some students to graduate from the last Durham High, four, maybe five, students can honestly say the did as they were told and stayed out of the tunnel.

The tunnel? Ask the ones who've been there.

They remember yesterday.

Teachers

One's debt to teachers is an acknowledged fact. Teachers in our schools first showed us the basics, then fine-tuned our talents, led us in the way.

Those who have taught in the Durham Public Schools system have left their mark on all of the students, and for that most are grateful.

When one attempts to single out particular teachers to profile in such a centennial book as this, it is most difficult to do, yet there is an obvious choice. . . Henreietta Geis.

Asked to give her summary of her school teaching, Mrs. Geis jotted a few notes, which in no way encompass the magnitude of ther work, but here they are.

"Taught Math and Science in Durham for 35 years, coached plays, and contest one-act plays, accompanied music groups, was advisor for the high school newspaper and annual. Retired in 1970, just to retire in a community where I taught for so long." "I have many grandchildren," is a post script.

Anyone who attended Durham High during those 35 years is sure to remember more of her giving goodness and her gift for teaching than such a concise and self-effacing notation provides. She was always interested in students' progress, and willing to give of her time whether it was playing the piano for yet another practice of a musical group, or sitting through a play rehearsal, in addition to the ongoing fine skills as a teacher of math and science.

Now active in the Durham Senior Citizens' group, she and her husband, Irwin, continue to participate in the community of which she was a vital part.

Henrietta Geis not only was a teacher of many, she had a busy home life, and her twin daughters' playmates were well-acquainted with the homemade cinnamon rolls and other kitchen delights she turned out. Of that family life, which included her in-laws, Solomon and Lottie Geis, themselves long-time residents of the Durham area, she recalls fondly, "We celebrated 45 Christmases with all of us together at home. We had some wonderful times."

Thanks to Henrietta for the memories. . .

Mixed Chorus

Henrietta Geis, at left, accompanist for mixed chorus, and other musical groups.

Another teacher who made an indelible impression on the girl students was Gladys Negley, for she taught many young women to cook and sew. They started out with varying degrees of ability, but under her patient tutlage the girls learned the skills required to run a home, even though there were early tendencies to sew the pajama leg-holes shut, and to throw out the good part of the split peas for soup! Thank you, Gladys! We use those skills you taught us every day!

Gladys Negley was also sponsor of the Kayettes. This photo was taken in the girls' lounge, upstairs in the old red brick school.

Gladys Christiansen Negley, fondly remembered from teaching many girls to cook and sew, as she was the home ec teacher at Durham schools.

Mrs. Gladys Negley, teaching the Foods I and Foods II classes home economics lessons.

First row: Mrs. Geis, M. Krotz, T. Dirks, J. Klein, J. Unruh, A. Unruh, S. Rediker, M. Steiner, P. Kaiser, J. Jantz, S. Jantz, Mr. Pennington. Second Row: N. Frick, J. Vajnar, M. McDowell, V. Steiner, K. Goentzel, W. Weibert, B. Klein. F. Dyck, K. Schwemmer, M. Christiansen, S. Becker. Third Row: J. Hein, T. Kerbs, T. Kraft, L. Frantz, G. Frick, L. Wedel, A. Hett, D. Wedel, G. Christiansen, C. Goentzel. DISTRICT III

1969 Cheerleaders; Connie Klein, Jacqueline Kerbs, Cindy Goertz, Barbara Christiansen.

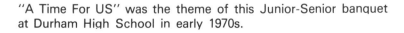

1970 class officers, with Henrieta Geis, sponsor, and Jim Catherman, co-sponsor. From left, Galen Unruh, Kim Oblander, Diana Rader, Eldon Kaiser and Susan Goertz.

"A Time For US" was the theme of this Junior-Senior banquet at Durham High School in early 1970s.

School Memories

That our Durham School was loved and idolized is a widely accepted fact.

But there is a generation of Durham students whose children are now in school at Hillsboro Unified Dist. 410, and who remember fondly the old days at Durham while seeing the vast differences that distinguish the older, smaller school from the trends in modern education.

Pointing out those facts, is Priscilla (Kaiser) Unruh, (Mrs. Robert Unruh) of Durham, whose daughter, Shawn, is a junior at Hillsboro High. Son Brent is in Junior High.

"Things have changed," observes Pricilla, herself a secretary at Hillsboro Schools.

"For one thing – dress is so different. When I was in Durham High in 1968, we girls wore dresses or skirts every day, except on baseball game days. Then we could wear jeans. Our dresses were gathered skirts we made in home ec, or matching skirt-sweater sets, or shirtwaist dresses. Now. girls wear jeans and slacks to school all the time."

"Also, there are no games during the school day. In Durham, our games used to start at 1:30 p. m. Also, in those days, teachers were always considerate of "game day". And the day after, too, because then was when everyone had a chance to review the game. The only method for reviewing games then was to look at the scorebook. Scorebooks were the only tools to determine past-played games, achievements or failures. Now, videos are played and the

1963 Pep Club and Cheerleaders. First row; J. Klein, M. Christiansen, P. Kaiser, J. Jantz, B. Bolte, V. Steiner, K. Schwemmer, T. Dirks.
Second row; F. Dyck, D. Schlehuber, J. Vogt, J. Vajnar, S. Jantz, N. Frick, M. McDowell.
Third row; M. Krotz, S. Becker, A. Unruh, J. Unruh, S. Rediker, M. Steiner.

video recorders catch every play, so that it can be studied and improved upon."

Practice now takes place from 3:30 to 6:00 p. m. every night, whereas during the 1960's, it was not unusual to have ball practice during the school days, she said.

Sports were for boys only in the '60; the girls were the cheerleaders and the pep club. Today being a cheerleader is not as prestigious as it was in the '60's. Then it was a popularity contest, with the student body voting, and now, they are chosen on the basis of gymnastics and ability by an unbiased group of experts.

"In 1962 and 1963, when Durham's teams went to the state basketball tournaments, players and cheerleaders stayed over in a motel at the school's expense. Today, whether or not you are in a tournament, there is no abbreviated schedule of the school day, and tests are given as usual. Students' attendance at the tournametn is at the student's expense, both out of pocket, and concerning classes."

"One thing that hasn't changed is lunch time. It is just the same as its always been. The boys always ran to the basement of the Red Brick School, to get in line for lunch, and today the kids were running again – the boys were – that hasn't changed. It seemed like in Durham, you had to run to get the lunch."

In Durham, after school, the high school boys would go to "Harry's," (run by Harry Nuss) now E and M Cafe, and play pool after school.

Another thing kids in Durham did, was they would try to run

across to Schneider's Service Station to buy candy bars before the busses left for home after school.

"Life was definitely less complicated then, " says Priscilla. "I know kids did ornery things in our day, but things seem different. "

"One thing I notice, having a teenage daughter, is I think she and her friends spend more time in homes, watching viedos and just being with friends, than maybe we did, because we were busy dragging up and down Main Street in cars.

"After play practice in the evenings, it seems we had to allow for time to run around so one of the social activities was play practice. It seemed like new romances would start or end then. "

"In your junior year, you usually wanted a creative sponsor to help with the banquet, whereas seniors needed a young, fun-loving person to go on the senior trip with them.

"There were no dances in Durham, after the junior-senior banquet. We went to movies in another town. Hillsboro has a prom, with dancing. Their decorations are elaborate. . . program books, certain glasses, favors, everything is ordered. In Durham, we would have made our own program and decorations,and done it all by hand. "

"Juniors had to sell Christmas cards, seniors sold magazines, and freshmen and sophomores had food sales, all to make money for the senior sneak.

"I'll never forget those hot sweaters, the Kelly green pep club sweaters, and if you were a senior girl, you had to carry the cakes around and sell chances on the cakes. You see, senior mothers made three or more cakes per game, and chances were sold on the cake, ten cents for one chance or 3 for 25 cents. I can remember getting frosting on my sweater lots of times, " she said. Drawing was at half-time of the A game.

Attending a basketball game on a Friday evening was a big social event in Durham. "The eyes of the young high school girls were either on the players, or watching the balcony (that's where visiting boys from other schools, or our own alumni members sat) in the old 'crackerbox' gym. " The pep club was on the side which looked out on the balcony.

"Christmastime is different now too. In Durham, every school room had a real Christmas tree, and we decorated them all. Now, trees are not allowed in school because of fire safety. In Durham, we had one in the music room too for the all school party, and we drew names for gifts. "

Priscilla attended country school until 6th grade. "When Square Top closed in 1956, you had to choose either to go to Grand Central or Durham.

"The bus came and picked me up, and Ben Goertz was driver. It was not unusual to get stuck on that road. When we did, Delton Ollenberger and Dennis Zitterkopf (the seniors) would get out and push. Square Top never had more than seven students when I was there. If I had one other person in my grade, that was something. "

Teachers remembered are Pearl Lawrence, Johanna Beltz, and Velma Dirks.

"It was hard to merge! Being a student at town school was scary. The first day of school was very frightening to us! There were too many kids!

"When I think back to our school closing, it was sad, but kids had to adjust to Hillsboro High School, just the way us country school kids had to adjust to going to Durham.

"Durham closed because of the lack of kids. If we had school there now, there would probably be just three students in my daughter's class. "

Do You Remember Senior Sneaks?

In the days of Durham School, the seniors traditionally "sneaked away" for a several day trip to a neighboring state.

In later years, the senior sneak was usually to Rockaway Beach, Missouri, and the class of 1962 members sent a group to the top of the Durham elevator at midnight, before they left for Rockaway, to leave a sign saying, "Rockaway, here we come. "

This brought town fathers to protest the risk and danger of such activities, but then, "seniors were always seniors. "

For seniors, this was a "really big deal, " because not very many families in those days had the opportunity to go on family trips during the year, and this was a chance to see some new sights.

Many Durham kids probably ate their first pizza during the trips to Rockaway, because of the Italian resturant that featured pizza. Also, they got a good taste of the "junk foods" that have since become accepted dietary fare.

Hallowee'n night was usually an important night for the high school boys, and usually the day after Halloween, businessmen would come to ask that the merry go-around, which was taken down to Main Street, please be hauled back up to the school.

The "Last Day of School Picnic, " was a Durham Schools tradition for many, many years. It was a covered dish meal, and everyone would bring food, and that is how the school year would end, it was a real high point.

Class of '71
Last students to graduate from the third Durham School Building were, back row, left to right, Kathleen Redger, Gladys Rhodes, Christina Wiebe, Jane Wedel, Wanda Winter, Barbara Hamm, Gene Oblander, Dudley Donahue, Wendell Wedel, Gordon Jantz, Marilyn Weibert; front row, left to right, Dwight Dirks, Keith Unruh, Ray Redger, Randy Redger.

Graduates of Durham High School

The Durham High School graduates over the years include the following persons, beginning in 1916.

1916
Gladys Eichenour
1918
Enid Powers
Flossie Smith
1922
Willie Savage
1923
Harry Borton
Howard Huenergardt
Eddie Weible
Walter Haas
Dale Walker
Mollie Heinrichs
Claude Eichenour
1924
Jane Belton
Roy Ehrlich
Irwin Geis
Carl Heinrichs
Palmer Miller
Ben Pankratz
Solomon Popp
Martha Smith
Ona Smith
Arnold Voth
Bernita Voth
Grace Williams
1925
Orrie Morlong
Manuel Oblander
Elsie Ratzlaff
Alva Schlehuber
Margaret Wardlow
1926
Evelyn Belton

Souvenir program from Geis School, many years ago, when Ada Ireland was teacher. Among the students listed were Dave and Martha Zimmerman (grade school)

Juanita Frick
Naomi Gant
Mamie Gant
Frances Jones
Theresa Lorenz
Roy Meier
Alberta Walker Miller
William Smith
Harold Snyder
Harold Voth
Wesley Voth
Madaline Williams
1927
Robert Belton
Jacob Dirks
Monroe Frick
Alice Geis
Abraham Heiser
Elmer Krieger
Ruben Miller
Bernice Schultz
Irene Smith
1928
Edna Davis
Irvin Dirks
Elviana Frick
Ralph Frick
Frances Geis
Juanita Geis
Alma Hefley
Edwin Herbel
John Kepl, Jr.
Ted Oblander
Edna Popp
Esther Rhodes
Adrian Savage

Edna Schmidt
Ruth Schmidt
Kenneth Seleske
Arthur Wohlgemuth
1929
Herman Brunn
Tobias Dirks
Wilma Duke
Lucia Eggleston
Edna Funk
Clifton Geis
Daniel Helmer
Margaret Krieger
Pearl Lorenz
Evelyn Meier
Clennis Miller
Christine Popp
Augusta Riffel
Virginia Weber
1930
Frank Brunn
Marvin Eggleston
Emily Frantz
Clara Frick
Mollie Frick
Theodore Hefley
Gladys Herbel
Alice Kaiser
Beatrice Lorenz
Lorane Meier
Margaret Niederhouse
Alvin Rotzlaft
Mildred Steiner
Harry Wohlgemuth

1931
Ruth Arbeiter
Harold Branton
Alice Christiansen
Alice David
Wesley David
Eldo Frantz
Clinton Frick
Viola Frick
Anna Gant
Ruben Hefley
Victoria Knybel
Elsie Lorenz
Lorene Ollenburger
Rachell Popp
Harvey Yauk
Edna David

1932
Goldie Arbeiter
Lucille Belton
Harry Belton
Josephine Davis
Edgar Erion
Melvin Frick
Leonard Haas
Virginia Herbel
August Klein
Lillian Krieger
Ivan Meier
Max Savage
Ralph Steiner

1933
LaVera Bessel
Alvin Brunn
H. Irvin Christiansen
Hulda David
Erlean Glantz
Erlene Hefley
Lydia Kaiser
Florine Rhodes
Edna Wohlgemuth
Edna Yauk
Elsie Goertz

1934
Dorman Becker
Erlean Frick
Alvin Klein
William Knaak
Elizabeth Knybel
Harry Miller
Abraham Peters
Selma Schneider
Adeline Seleska
Gilman Smith
Lewis Steiner
LeRoy Wasemiller
Raymond Berg

1935
Irene Belton
Georgia Mae Davis
Ethelyn Ewert
Elda Frick
Eunice Geis
Willard Goertz
Louise Hatfield
Alvie Hefley
Louise Hoeffner
Wilbur Krieger
Gerhard Peters
William Popp
Beatrice Schlehuber
Francis Steiner
Arnold Yauk
Evelyn Wohlgemuth

1936
Florence Belton
Clifford Beltz
Harold Berg
Geraldine Christiansen
Elsie Fast
Julia Frick
Melvin Fritsch
Arlo Garrett
Nettie Weiss
Leona Geissler
Harvey Hefley
Barbara Herbel

Fernetta Jacobs
Elizabeth Popp
Emily Steiner
Paul Weinmeister

1937
Leonard Bartel
Genevieve Becker
Rozella Beltz
Cecil Bergman
Evelyn Bessel
Zella Borton
Obed Brown
Gust Dirks
Quenton Geis
Vernon Geissler
Verna Hein
LuElla Hoffman
Leland Kaiser
Bernettie Krieger
Herbert Neiderhouse
Matthew Rudolph
Laurence Tajchman
Elmer Wasemiller
Edwin Winter

1938
Carroll Christiansen
James Davis, Jr.
Delphia Frick
Orlean Geis
Clinton Haas
Frederick Hein
Lloyd Hein
Olinda Mohn
Edna Peters
Arthur Wayne Pope
Raymond Ratzlaff
Elsie Peters
Willard Schlehuber
Levi Seleska
Alfred Steiner
Edwin Weibert
Burtis Weible

1939
Lester David
Floyd Funk
Edith Helmer
Dan Goertz
Fern Schafer
Menno Unruh
Ralph Unruh

1940
Dorothy Dick
Leon Fast
Mildred Frick
Betty Geis
Maynard Hefley
Eugene Herbel
Junice Herbel
Marvin Kaiser
Loreece Lorenz
Marcella Lorenz
Vernedda Lorenz
Virginia Lorenz
Warren Pope
Lupe Rosas
Genevieve Schlehuber
Orval Schmidt
Lorene Schafer
Arthur Schultz
LaVern Seleska
Pearl Steinle
Reed Unholz
Dave Weibert
Ruth Ann Wasemiller
Raymond Zimmerman

1941
Velma Christiansen
Roland Frederick Geis
Harold Fritsch
Delmar Gardner
Gaylord Hamm
Fiennes Jantz
Mae Marie Laclair
Wilma Meier
Hester Savage
Alice Steiner

Gladys Tajchman
1942
Clarence Bartel
Donald Ewert
Eddie Frantz
Lamar Geis
Bernice Goertz
Doris Lais
Harold Miller
Lucille Pope
Fred Riffel
Walter Schmidt
Howard Schultz
Betty Smith
Bernice Steiner
Joyce Unholz
Eleanor Yauk
Lois Jean Geis
1943
Merle Dick
Wesley Eilers
Frances Frick
Robert Geis
Harry Garrett
Arlene Hamm
Geneva Jantz
Arlene Kaiser
Nadine Merilatt
Duwane Miller
Paul Pankratz
Victor Riffel, Jr.
Helen Schafer
Helen Steiner
Vera Tajchman
1944
Merrill Christiansen
Howard Geis
Jane Geissler
Nadine Klaassen
Virgil Oblander
Dean Ollenburger
Althea Pankratz
Jean Peters
Ruth Rhode

Bernice Tajchman
Max Unholz
Oliver Unruh
Joan Rhodes
1945
Wilma Geis
Benjamin Goertz
Florence Hefley
LeeRoy Hein
Manford Jantz
Margie Krotz
Evelyn Steiner
Bernice Unruh
1946
Junior Medley
Dean Bartel
Alice Tajchman
Geneva Rhodes
1947
Mary Emma Clark
Robert Dick
Donald Duke
Josephine Frantz
Virginia Garrett
Marcella Hamm
Helen Gray Hein
Joyce Janzen
Milton Kaiser
Georgia Peters
Anna Mae Senner
Loretta Steiner
1948
Alma Fritsch
Delores Jantz
Florian Krotz
Jack Kerbs
William Medley
Vivian Pope
Mary Kathryn Rhode
Joyce Schneider
Lowell Rhodes
1949
Virgil Kaiser
Keith Mueller

Luella Pankratz
LaDell Oblander
Howard Wolf
Dorlene Schlehuber
1950
Marvin Frick
Pearl Hein
Evelyn Jantz
Donald Klein
Shirley Kaiser
Lorraine Laubhan
Randall Pope
Eugene Steiner
Loren Nuss
Lois Zimmerman
1951
James Donahue
Joan Dirks
Delmer Klein
Donna Jantz
Henrietta Steiner
Donald Schlehuber
Junior Unruh
Ronald Unruh
Jenny Lee Unruh
Janet Rhode
1952
Patricia Ahlstrom
Ronald Duke
Joan Kaiser
Alma Laubhan
Gustav Hamm
Joan Schneider
Lucille Schwemmer
Beatrice Steiner
Robert Unruh
LaVonne Nuss
1953
Clinton Ewert
Carol Laubhan
Joan Jantz
Donald Garrett
Adam Hill
Neda Haas

Kathleen Dirks
Edward Krotz
Dwaine Klassen
Morene Zimmerman
LaDonna Schlehuber
1954
Joyce Decker
Donna Geis
Doris Geis
Charles Hill
Dela Rose Johnson
Richard Klassen
Kenneth Klein
Evelyn Laubhan
Jean Unruh
1955
Alvin Bergman
LaVern Dick
DeWayne Dirks
Janice Frick
Shirley Jantz
Calvin Mohn
Marvin Hamm
Robert Hein
Dean Nelson
Judy Peters
Kathleen Steiner
Ralph Vogel
1956
Betty Base
Tom Belton
June Bergman
Tobias Dirks, Jr.
Sharon Frick
Joyce Gill
Clara Jantz
Gary Kaiser
Dennis Klein
Soren Medley
JoAnn Negley
Wayne Ollenburger
LaVern Laubhan
Joyce Steiner
Larry Unruh

Deanna White
1957
Richard Dirks
Duane Jantz
Gerald Jantz
Weldon Meier
Delton Ollenburger
Loretta Schneider
Louise Unruh
Mary Jane Unruh
Muriel Yauk
Shirley Youk
Dennis Zitterkopf
Merna Zimmerman
1958
Gary Ahlstrom
Wendell Dirks
Gary Frantz
Nancy Kaiser
Larry Klein
Jim Ratzloff
Frank Steiner
Carolyn Youk
1960
Patricia Kaiser
Margie Youk
1959
Larry Bergman
DeLoyce Dirks
Kenneth Jantz
Delores Krotz
Glenn Laubhan
Rodney Negley
Delores Ollenburger
Larry Rader
Philip Schmidt
Virgil Wiebe, Jr.
1961
Gerald Bergman
Glenda Bolte
Robert Christiansen
Jolene Decker
Stuart Dyck
Vernon Frantz

Janet Frick
Danny Jantz
Manfred Hein
Richard Laubhan
Dianne Negley
Dennis White
Warren Winter
1962
Richard Belton
Gloria Dirks
Edith Frick
Flora Jantz
Sharon Klein
Sherman McElhiney
Owen Meier
Barbara Steiner
Robert L. Unruh
Willard Unruh
Sheryl Weibert
1963
Mona Christiansen
Lauren Frantz
Galen Frick
Vernon Henry
Jerrie Jantz
Priscilla Kaiser
Larry Kerbs
Judy Klein
Dwight Negley
Jeanette Vajnar
Judy Voth
Larry Wedel
1964
Barbara Bolte
Theresa Dirks
Feryl Dyck
Kenneth Goentzel
Sharon Jantz
Robert Klein
Mary Jane Krotz
Mary Agnes McDowell
Lloyd Meier
Kenneth Pankratz
Rick Riffel

Vernie Steiner
Janice Unruh
Norma Frick
Warren Weibert
1965
Gordon Christiansen
Charles Goentzel
Terry Kerbs
Robert Lang
Kathy Schwemmer
Anita Unruh
Douglas Wedel
1966
Sheryl Becker
Leonard Frantz
Robert Frantz
James Hein
Alvin Hett
Janice Jantz
Kirby Rector
Sharon Redeker
Margaret Steiner
1967
Verlyn Bergman
Sharon Hein
Thomas Christiansen
Mary Lang
Dennis Ewert
Shirley McDowell
Kathleen Miller
Jerry Rader
Marlin Miller
Jimmy Redger
Sherilyn Pankratz
Gerald Unruh
Steven Wedel
Terry Unruh
Beverly Weibert
Galen Youk
Rosalie Redger
Sheryle Wedel
1968
Jim Bernhardt
Frances Bolte

Robert Goentzel
Bonnie Hamm
Deanna Jantz
Rodney Jantz
Stanley Jantz
Duane Kaiser
Myrna Klinkerman
Allen Longstreth
Linda Miller
Burtis Oblander
Virlin Richert
Harry Rhodes
Eugene Schafer
Dennis Unruh
Sherry Unruh
Larry Winter
Norman Winter
Meredith Yauk
1969
Barbara Christiansen
Dale Christiansen
Rick Drake
Jonas Frantz
JoAnn Frick
Cynthia Goertz
Sharon Kaiser
Jacqueline Kerbs
Connie Klein
Loralie McDowell
Ruth Ann Miller
Carolyn Ollenburger
Doneta Rader
Kelly Rector
Valora Redger
Dieter Schock
Stanley Ray Unruh
Irma Winter
Glenda Rhodes
1970
Kent Becker
Lane Dyck
Carolyn Ewert
Richard Frantz
Patricia Hein

Wanda Hein
Betty Kaiser
Kala Klinkerman
Rhoda Kraft
Rhonda Kraft
Thomas Krotz
Brenda Medley
Wendy Oblander
Ralph Steiner
Richard Unruh
Melvin Winter
Wayne Winter
1971
Dwight Dirks
Dudley Donahue
Barbara Hamm
Gordon Jantz
Gene Warren Oblander
Kathleen Redger
Gladys Rhodes
Keith Unruh
Jane Wedel
Wendell Wedel
Christina Wiebe
Marilyn Weibert
Wanda Winter
Ray Redger
Randy Redger
1972
Tom Donahue
Gayleen Miller
Susan Goertz
Eldon Kaiser
Autumn Kaufman
Charles Nesser
Mark Nuss
Kimberly Oblander
Diana Rader
Krystal Richert
Galen Unruh
LaDonna Unruh
1973
Glenn Ewert
Betty Frantz

Norman Frantz
Curtis Frick
James Hamm
Lynette Medley
Gary Nuss
Marolyn Ollenburger
1974
Debra Donahue
Danny Joy
Kim Kaufman
Brenda Unruh
Marlene Unruh
Karen Wiebe
Teresa Youk
Laurel Bernhardt
Ervin Dickie Hein
1975
Herman Bolte III
Karen Christiansen
David Hein
Alan Miller
Brian Nuss
Roy Steiner
Linda Winter
Jayne Wiebe
Norman Miller
1976
Tim Donahue
Dale Geis
Shawn Miller
Donna Pankratz
Annette Richert
Gene Unruh
Jeff Youk
1977
Tamara Becker
Jan Christiansen
Tim Kaufman
David Redger
Kevin Redger
Debra Kay Unruh
Galen Unruh

1978
Merrill Base
Eileen Duggan
Wayne Geis
Shelley Goertz
Melanie Mayfield
Synita McGehee
Perry Steiner
Kimberly Weibert

1979
Coleen Dirks
Elain Duggan
Tom Harmon
Shirley Klein
Rick Shriver
Terrie Bolte

Main Street in Durham after a heavy shower, spring, 1907.

Floods (and Fires)

The Funk Creamery was located just west of the old wagon bridge, west of Durham. It burned in 1916. Claude Unruh has some metal milk labels taken from the ruins in his 'relics' collection.

May 13, 1953, after the disastrous fire which destroyed Charles McDowell's grocery store, on the main intersection of Durham

Fires

The entire east side of Main Street in Durham was destroyed by fire in 1911, wiping out four businesses. Another fire in December 1935 took the Blue Goose Hotel, also called Durham Hotel, which was on the east side of Main near the Railroad tracks. And in 1953, Charles MacDowell's grocery store and locker burned to the ground.

On November 23, 1911, Durham had one of its most disastrous fires. Nearly a quarter of a block of business places were destroyed by fire.

George Youk, who lived in the north part of town at that time was on his way to the depot with his sister-in-law, who had planned to take a west bound train for Oklahoma, when he saw Wyant's General Merchantile Store on fire. Immediately he started shouting fire, but all too late, Durham had no fire fighting equipment - only the "Bucket brigade."

The fire burned with vengence, leaping first onto one building then another, yet the wind seemed to be very calm. In a short time it had consumed Wyant's Store, a twonship building, Power's Drug Store, Jone's Barber Shop, Jone's Dry Goods, and Grocery Store and Meschkes' General Store.

Tor awhile it appeared that all of Durham was doomed to burn for when the fire was burning at it's greatest height something inside Wyant's Store exploded sending flames and glass completely across the street.

The frantic townsfolk saw there was nothing they could do to save anything on the east side of the street, not even a little of the merchandise, so they set to work with their buckets to save the west side.

At last after the angry flames had reached the corner building it burned itself out for all the buildings across the street had been thoroughly soaked with water, although the fronts of them were badly scoarched from the heat.

When the Blue Goose burned, the Goertz Hardware and Implement frame building, about 50 feet away, was saved by volunteer fire fighters who crawled onto the roof with a bucket brigade and poured water onto the roof to prevent it igniting from flying sparks.

On the morning of May 13, 1953, Mac's Grocery Store was completely enveloped in flames before anyone knew it was on fire. The locker plant, cream station and Schultz filling station, were also a total loss. Nothing was saved out of any of the buildings.

The following account was from a letter written to the Rock Island Railroad Company regarding the flood damages done to the City of Durham on the eleventh of May, 1929:

I am a merchant located at Durham, Kansas and have been in the merchantile business for the last past 33 years. My store is located in about the center of the block between 4th and 5th Street on the east side of the street facing the west on Douglas Ave. The building occupies for a store room is a frame structure one story about 14 x 24 feet and have been in present location about 8 years. I carry a general line of groceries.

On the night of May 10th, I happened to be out until about 11 o'clock returning to my home about that time and soon after retired. My house is located on Lawrence Avenue, which is about 3 blocks northeast of my store, which is probably 8 feet higher than the level of the ground where the store is located and the high water did not reach my residence. At or about 4 a. m. of May 11th I was awakened by sound of people calling for help and I was somewhat confused thinking probably I had been dreaming although I got up and went to the window but did not see anything unusual and called to my daughter who was up on the 2nd floor and we both dressed and started out to investigate the cause of the trouble. And both leaving the house together walked towards town. My daughter suggested that she go ahead and determine what was the trouble so she walked on south and turned west around the corner. She had only gone a short distance when she ran into water. It was not raining at that time but had been a short time before. After we discovered that the excitement was caused by flood, we remained together about 30 minutes and then both returned home. It was just getting daylight. It is my judgement that the water rose about 12 inches after we first saw it. The water remained at the high point probably 30 minutes and then suddenly started to go down. It went down gradually. By 8 o'clock the water had entirely left my building. The water had been about four and one half feet in my store. Everything below the waterline in the store was ruined, especially the sugar, coffee, beans, lard, the refrigerator, cash register, counter scales, cigars, smoking and chewing tobacco, candy, washing powders, soap, vegetables, a small amount of fruit, flour, and show cases. The water ap-

parently seemed to have two currents, one going south on Douglas and another current coming from the south through the alley between Douglas and Lawrence, Lawrence being the first street east of Douglas. This current was going north and my solution is that when the water struck the railroad embankment near the depot it turned up the drain to the east paralleling the railroad tracks on the north side seeking an outlet. This drain is probably 8 feet wide and an average of two feet in depth. This drain is on the right-of-way and is something like 75 feet north of the depot. The high point where the water divided is about half way between 5th and 6th Street on Douglas Ave. At the railroad crossing on Douglas the embankment is probably 4 feet higher than the level of the street in front of my store and the only outlet the water had was through the little ditch running parallel with the railroad on the north side of the track and which carries the water off into the Cottonwood River. This ditch is sufficient to carry off an ordinary rainfall, but in this instance the water could not escape because the river was too high to permit the water to escape. While I have no personal knowledge of the point where the water first broke over the river bank, it is only fair to assume that it came over through Mr. Haas' property, there being a depression or low place through this property. This depression runs to the northwest from the north end of Douglas Ave. extending to the river.

I have no way of determining the amount of rainfall in the vicinity of Durham but I heard it and knew that it was a terrific rainfall. This heavy rain fell to the best of my judgement between the hours of midnight and 3 a. m. and estimated that it was a rainfall of 10 or 12 inches. I have no personal knowledge of any water spout or cloud burst in the water shed north and west of Durham but I understand there was.

I was located in Durham in business during the 1903 flood and it is my judgment that the water in May of this year was 18 to 24 inches higher than in 1903. Although the same section was flooded in 1903 as was in 1929. The only difference being the depth of the water. While I am not positive as to the time the embankment west of the Cottonwood River bridge went out, I am under the impression that as soon as this embankment went out it relieved the situation is the town and the water began falling immediately. In my judgement there was about one half mile of the railroad fill or embankment washed out and the tracks were washed off the embankment onto the south side. The water ran over the tracks between the depot and bridge but as to the depth, I am unable to say but it washed out the ballast and the fill. It is my opinion that the bottom of the bridge was possibly two feet or more above the level of the high water. I believe that it will take an additional opening on the west end of the railroad bridge of 200 feet to prevent a re-occurance of the 1929 flood. I think this would be money well spent on the part of the railroad company as it would no doubt prevent any farther destruction to their fill and tracks. There is no doubt in my mind but what the bridge is inadequate to carry off this great volume of water, while it is true this was a very unusual happening and may not occur for 25 years. But when it does occur it destroys not only the railroad property but individual and personal property and it requires a very large expenditure to repair the damage.

During the many years that I have been located at Durham there has been frequent occurences of high water and the water has gotten into the streets many times during that periods but the various dates I am unable to give for I do not recall them but there has only been two times in the last 26 years or to my knowledge that the business section of the town has been overflowed and damaged by the high water.

There is a highway bridge over the Cottonwood River on 5th Street. This bridge is constructed of steel and concrete and is considerable lower than the railroad bridge although I do not know definitely the height of either bridge. The highway bridge has a cement floor and a steel frame which projects above the floor of the bridge higher than a man's head. On the east end and the south side of the highway there is a row of trees extending east from the bridge to a point possibly 200 feet. There are also trees on the west side of the bridge and trees on the river banks north of the county bridge.

The Cottonwood River heads in the vicinity of Canton and traverses through an irregular route probably traveling a distance of 40 miles and in the distance of course it has a number of tributaries. The north Cottonwood River is rather deep and narrow stream and ap-

parently a pretty good fall. I don't know how long the railway or highway bridges are but I am under the opinion the bridges are about the same length but there has been some addition added to the railroad bridge on the west since the 1903 flood and I don't know just what that was. I don't consider that the small dam across the river below the railroad bridge had anything whatever to do with the flooded condition of the town of Durham for the reason that opening in my judgment was inadequate to carry off the water and did not have a chance to escape. It is quite evident that the water on the north side of the railroad tracks was fully 18 inches higher than on the south side and possibly more than that no doubt was due to the fact that the water was held back by the embankment.

My stock of goods was damaged, also the building between $350 and $500 dollars, the plastering had to be removed and the building be replastered.

I have not made any claim against the railroad company or have I any intention of making a claim for this damage and loss for the reason I do not feel that the railroad company is entirely responsible for this damage. Although I do feel that they are partially responsible.

No doubt with a larger opening through the railroad embankment the water would have gotten into the buildings some anyway for the reason that this was the most water in volume that I have ever seen. This is the greatest amount of rainfall in this section that I have ever known in the short period of time in which it fell.

In addition to the things I have enumerated as lost and damaged, my seven ton platform scales were absolutely destroyed by the current of the water. They were 7 ton Fairbank scales and had been in use about 10 years.

I recall now as I walked home the night of the flood that it was extremely dark and observed one of the most severe electrical storms that I had ever seen. The entire skies were filled with lightening flashing from every direction.

This is all of the information that I am able to give concerning this matter.

Very truly yours,
L. A. Jones

Floods

Several devastating floods have hit the town of Durham, including one in 1903 (see letter about flood). A flash flood in 1929 caught people by surprise, because it had not rained in Durham, and area residents got the flood water from heavy rains northwest of town. The Rhodes Ranch had just received a hugh shipment of cattle at the Durham stockyards the day before, but they came through without loss.

The year 1941 saw another destructive flood, but the biggest of all, and the most destructive, hit the town in July, 1951, causing major losses.

Some of the threats, problems and losses from high water can be best described by reading the Durham column in the Hillsboro Star newspaper during July, 1951, The columnist is not identified, but she describes the dilemma of a town facing high waters very graphically. Some of her material follows.

A drive down Main Street of Durham required special equipment during this Oct. 2, 1941 flood. Try a boat!

Harvey Yauk, Postmaster, with J. Zitterkopf, ponders the clean-up after 25 inches of water came into the post office during the July 11, 1951 flood of Durham.

Taken from the top of the elevator, partly submerged equipment, and inundated homes, are seen in this photo of the 1941 flood of Durham.

Waters over roads...a too-common sight around Durham some years. This is Spring, 1951.

The Durham News correspondent at that time for the Hillsboro Star describes the '51 flood firsthand.

Second Flood in Month of June

Durham was under water again Friday morning after a four inch rain Thursday night and Friday morning, bringing the water out into the streets about 10 o'clock Friday morning. The water lacked about 10 to 14 inches of being as high as it was the 7th of June. Sandbags were used and the water didn't get into but one or two business places and then not over two or three inches.

Again we were lucky. A number of basements filled again, including the one where we live. The only casualty that I have heard of was the one at our house when one of our chickens got tired of living and hung himself, we had them penned up in a chicken coop.

The wheat harvest has been delayed again and again on account of heavy rains and the weatherman is predicting more of the same. A lot of the wheat is ready to harvest and much more rain will be a greater loss to the farmer and he has already had enough for one year. You can't tell the garden from the weeds as it's been impossible to get it hoed between rains.

The 1951 flood devastated Durham. Apprehension at the weather was noted in the Durham News column in the July 19, 1951 Hillsboro Star.

We are almost afraid to turn on the radio and listen to the weather forecast anymore as it is always the same, scattered showers and even if they say fair and warmer it still rains. Yesterday morning, Sunday, we had a severe wind and electrical storm with some rain. Becker's store was hit, knocking out the light meter and telephone, ruining the phone completely. Several report their electric clocks being put out of working order. The forecast is for more showers for tonight and tomorrow. The wheat harvest is still being delayed with the greater number of fields still standing untouched. All that has been harvested is on the high land.

The next column, July 19, 1951 tells of the actual flood.

Durham Has 4th Flood in 5 Weeks

Durham suffered its fourth flood in 5 weeks on Thursday July 12, but the one July 11 was the one that nearly got everyone in the flood district. The flood came up fast and stayed up, going down slowly as there was so much water below us it could not run off. It ranged

from 2 inches to 6 feet or better in the residential districts. In some places the water was higher than in 1929 but in our house it lacked 14 inches of being as high as in '29. Another inch and it would have run in and out of the windows. It was 21 inches deep all over the house. Alex Becker had about 36 inches, Ed Becker 45 or 46 inches and in the south part of town it was higher, I haven't had time to inquire. Across the tracks it was higher in Ed Klein's house than in '29. They had 6 inches in 1929 and 18 this time. It was higher most everywhere than in 1941. We still think we were lucky in Durham, most everyone got things up so they didn't have too much loss in furniture and merchandise but of course we had the full clean up job of mud and slush. In fact, we are still cleaning and trying to get the walls and floors dried out and then comes the cisterns, wells and outbuildings. You that never have had this clean up job to do get a bang out of riding thorugh the streets and enjoying the water but if you were in our shoes, you would sing another tune. Thanks Hillsboro for the food sent over, we really appreciate it more than words can express and thanks so much to all of you that came in with your working clothes on and helped the merchants and in the homes. We will never forget your kindness. One kind friend called me up and asked me if I wouldn't like to come up to her home and have a nice hot bath, and boy, I didn't turn that down. I felt like a new person after battling mud and filth for three days. A little thing in itself but something I will never forget. Yes, we had water everywhere but not a drop to drink or use and still have to carry water and again thanks to our friends on the hill for letting us get water. Thank God it wasn't any worse.

The October 1941 flood was memorable. Reuben Funk, with merchandise that was taken out of the cellar before it filled with water, pulled to sidewalk in front of the store.

Durham after a flood in the 1930s. Photo taken from the elevator top.

The flood, June 31, 1965, brought 8" of water into the post office. Photo was taken from the top of the elevator.

Even the dogs of Durham were impressed by the floodwaters

Alex Becker's alfalfa field, flooded June 31, 1965.

Farming and Ranching

About Durham Cattle

Grolier Enclyclopedia -- Shorthorn - Breed of domestic cattle. Its merits and remarkable adaptability to almost any climate have caused it to become distributed throughout the world. It is of considerable antiquity, though not so old as the Longhorn, but it was not until the close of the 18th century that the Breed was developed. The breed is still widely known as the Durham.

Shorthorns vary in color from pure red to white, but a roan blend is now the most popular. The horns are short, curved, and flat and may tend to turn either upwards or downwards.

The body is symmetrical and very bulky in proportion to the size of the skeleton. The breed is of the general utility type, ranking high as a milk producer, and yielding milk of the highest grade. It matures speedily and attains great weight.

Book Of Knowledge

Cattle - The shorthorn, or Durham, is a popular breed, especially on farms or where the farmers grow crops and have only a few cows. They are large animals, usually reddish white, or a mixture of these colors, and they make fine beef. Some varieties are also good producers of milk and are known as dual-purpose cattle.

G. E. Durham
County and City in the county of England
Noted for horses and shorthorn cattle, and sheep rearing.

Farming and Ranching in Durham

Farming and ranching in the Durham area has had a long and varied history. The land, which was once considered a part of the Great American Desert, came to be highly prized as fine agricultural land, and was settled and acquired by those who tilled the land, in a number of ways.

Everything from fruit to tobacco to grapes to silkworms and honey has at one time or another been grown in Marion County, but of course the regular crops such as wheat, corn and cattle have been the prime crops.

In 1872, the principal crop in Kansas was corn, and it was known as "The Corn State," with wheat being the least profitable crop. But in a few years, (through problems with drought and low prices for corn) the farmers began growing wheat, which eventually came to rank in first place for national wheat production.

The Mennonite immigrants introduced the Turkey Red wheat, which they had brought with them from Russia, and this crop was much superior to the soft wheat varieties which had previously been grown. The Mennonite immigrants came to the area between 1872 and 1874, and their contribution to the state's agriculture, and to wheat production, and therefore, feeding the nation, and the world, with bounteous wheat crops, can never be forgotten.

But farming, and wheat production and harvest, was then a far cry from what it now is. It was tedious, dangerous work, with horses pulling the equipment to tend and harvest the wheat, as well as other crops. And early machinery had hazards.

Anyone familiar with farm machinery knew the dangers of the equipment; the tendency to injure the workers. One nurse who tended injured brought into hospitals in a rural area, said she could tell the advancement of the farm equipment, by the extent of the damage, usually to a farm worker's arm or hand, and the development of better equipment.

A man's arm, caught in a corn picker, or some other farm machinery, would be completely lost from early equipment, whereas later developments meant lesser injuries, down to a hand or fingers missing. Those farm tragedies were part of the lot of farming in those days and accepted with stoicism. Several men from the Durham community were fatally injured when their tractor overturned on them while working ground.

Elsewhere, it has been mentioned that much of the Durham area was farmed by farmers who leased the Scully Estates, and that influence was felt for the entire history of Durham, with Scully just now bowing out of major landholdings.

Land was acquired through several methods, when the county was opened for settlement after having been officially surveyed in 1859.

In 1863, the Kansas government reserved about one-third of Marion County land for the Santa Fe Railroad to sell, and buying was relatively simple with several payment options available.

There was a five-year residence and improvement requirement, but this could be circumvented by the Timber-Culture act, which stated that if trees had been growing for two years, the homesteader could reduce the time requirement. . . an example of the need for, and encouragement of, tree production to change the face of this "desert/prairieland."

Within seven years after the Civil War ended, nearly all the government land was claimed in Marion County, with about 90% of it available for crop cultivation.

The Cottonwood River near Durham was prime land because of its quality and the water rights and accessibility, and so Durham early had a number of successful farmers in the business of producing food crops.

Everyone has a memory of the pantry or cellar for storing one's garden produce, and making preparations for winter, (or until the next growing season). One of the heaviest blows to those earliest settlers who were eeking out a subsistence with their primitive growing of crops, in their precious gardens, was the invasion of grasshoppers, in the year 1874 (see story elsewhere in this book). That set people back, and used up their store of food before it was harvested. But survive they did. . . to become some of the most productive farmers in Kansas.

As mentioned earlier, the Crane Ranch was a large user of early grain crops to feed the stock at the ranch, and farmers from the surrounding areas had a lively market once they got the crops produced.

Grinding of wheat was an early concern, and one of the first mills was in the Durham area.

Beef cattle have been mentioned previously, and the dairy industry also prospered in the Durham area, with farmers usually having multi-crop plans for their farms, to insure against total loss in event of some crop disaster.

As some information is presented concerning certain ranches and their role in Durham's history and economy, this record will not elaborate on that, except to say that Durham was, and is, a typical farming community.

Even though farmers have seen hardships, and economic disasters in recent years, in looking at their history and heritage, it is noted that they triumphed before and no doubt even if the face of farming changes, there will be many Durham area farmers and ranchers who will continue to raise that most vital of all crops. . . food for the world.

Grasshopper Plague

Marion Record-Review, October 5, 1944
Ferdinand J. Funk Records His Memories Of
The Great Scourge of '74,
The Grasshopper Invasion

In the "Kansas Teacher" for October, 1944, Ferdinand J. Funk, former resident of Marion, writes his version of the grasshopper invasion. Ferd Funk has just emigrated with his Mennonite family from East Prussia in the spring of 1874 to Marion county. The event made an indelible impression on the fourteen year old lad.

E. S. Hannaford received the clipping from a friend and shares it with Record-Review readers. It follows, in part.

"The opening date of this devastating experience was the sixth of August, as bright and sunny a day as any summer day ever was in Kansas. Not a cloud in the sky above, nor even a hint of a cloud on the low horizon. That's the way it was until about 4 o'clock in the afternoon. Then the sky suddenly became hazy and speedily darkened until in a matter of a very few minutes, it was so dark that it not only frightened me but also did something to the chickens. I can't say whether they were frightened or whether they just did the best they knew how under the circumstances – they hastened to their roosts as fast as they could. They had never had occasion to go to roost in such a hurry at such an unseemingly early hour.

"All this happened in such an incredibly short time that it hit my youthful mind with an indescribable feeling of awe and consternation, as of some terrible and disastrous catastrophe impending. I am sure everybody there had the same sort of feeling. That mysterious phenomenon of nature. What could it be that could transform the brightest day into the blackest darkness of night in so short a time? We quickly found out what it was that so appalled and terrified us. It was grasshoppers. With a whizzing, whirring sound they came from the northwest, and they came in unbelieveable numbers – 300 billion, at least. They hit on everything, and they were no respectors of person. In less than no time I was covered from head to foot, and where they hit the face or hands, they hurt like a impact by hard missiles, and they immediately commenced to eat on me and took several bites out of my ears before I could brush them off. They covered everything exposed, and the ground was covered in some spots to a depth of four or more inches, and trees along the creek were loaded with them so thickly that sizeable limbs broke with the weight of them.

"They fell into the creek that ran through our farm in such vast numbers as to form a high dam by drifting with the current against obstruction and damming up the water so as to form deep swimming holes in the normally shallow stream. But I could not make use of those swimming holes because the water was made too foul by the dead hoppers. It turned brown like coffee and cattle refused to drink it. Even the fish could not take it; they added to the foulness of the water. Not until after the creek had been flooded by heavy rains did the water become normal again. When I now think of the way those hoppers sent the chickens to their roost in a hurry, I can see something funny about what seemed so terribly frightening at the time. It was but a very short time until the hoppers had all come down out of the sky, and the sun was shining as bright as ever. Thereupon, the chickens immediately left their roost and at once pounced upon those hoppers with a voracity that was not only fierce but positively funny to behold. They gorged themselves with those hoppers until their crops bulged out almost as big as their bodies and when they could not take on any more, they stood around in a sad and mournful fashion as if grieving over their lack of capacity for taking on all there was before them.

"My father had bought out a homestead claim with a small shanty on it for about $12 an acre instead of buying as good Santa Fe land at $3 an acre, and he did so because the claim had about 15 acres of wheat and 15 acres of corn on it. Wheat was worth $1. 50 a bushel and corn $1. 25, and at that price the crop promised to just about pay for the farm. We looked forward to having wheat and corn to sell instead of buying the same. The wheat was harvested and threshed before the hoppers came, and the corn looked good for 50 bushels per acre until the hoppers lit on it about 4 p. m. that fateful day in August. By nightfall, there was nothing left of it except about two feet of naked stalks, and by sunup the next day even those stalks were gone.

"On nice nights I picked my sleeping quarters on the strawstack, out under the starry sky. That's where I went to sleep on that grasshopper night. When I awoke in the morning, I found that the hoppers had eaten part of my straw hat. There was plenty of straw in the stack, but they liked my hat better, at least that part of it where the brim joins the crown. There they found the hat sweeter to their taste, by the sweat of my honest young brow. The hoppers feasted on that part of the hat so that when I went to put it on, I found it in two parts – brim and crown – both quite useless. For voractiy and capacity of eating, there are no creatures on all this earth like the hoppers. They ate many times their own weight in a day and ate everything green except the grass. They just hopped that, and I suppose that is why they are called grasshoppers. They ate the harness on the horses' backs or hanging in the barn; they gnawed the wooden handles of forks and shovels, probably because of the taste of the sweat of hands found on them and which they seemed to like. They were not only most greedy and voraciuos, but they were also cannibalistic in their eating, and when they had devoured everything else, they devoured one another.

"In the fall they deposited their eggs in the ground, which produced a new brood the next spring to eat up the growing crops to the last leaf or sprout. After that they somehow disappeared, but they had done enough damage to cause some of the new settlers to pull out and move elsewhere or go back to where they had come from. As for my folks and myself, we could not do that, and therefore stayed 'put', to go through other experiences that were plenty discouraging and distressing and some of them appeared to us as superlation in their nature."

Mid-harvest on the Cameron Smith farm. Binder was method of cutting and wheat was shocked. Grandpa Weimer on binder, Cameron Smith leaning on binder, Alex Weimer driving Fordson and Buz Smith sitting on tractor.

SCULLY LAND

The Scully estates, as they were called, were being leased and worked by many of the farmers, although other farmers owned their own land, too. The Scullys owned more property in Marion County than any other person in the county, and for that reason, information on Scully is included in this book.

Scully Leases Farmed Locally

William Scully, an Irish landowner, sold off most of his Irish holdings around 1850 and came to the United States to purchase western lands. Having bought land in various states, he would eventually own more land in Marion County than any other individual or company.

From Scully's largest holdings in Marion County of 55,666 acres, in 1886, the estate was only somewhat depleted by 1942 when it was appraised at 53,491 acres. A large change in the estate was occasioned by the building of the Marion Reservoir in the 1960's when about 3,400 acres of Scully land was submerged for the reservoir use.

Scully bought all of his Marion County holdings between 1870 and 1885 by various methods. He was able to accumulate a large portion of lands through the purchase of "warrants" (each good for 160 acres) from soldiers who had been in the Mexican War. Other parcels were acquired from the United States government, the railroad and some individuals.

"Scully leases" have always had to be renewed annually. Initially, leases made rents due only once a year, but a twice-a-year arrangement was necessitated by increased assessments on the land for such services as roads and schools. Later the rents were made due on August 1 and December 1 and included as part of the rent the total amount of all assessments and taxes.

Generally, the lease agreements have been satisfactory. The arrangements have been so desirable that there is even a sizeable cash value accorded to the ownership of a Scully lease.

While many tenants have kept their leases for long periods of time, when a tenant does give up a lease, he sells the improvements to the new tenant, having paid for the house and outbuildings himself.

One tenant who remained a lifetime was W. E. Carter of Durham, whose lease of 53 years went to his grandson.

Rhodes Ranch.

The Rhodes Ranch

Ranching enterprises have been an important part of Durham's agricultural scene ever since the early 1870's, when Albert Crane dreamed of cross-breeding cattle from the British Isles with Texas longhorns he acquired, from herds being trailed up from Texas to the rail-head town of Abilene, Kansas.

Ranching and farming operations have been a backbone of Durham over the years. Several large, successful ranches operated in the Durham area, but no one single ranch has had a longer history than the Rhodes Ranch, north of Durham.

Harry Walter Rhodes bought the land, a Scully lease, from Mrs. Pete Schnieder, in about 1906, prior to Harry and Lillie Rhodes' marriage on June 3, 1908.

The young couple lived at several locations before settling on the ranch in October, 1923.

The ranch received cattle into the Durham stockyards, grazed them through the summer, and then drove them back to Durham, shipping them to markets in Kansas City, St. Joseph, Missouri, or Chicago.

Among the huge shipments of cattle received was a notable one, that of 1100 Brahma cattle (see photo) which came into the Durham stockyards in 1929, just before the big flood. According to recollections, family members stayed up all night, remaining at the stockyards in event of high water endangering the animals, but none occured.

Harry W. Rhodes passed away in 1932. After his death, his sons managed the ranch. Harold, Dale and Jack all managed at different times, until they married or moved away. Robert and Dean Rhodes managed it for the last thirty years.

Lillie Rhodes stayed on the ranch, helping with the management, retiring in later years.

The Rhodes family included eight sons and five daughters.

Just this year the ranch was sold and operations discontinued, drawing to a close one of the most glamorous, exciting eras of Durham rural life.

The cowboys are Harry Walter Rhodes, ranch founder, with eldest son, checking the stock.

Lillie Rhodes on her 80th birthday.

The most cattle ever unloaded at one time was 36 cars at Durham stockyards, in '29-30 for Rhodes ranch. They operated 3, 000 cattle on 10, 000 leased acres acres at the ranch 's peak in 1929.

Rhodes family gathering.

Chore time on the Henry Christiansen farm. Mattie Christiansen, standing, Geraldine on the water barrel, and Velma in the bucket. Alice is leading the horse.

A threshing crew

The Christiansen Trucking equipment, part of a successful farm operation.

Hay-baling on the Christiansen farm. There are 1,610 bales in this one stack. Over 1900 bales were taken from one hayfield.

Activity at the Durham stockyards was brisk during the years of railroad cattle-shipping era.

Ratzlaff threshing crew.

20, 000 bushels of grain, piled up in the winter of 1915. Skyline from left includes elevators, two-story depot and the railroad water tower, looking southwest along road by railroad track.

Silo filling -- the Christiansen farm.

The windmill at a Rhodes ranch farm pond.

Cattle was the important crop of many Durham farmers.

Farm work was never done, it seemed. Dave Zimmerman, at right with father-in-law Pete Ratzlaff, 1946.

Farm conditions dictated life's pleasantries in a family farm operation. There was a bumper crop of wheat in 1946, and sisters Morene and Lois Zimmerman were asked to stand in the wheatfield to show just how tall the wheat was then!

Harvesting
Letter to the Centennial Committee

Ethelyn Jantz of McPherson provided this photo of 'Dad' Ewert and his threshing machine and crew, about 1926.

Lunchtime for the threshing crew of Mr. Ewert, 1926.

I noticed in the Hillsboro Star-Journal that you were wanting pictures concerning Durham history. Here are two pictures taken in approximately 1926 near Durham, Kansas.

My father (Frank Ewert) and his brother, Henry Ewert, owned a steam engine and a wheat separator. They would travel from farm to farm in wheat harvest time and thresh wheat for the farmers.

Wheat was cut with binders which made bundles and the bundles were stacked in small shocks of 10 or 12 bundles. Threshing crews would pick these shocks up in hayracks and pitch the bundles into the separator.

The wheat kernels would go into wagons or trucks and the wheat straws formed large straw stacks. Water for the steam engine was hauled from the nearest creek or pond.

Two horses were used to pull the water tank. Coal was used to fire the engine. A large, long belt connected the engine and separator. This enabled the separator to thresh the wheat.

Ethelyn Jantz
McPherson, Kansas

Family fun at the Irwin Christiansen's, rural Durham.

Henry Christiansen and grandchildren.

Lunch time at Elm Springs. Christiansen farm hands seek the only shade on a hot day, sheltered by the boards from the corral.

What was the west without the horse? The territory could not have been settled without horses, and they were the means of transportation for many years, before the horse-less carriage made real horsepower secondary.

Irwin Christiansen, and his trick horse, Buster, who takes a bow.

"To Work Is To Pray"—

As we write the closing of Durham's Centennial book, we wonder what the future holds for Durham and for all of us. Small town and rural America as it has been known for generations, is passing away. A whole culture, a whole way of life, is dying out. Someday this will be recognized as a terrible loss to our country.

Much of the difficulty lies with politics – with administrations who are dedicated to a "cheap food policy" regardless of the needs of America's food producers. The last decade has been hard for farmers, with drastic financial conditions of which most people in 1987 are well aware.

Yet, we know that an agrarian society provides self-respecting, self-supporting people – whose close-knit families were created by working and spending time together in a rural setting.

The essence of Durham remains, even though times change. And perhaps when people are sickened by fast-paced city living, Society will "re-invent the rural life," and Durham will enjoy a new zenith.

At any rate, Durham will abide. It is assured of its citizens' loyalty, allegiance and continued support. For it is Home.

Silo filling crews were community efforts in some cases.

What's Happened Since...

Readers having followed, in this book, the early years leading to Durham's founding, plus the complete history of Durham, carried to its 60th anniversary, (pages 111-123), naturally want to know "What's happened since then?"

That question is answered on the following pages by Ona Donahue, who contributed a brief update on the last forty years, entitled "In Recent Years." Photos from the present-day enhance her story, which begins on the next page. Together with information contributed by businesses of their highlights, and other features, one can "catch up" on new happenings, and put Durham's recent past into the total perspective. Mrs. Donahue has thoughtfully included a section, "What Centennial Visitors Will See", that's new and different about town.

Gradually, times have changed since the era of Durham's "heydays". The town reached peak population (before 1950) of nearly 400 persons. But mobility and social trends led people to go beyond their hometown for needs and entertainment.

Over the years, the image of Durham has changed. Some businesses closed, although several active businesses remain. Several of the original or long-standing firms are enjoying success, along with new businesses – all mentioned on these pages.

But farming has changed, and with it the face of farming communities such as Durham. The population now stands at about 150 persons, yet counting all those of us who lived in and fondly cared for Durham, its inhabitants number many, many more. . . in spirit, if not in person.

The Marion Reservoir, built southeast of Durham, has created some tourist influence. There are modernizations, as well as attempts to retain the original atmosphere with sentimental and cherished artifacts.

The town remains unique, and nothing will take away its wonderful historical status, nor its great asset, the friendliness of this unique community.

Durham "lives on" in each of us who count it as "home", each of us gained something positive by association with its people and the town. The Centennial Celebration provides a welcome opportunity to show those feelings.

In Recent Years
An Update
Ona Donahue, Contributor

Marion County co-op building on Highway 15, Durham, today.

The last quarter of Durham's 100 years has seen changes similar to those experienced by our neighboring small towns, but it is still an agricultural community.

The Rock Island Railroad, after falling on hard times, had to give way to the Southern Pacific. The Rock Island trains, exclusively freight, were having to go 10 miles an hour over the rails, although in 1957 new tracks had been laid, and again in 1960 a ribbon rail had been laid.

Charles McDowell brought to our attention that in front of the elevator there is a rail dated 1903 that is a reminder of the Rock Island sending fast passenger trains through Durham, such as the "Golden State."

By the spring of 1980 the Southern Pacific has assumed ownership and laid new tracks, and their fast traveling freight trains were hurtling through Durham. This is a boon to farmers who have to get their grain to market.

One bad interruption occured in the spring of 1985 when a nighttime cloudburst caused a freight train to derail a few miles north of town. Forty-one of 69 cars were derailed as were two of the three diesel locomotives. There were many sightseers for this spectacle.

CHURCHES

Of the original churches in Durham, there still remain Church of God, Baptist, and Lutheran. The Adventist Church was sold and torn down. In the adjoining rural area there are the Morning Star and Central Heights churches which a number of Durham people also attend.

Each church still has its Ladies Aid, Missionary Societies and Auxiliary groups such as the Baptists' "Kings Daughters" and Young Peoples' groups. The Baptist Church enlarged their facility, remodeling it extensively in 1979.

SOCIAL

Organizations of a strictly social and service nature for women are the Home Circle and E. H. U. For men there is the Lions Club which annually puts on a sausage and pancake feed all day long at the opening of pheasant season.

The Senior Citizens are also an active force in the community. Under the Golden Years Inc. grant by the Ford Foundation, Durham, in the late 1970's was one of the community-based groups to be added in the county. The Senior Citizens meet once a month for potluck dinners and varied programs. The average attendance is 40. Vernedda Klein is current president. From time to time they serve soup and pie suppers.

The centennial project is a log-cabin quilt that was pieced by Ella Schuber and Ruby Yauk. There is a drawing for it on July 18 in case you gave a $1 donation. You don't have to be present at the drawing.

BUSINESSES IN 1987

A huge, tall elevator that has replaced two older and smaller ones is the first building to be seen as one approaches Durham. It has a capacity of 350,000 bushels. Durham merged with Tampa's elevator operation.

In July of 1975, Durham State Bank was remodeled and the grand opening was July 27, 1975. Dorman Becker is President.

Earl and Margaret Frick became the owners of the E & M Cafe on Main Street, January 1, 1968 and are still serving the huge, juicy hamburgers known around a huge area. The hamburgers have been publicly lauded by a well-known News Editor, Henry Jameson of the Abilene Reflector - Chronicle.

Jim Donahue set up his trailer manufacturing plant in the old lum-

Durham Businesses Today

Meier family operates the coffee shop on Highway 15.
It was previously owned by Fred Schneider. Some of the family members are shown.

ber yard in the spring of 1961. With the growth of the business, a new plant was built one mile out of Durham, situated on Durham-Lincolnville Road, in December of 1972. The official and grand opening was in January of 1973.

Bruce and David Hein are in their shop and repair business on Main Street still servicing the farmers' machinery and vehicles. They have been in business there since 1951.

Durham has a Marion County Co-op business on Highway 15 that services tires and has new modern fuel pumps using the card trol for individual use. The firm also distributes propane to urban and rural areas. Fiennes Jantz has been with the Co-op for 12 years.

Dieter Oil Production has an office south of the tracks and will be remembered as formerly occupied by Riffel's K-T oil station on Highway 15. Those returning after years of absence will be very surprised to see the numerous oil wells that have sprung up west of town. Dieter's orange office building is a most attractive addition for the town.

Ben Goertz has a hardware and implement store at the south end of Main Street. He has the dealership for White farm equipment. He is carrying on the family business begun in 1927.

A Coffee Shop located in the north part of Durham and on Highway 15 is the original filling station of John Bessel, subsequently owned by Fred Schneider. It is now owned and operated by Lloyd and Linda Meier. It has become a very handy stopover for Highway 15 travelers.

LaDonna's Hair Styling, operated by LaDonna Klein, was begun west of town in August, 1969. In July of 1974 it was moved to east of town on the Durham-Lincolnville Road where it is pationized by many from the surrounding communities.

Occupying the space that was formerly Riffel's K-T oil station, is Dieter Oil Production on Highway 15.

LaDonna's Hair Styling is owned by LaDonna (Mrs. Bobby) Klein and enjoys a loyal clientele.

NEW SIGHTS FOR CENTENNIAL VISITORS
RETURNING HOME

Some new sights that will greet the visitors and former residents who haven't returned for a number of years:

* Arriving into town from the west you will cross the new two-way town bridge over the Cottonwood River which was built in 1973. The old iron one it replaced known as the Wagon Bridge was built many years ago.

* The old fire bell is now on a solid cement block and beside it is the flag pole that was in use at the school. Appropriately, it is found near the fire station downtown. Bob Gordon, an adopted Durhamite, has been the brain-child of this project.

* At the north end of town on the hill you will see a new shelter house and restrooms. Placed at the east end of the shelter house is the old school bell that rang for many years. . .

* On North Main Street is a new fire station. Bruce Hein is the fire chief. Quoting Bruce, he has "been there since the first fire engine was purchased." There are no salaried firemen. Local people have always volunteered.

* As to the local government, we have a Mayor and City Council. Ben Goertz is the present Mayor and the Council includes Kent Becker, Bill Harmon, Jim Hein, Bruce Hein and Galen Youk.

* We have had our own water system since 1966. We shouldn't forget that Emil Schwemmer and D. D. Regier were the pushers and planners for this project and moreover were instrumental in getting our road blacktopped through Durham. The road extends from Nebraska to the Oklahoma line.

* The post office location has been moved over to the east side of Main Street. The building it now occupies was formerly known as Dick's Restaurant and then Vogel's Cafe.

* One of the most striking changes that will be observed is the Durham Community Center on the west side of Main Street. It will be remembered as Becker's Butcher Shop, Grocery and Dry Goods Store. The Nessers' and the Harmons' subsequently were the proprietors of this grocery store.

* In February of 1977 the city purchased it to be used as a meeting place for Durham's civic and social organizatons and for private use. This has appropriately filled a void created by the closing of our school facilities. It has become the regular meeting place for Golden Years group. It really can be called a multiple purpose place for the whole community.

Durham's present day Main Street, looking south.
The old Valley Hotel is the first building on the right.

* One will also particularly notice that Durham has officially named streets. They are Park Avenue, Santa Fe, Abilene, Douglas Avenue and Lawrence. Named streets run north and south and numbered ones east and west. Main Street really should be called Douglas Avenue.

AND NO LONGER...

As the years catch up with us it's one's nature to want to hold on to people, places, and things of our past. But they do pass on and give way to the new. Our only centenaria, Amelia Smith, after observing her 100th birthday in October, 1986, has passed away.

The Rhodes Ranch, so long a vibrant part of our community life because cattle were associated with it – it too after many years is no more. This year marks the finale for that picturesque operation, the Rhodes family having sold it in early 1987.

The old depot and old hotel, at the south end of Main Street and north end, respectively, no longer serve a purpose, but there they stand as a reminder of what was.

Thus time passes but it can't take away our memories.

SCHOOLS

* The second Durham school was a fine brick structure built in 1910, which housed both the High School and Grade School for many years.
* The first high school principal was Ben McIntosh and the first high school graduate was Gladys Eichenour in 1916. The next graduates were Flossie Smith Unholtz and Enid Powers Pope in 1918. Since then, until 1972, classes graduated each year, when consolidation occurred.
* Originally basketball teams practiced and played in a low-ceilinged hall over a pool room downtown. In 1925 a fine new gymnasium was added to the red brick building. (See related articles)
* As years passed and the old red schoolhouse became inadequate, a fine new one-story building was constructed and the high school moved into the new one in 1956. Athletics and dramatics continued in the old gym.

  When the old red brick building was razed in 1974, many fond memories went with it, but the sound of happy students running up and down those wooden stairs still resound in our memories.
* Through the years Durham High School students have won many local and state honors in music, track, drama, baseball and basketball. In 1963 our basketball team won the state championship. The whole town evacuated each game night to follow the team, wherever they played, and however far away.
* In 1971 the last class graduated from Durham High School as unification of school districts took place. More than 600 students graduated from the school during the school's 61-year history.
* Local high school students began attending the high school in Hillsboro after 1971 but grade school kept our school alive for another 9 years before the final closing in 1980.
* To name all the principals and teachers of Durham schools would be an impossible task, but those principals who because of tenure are remembered best are Paul Loveless, D. D. Regier, Earnest Toland, and C. J. Ahlstrom.

  Our school is gone. The last high school now stands empty, desolate, windows starting out at one. When a school goes, something happens to a town's spirit, but thanks for the memories of those school days.

Contributed by Henrietta Geis
(formerly a teacher in the Durham Schools)

The schoolground of the old red brick school featured a small building popular for "ante-over" games, and a tall slide. Taken at the time of the building's razing in mid 1970s.

Twenty Years For
E & M Cafe

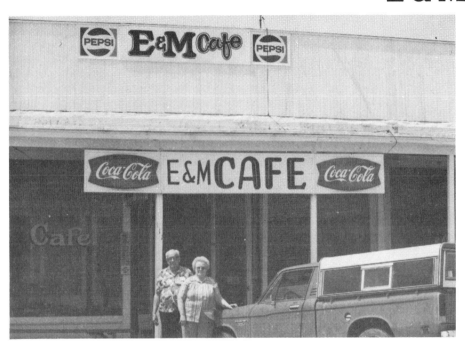

Twenty years For E & M Cafe

"Sombody had to do it!" That's the way Earl Frick describes the way he and his wife Margaret ('Blondie'), became the proprietors of Durham's E and M Cafe twenty years ago.

"When Harry Nuss quit, there wasn't anyone to take over, and we needed a cafe in town, so," says Earl, "here we are."

Although the building is still essentially the same as when it was built in the early 1900's, and "folks like it that way" the clientele is eager and the menu is top-notch.

"We feature hamburgers, (priced about $1 at present), that are second to nobody's, and a wide variety of good meals.

"Our specialities," says Earl modestly, "are just about everything we make. . . old-fashioned pan-fried chicken, (no comparison to that deep-fried junk), and old-fashioned beef roast. Our shrimp goes over pretty well, and we feature homemade cinnamon rolls and homemade bread. These are very good drawing cards," he says.

They regularly have customers in from surrounding towns, and are open 7 a. m. to 7 p. m. , six days a week (closed Sundays).

Asked about the recipes for the cinnamon rolls, the breads and other items, Earl has a two-word answer. . . "Have you ever heard the words, 'trade secrets'?" he quips.

Blondie had been working for Harry Nuss in the cafe, and had fifteen years experience in the restaurant and food service business, having also worked for the Durham Schools as cook.

They have six part-time helpers, all women who help with the cooking, waitressing, and other work.

Earl says, "I bake the cinnamon rolls, and take care of the coffee and tea."

Married in 1941, the couple say they enjoy working together in the business. They feed upwards of 60 people a day in the cafe, not counting the short-orders and coffee-drinkers. (The jukebox is gone, that used to be a feature years ago, when Riffels ran the cafe).

Fred Riffel, Vic's dad, started the first restaurant in the store in 1926, the building having previously had a department store owned by John Borton, and another store owned by Kroger.

"My dad, Conn Frick, bought the building from Kroger in 1926. Now I own it. Meantime two or three others have owned it."

Earl's father bought it as an investment, and made two rooms of it, one part a meat market, which ceased operation years ago.

Asked what he's seen occur in Durham life since starting in business, Frick said, "Losing our two schools was a big blow to our town. Farming has changed, too. People now want to go someplace else to get a job, so there's less people and less traffic. However, we do have a loyal clientele."

Formerly a farmer, Earl (pictured elsewhere in this book as a one-year-old, with his twin sister Earlene, Mrs. Walter Ramsden of Wichita) and other family members, Earl is a good source of history about Durham.

Yet he knows a lot of the good stories will now never be told, because "a lot of the old-timers have died off."

Are they planning anything special for the Centennial days? Knowing Earl and Blondie, you can bet on it.

"Drop by and see us," is his invitation.

Hein's Repair is 36 Years Old

LeeRoy Bruce Hein has owned and operated the Hein Auto Repair in Durham since 1952, and is now celebrating 35 years in business.

"My specialties are work on cars and trucks, " says Bruce, whose two sons have followed in the family tradition of auto mechanics set by their dad. James, the older son, started apprenticing before he was in high school, later graduated from Emproria State, and now teaches auto mechanics at Hillsboro Schools.

David, the younger son, is in business with his father, and is able to rescue a car from a ditch with the handy wrecker, or fix whatever ails the automobile or truck, in other words, "he's a good worker and all around mechanic, " says dad.

Hein got his start working for Mr. Ed Becker, in his Kaiser-Fraser Automotive Agency in Durham. When Mr. Becker passed away in 1951, Hein started in business for himself.

The family also operates two hundred acres of wheat, milo and feeder cattle.

What's the secret of success? "There's an awful lot of good farmers around here, and I've done work for them, and they've been very good to me, " says Hein.

In early years, Becker gave Hein an edge in mechanics by sending him to "school, " a week at a time, in the Kaiser-Fraser dealerships at Salina and Wichita. Now, with computer chips a part of automotive repair, Hein has had to study some new techiques again.

Hein also has a daughter, Wanda (Mrs. Dwight) Schroeder, whose husband farms, and also is a diesel mechanic at Newton, keeping the skills all in the family.

After his wife, Helen Gray Hein passed away, Hein remarried, Shirley Vogel of Marion. The memorial fund for Helen Gray Hein was used to help the Lion's Club build the shelter house and picnic area in the Durham Park since two of her lifelong concerns were occupying children and family enjoyment.

Bruce Hein is also the town's fire chief, supervising a volunteer fire department, which has a new metal building, (in the approximate location of the old livery stable for the Valley Hotel). In front is the fire bell that used to stand on the tall tower to alert residents of a fire.

The old fire bell now resposes on a stand in front of the new fire house, on Main Street in Durham.
LeeRoy Hein (known as Bruce) is the fire chief.

Lions Club is Thirty Years Old

The Durham Park with shelter and picnic area, includes the old school bell, and was created through the efforts of the Durham Lions Club. Monies from the Helen Hein Memorial Fund were used to improve the park.

The Durham Lions Club was founded thirty years ago as a civic organization to work together on worthwhile projects.

Current president is Kent Becker, and the incoming president is Irwin Christiansen. There are presently sixteen members, and the group meets twice a month.

A highlight of the Lions Club activities is the annual "Pancake Feed," held on the first day of pheasant hunting season, in November each year, as a money-making project to enable financing of other improvements and beautification projects in the town.

The Pancake Feed starts at 5 a. m. and runs until 3 p. m., and brings many hundreds of hunters and others to the town to enjoy "breakfast" and partake of the local hospitality in the friendly little community and recognize Durham's uniqueness. "We have hunters here from Wichita, Salina, and many other areas all around Kansas," a member said.

One of the Lion's earliest projects was the purchase of an artifical limb for a local person. The group is always on the lookout for positive, helpful things they can do.

One project is the annual Christmastime visit of Santa Claus, who comes on a Saturday before Christmas, to make an appearance and hand out candy and nuts to children. That project was taken on as soon as the Lions Club organized.

Upkeep of the Durham Park Cemetery is another effort. In return for a small donation to their club, the Lions Club maintains the cemetery, with members getting together on a regular basis to mow the grass and tend the cemetery grounds.

Among recent projects is the completion of the picnic and shelter in the Durham Park (on the schoolgrounds), with installation of the original school bell from the Red Brick School.

The group works together with other individuals and organizations to further its goals and help the community.

"Consider Durham For Retirement"

Bob Gordon, a Salina native who chose Durham as the retirement home for himself and wife, Velma, is chairman of the Durham Centennial Committee, and he's "really up on Durham."

"The history of Durham is just fascinating," says Gordon, who came to town about ten years ago, and purchased the former Maude Savage home, which he has since remodeled.

"I think this town is really fascinating. We're interested in preserving as much as possible of the original history. Recently we got the flagpole from the old schoolhouse erected at the fire station, and the fire bell, too. The bell from the red brick school has been placed in the park on the old school grounds."

Gordon and Velma, (who was raised six miles south of Abilene) raised their family of one son and one daughter in Salina, when he was with the Post Office. He has started as a carrier, then clerked, and spent the last fifteen years as vehicle maintenance supervisor. After retirement in 1973, the Gordons brought their travel trailer over to the Marion Reservoir near Durham, "We enjoyed camping and boating over there, and real good fishing," he said.

In 1978 they purchased the Savage home, and after remodeling it, moved permanently to Durham. "The reason we chose Durham is because of the nice friendly people, the city water, city sewer, and reasonable taxes. It's just a really nice place to retire," he said.

Durham is also centrally located to a number of larger towns. They enjoy the small community real well, but for health reasons spend winters in the South.

"The fishing is the greatest around here," says Gordon. "White bass, walleye and crappie are popular, and people come from all over the state to fish at the Marion Reservoir, (just southeast of Durham) for white bass"

He said they enjoy the Senior Citizens potluck dinners and bus tours, among other civic events.

Gordon recognizes people's curiosity about how he has re-done the old Savage place. Some walls were taken out, bathrooms installed, and carpet and paneling put in. "I've had people here from California who used to live in this house stop and ask to see it."

For this reason, the Gordons are making their home open for public visiting during the Centennial in July. So if you're interested in visiting the old landmark home, (if, for instance, you were a piano student of Miss Savage' during her later years) you're invited to drop in and meet the Gordons and see the home.

———————

Note: Credit should be given to Terry Shaw and his wife, the late Linda Yauk Shaw, for donating the flagpole so it could be incorporated into the Durham decor. The Shaws had purchased the school facilities from the city after it was no longer in use.

The Cottonwood River's path has changed through the years, and recent flood prevention measures have made it less of a threat to the community. The construction of Marion Reservoir southwest of town was a major step in controlling the river.

Present directors of the Durham State Bank are Dorman C. Becker, Benjamin A. Goertz, Virginia Frick, Mary Helen Becker, and Kent D. Becker.

The Durham State Bank, present day.

Durham State Bank
Durham, Kansas

The Durham State Bank was organized and started business on June 28, 1904. Officers consisted of S. L. Armstrong as President; J. C. Fast, Vice President; A. W. Frick, Cashier and H. B. Kliewer, Assistant Cashier. Directors elected at this time were: S. L. Armstrong, J. C. Fast; A. W. Frick; J. M. Clubine; and G. Meschke.

Original capitalization of the bank was $10,000. The bank has continued to serve the community over the years even though it has encountered some severe economic times, especially during the depression era of the early 30's when many bank closings occurred.

A number of individuals have served as President of the Durham State Bank and all were local stockholders living in the community. Starting with S. L. Armstrong as first President, other Presidents include: W. H. Popp; J. J. Benjamin; Floyd White; John Frick; Henry P. Goertz; E. M. Becker; Elmer C. Frick; Ralph Frick and Benjamin A. Goertz. At present, Dorman C. Becker serves as President.

The bank has made steady growth over the years and has built up its Capital Structure to $730,000 from its profits starting with the original Capital of $10,000.

Over the years improvements have been made in the Bank building and in 1975 major improvements were made. The entire interior of the bank was remodeled and an addition of two offices along with an entirely new vault and vault door built to FDIC specifications were added.

Mary Helen and Dorman Becker started working at the Durham State Bank on January 1, 1947. Their son, Kent, joined them in August of 1978.

At the time the Beckers started their employment, the total resources of the Durham State Bank was $300,000. In July, 1975, when major remodeling occured our total resources stood at $2,500,000. As of December 31, 1986, the total resources were $6,350,000.

Present officers of the Durham State Bank are: Dorman C. Becker, President; Benjamin A. Goertz, Vice President; Kent D. Becker, Cashier; Dwight A. Dirks, Assistant Cashier and Data Processing Officer; and Janice Mayfield, Asst. Cashier.

Present Directors of the Durham State Bank as of January 1, 1987 are: Dorman C. Becker; Benjamin A. Goertz; Virginia Frick; Mary Helen Becker; and Kent D. Becker.

From left, Mary Helen Becker, Dorman Becker and Veona Popp. Mrs. Popp worked at the bank from 1962 to 1984. This picture was taken July 27, 1975 at grand opening after bank remodeling.

Dorman Becker, bank president, is standing with Dwight Dirks, assistant cashier and data processing officer with Kent Becker, cashier and Janice Mayfield, assistant cashier is seated.

Janice Mayfield, assistant cashier, Dwight Dirks, assistant cashier and data processing officer, and Kent Becker, cashier, with bank president Dorman Becker. Ben Goertz is vice-president.

April 28th, 1972, Harvey Yauk signs retirement papers after 30 years of work as Postmaster of Durham.

October 31, 1972, Ruby Yauk signs her retirement papers after 30 years as clerk in the Durham Post Office.

Durham Has New Post Office
January 25, 1968

The Durham Post Office has moved across the street from the old location into its newly remodeled modern building. The move was made Thursday according to Postmaster Harvey E. Yauk. The new Post Office has mostly new equipment including the new boxes with keys. Ruby A. Yauk was the clerk. Joan Donahue substitute clerk.

Postmaster Harvey E. Yauk received his commission on the death of President Franklin D. Roosevelt in 1945.

Saloon in Durham Again!

In its early days, there were some saloons in our little town, and one will live again, for the few days of the Centennial, if plans of the Committee are approved. The old post office building is expected to be converted to an "old-time saloon", complete with the usual decor and menu. Barring any problems, folks can look forward to saying to each other, "Meet ya at the saloon!"

Its intention is to re-create a vignette of the old-time element of the town, and should be a popular spot for visitors.

The old Dick's or Vogel's cafe became the post office building in 1968. Lila Unruh is now Post Mistress

Perched on the old wagon bridge are Donna Geis, Pat Nelson, Doris Geis and Phyllis Yauk.

The old wagon bridge at floodtime. Looking west, the 'narrow bridge' sign is submerged, and the bridge top shows.

About The Bridge
From Durham Journal, June 13, 1907

The report is going the rounds that the parties who are opposed to locating the new $3, 400 bridge on 6th Street, have agreed to donate sufficient funds and labor to construct the entire grade, if the bridge is located on 5th Street, where the old bridge now is. This, no doubt, will cause many to think their taxes will be heavier if the bridge is located on 6th Street than if it should be located on 5th Street to be raised only three feet above the level of the old bridge, while the 6th Street site calls for a seven foot raise, making a difference of 4 feet between the two grades, thus putting the 6th Street grade above high watermark and the expense of keeping this grade up will be less by far than the 5th Street grade. And besides, the County Commissioners have already let the contract for the construction of a $3, 400 bridge.

However, the height and cost of the bridge and grade at either location is a settled fact, and the election to be held in the township building in Durham, Tuesday, June 18th is not to decide the height and cost of the bridge and grade, but where the majority of the qualified voters of Durham Park Township want the same located. It is to be a high bridge at either location, and at the same expense, so when the time comes case your vote for where it will be a benefit to the most people, and 6th Street will get the new bridge.

Following is a letter under date of June 11, 1907, from G. H. Rood, which will explain clearly the misunderstanding as to the difference in the cost of the bridge at either location:

Editor - Durham Journal,

Dear Sir:

The bridge engineer, who took the levels for the grade at the Durham bridge, was called here to-day on other business, and I asked him to go over again the grade levels of the Durham bridge, and in checking up the same, finds that we have made an error, and finds that the cost for grades will be practically the same at either place.

G. H. Rood,
Chairman

(However, 5th Street won out to have the bridge located there, where it still stands swept over time after time by the high water).

New Bridge Replaces Old Wagon Bridge

October 6, 1974, the new bridge west of Durham is under construction. 'Ralph, Skeeter, Daisy, and Harvey,' are pictured.

Durham as seen from the new bridge, looking east into Durham

A Local Treasure Gone

The Old Wagon Bridge served the Durham community for over sixty years. It was on the only road west out of town; it served as a fishing place and climbing spot for kids, and it was a measurement of the floods. . . "How high's the water over the bridge?"

When it was finally replaced, it took with it many memories of early day adventures. Information on how it came to be built is contained on the facing page.

November 11, 1974, the new bridge west of Durham was finished. This replaced the picturesque old wagon bridge that had been is use for over 60 years. Looking west from Durham.

G & R Implement
60 Years in Business

In 1927 Henry Goertz started Durham Hardware and Implement Co. He purchased this business from Adam Youk. He sold John Deere farm equipment plus a full line of hardware, trading grain, livestock and eggs for farm equipment and hardware in early days.

In 1938 he started selling Minneapolis Moline, then in 1940, the Oliver line of farm equipment.

In 1957 he retired and his son Ben, with a partner, Carroll Rhodes, bought the entire business and it became G & R Implement Company. In 1968 Ben bought out his partner Carrol Rhodes and became sole owner.

This business has won numerous awards from White Farm Equipment Company for sales, including a plaque, presented to Ben and his wife Anna Mae in 1984 at ceremonies in Scottsdale, Arizona, for "the most White farm tractors sold in the Western (half of the) U. S." that year, plus three other major awards.

G and R Implement Co., 1952 Farmer's Day, left to right, Walt Fritsch, Ben Goertz on 'Oliver', Ed Fritsch, and Rudy Fritsch.

G and R Implement, the business founded by Henry P. Goertz in 1927 is celebrating its 60th year in business in 1987, along with the centennial. Note old hitching rail, still in place in front of store.

Henry Goertz, local businessman.

Donahue Corporation

It all began with a good idea

The Donahue Corporation officers include Jim Donahue, at right, with Joan Donahue, Tom Donahue, and Richard Dirks in front of their present facility northeast of Durham.

When Jim Donahue was able to convert a good idea into reality in 1962, Donahue Manufacturing Company was born, and Durham had a new employer.

While welding at The Boeing Company in Wichita, Jim got the idea to build a better farm implement carrier. Jim conceived the idea while commuting to work, cogita ing on problem-solving he had seen, back in Durham where area farmers would often bring their equipment repair problems to him, sharing their equipment needs and concerns.

Jim started work on the carrier in the summer of 1962, and in a short two week period, the first Donahue Implement Carrier was completed. It had a patented feature that allowed a long, flat bed to be pulled forward of the wheels and axle, at ground level, so machinery could be driven or towed onto it. After loading, the bed could be backed up over the wheels and locked in position for transporting machinery.

From its first location in Durham, to the old Badger Lumber Company building, the company's growth was steady.

As production increased, the lumber yard building eventually became hopelessly overcrowded. So another vacant building nearby was acquired downtown in Durham. More employees were hired.

As new products were developed and production continued to increase it soon became apparent that even two buildings were not going to be large enough to accommodate the growing company. So, periodically, additional ones in the downtown area were acquired. Eventually Donahue Manufacturing was operating out of six separate buildings in Durham, in addition to contracting for considerable sub-assembly work being performed out of town.

The new 40,000 square foot office and manufacturing facility, completed in December, 1972, permits consolidation of all Donahue manufacturing activities under one roof.

Donahue Corporation's sign is seen on Highway 15 in Durham.

Donahue has built a sound, viable firm. One successful patent has led to another – a credit to his inventive ability and his managerial know-how. The company's line of products reflects a time, money and labor-saving approach to farm equipment carriers and includes a swather carrier, combine carrier, stock and grain carrier and bale handling system.

Originally, products were sold through dealers, and later through distributors. Now, products are sold in three ways; selling direct to dealers on some products, selling through original manufacturers, such as John Deere and Allis Chalmers, and selling through distributors for short-line products.

In the words of James Donahue, "From the beginning, we've been fortunate in getting excellent financial help and counsel. Since 1962, we've had an abundance of hard-working employees. People with pride in their work have made it possible to establish a reputation for quality products throughout the country. We've been blessed with an excellent group of people to handle sales and distribution."

"There have been many factors to facilitate success, and above all, my wife Joan, who was a classmate at Durham High School. She has done about everything but weld, since the time we first started the business, and today she still works full-time in the office," Donahue said.

Donahue also credited his brother-in-law, Richard Dirks for his efforts. "Richard started out with us in the beginning, and today plays a very important part in the managing of the company. Without the help of Joan and Rich, the accomplishments of the Donahue Corporation would have been very difficult."

Recently, Tom Donahue, son of Jim and Joan, has assumed a major role in the operation of the Donahue Corporation.

The Donahues also operate a ranching operation of about 8,000 acres in two locations. One is three miles northwest of Durham, which is managed by Dudley and Melissa Donahue. The other ranch location, is approximately twelve miles southeast of Lincolnville, and this unit is managed by Tim and Lisa Donahue. Debbie, Jim and Joan's daughter, is currently an accountant in Hutchinson, Kansas.

And those acquainted with Jim's relatives, his uncle and grandpa, Marion and Cameron Smith, knew well the creative genius and abilities of the family. Uncle Marion Smith's construction of many of the county's bridges made him a local legend, and grandpa was highly inventive also.

Due to Jim's innovation and the success of his company, his story has been told in many publications, including nationally distributed magazines, such as the Chrysler Corp. Magazine, which applauded Jim's inventive, entrepreneurial spirit. But in spite of these accolades, Jim is still approachable, and very much a part of, and dedicated to, his home-town of Durham, serving on the Centennial Committee, and describing Durham as a good place to be.

Tom Donahue and his wife, Rhonda, live in Durham.

In foreground, a Donahue implement carrier, the brilliant invention that sparked the Donahue Corporation, brain-child of Jim Donahue.

SBA Award
Small Business Administration Award

In 1982 James Donahue was honored as Small Business Person in Kansas by the Small Business Administration. Jim and Joan Donahue went to Washington D.C. to be honored as the Kansas winner in the national competition.

Amelia Smith, in antique chair, near her lifelong home, at age 100.

Few Towns Have A Centenarian

Durham's only Centenaria, Amelia Smith passed away in October, 1986, after reaching her 100th birthday. Her family and friends enjoyed her reminiscences of early days in Durham, with her husband, Cameron Smith.

She used to say, "When Cameron moved here, he recalled how the white bones of buffalo were still most visible, and scattered all over the prairie. " (Much of the slaughter of buffalo had been for the Army's purpose of removing the Indians' source of food.)

Recollections of early-day life in Durham included the memory of a saloon, located north of the present Goertz store, G and R Implement. "The dance hall was where the store is now, and the only entertainment in town was the dance every Saturday night. That's where I first saw the Christiansen boys swinging the blondes, and they seemed to be very modest, " she added.

One of the highlights on Sunday was to be at the depot to meet the train Sunday morning, called the Plug, which came at noon from the West going East. Then at 4 p. m. it came through going West.

The depot was very usually crowded, and only just to see the train. Sometimes very few passengers were getting on or off.

The Water Tank was recalled too. "Trains stopped in Durham for their water, as it was the best between Pratt and Herington. The water tank was also a "haven of rest" for the vagrants, or 'bums' as they were called them.

Amelia Smith passed on to her daughter, Ona Donahue, many of her recollections and notes.

Those Who Have Helped

Emil Schwemmer is remembered for his devotion to town projects and sports. During the mid-40's, when a grade school basketball team wanted to play, but had no coach, Emil volunteered his services as a coach. Schwemmer had previously coached the successful Durham Bulls basketball team. He also 'pushed' to get Durham its own water system. Water from wells near Waldeck is piped beside the railroad track, to a standpipe in town.

Other civic-minded individuals include Irwin Geis, who served on the school board for a number of years, and contributed to the town's advancement in many ways.

D.D. Regier, now retired and living in Hillsboro, was principal and superintendent at Durham High Schools from 1945 to 1951.

During that time, he recalls working with others on behalf of the town that included "politicking" to get K-15 Highway through Durham hard-surfaced. "This required visiting every Chamber of Commerce group between Abilene and south of Wichita, and making trips to Topeka to talk to politicians," he said. (In the late 1940's, the group was successful in getting the gravel road hard-surfaced.)

In addition, Regier recalls a time when Durham's streets were either dusty or muddy, much of the time, and the road past the school was in need of some rock. "So some of us local people donated truckloads of rock, so that we could get a better road. We 'rocked' the main thoroughfare, from the first road into Durham on the north side of town, past the school, and on down through Main Street, and then south out of town. At that time, truckloads of rock were $15 each, and many local persons contributed, in order to get the streets in better condition."

Ona Smith Donahue, a source of local lore, as her family were all Durham natives or residents..

Ona Smith Donahue, now 80, and a 40-year teacher in schools in Wyoming, Nebraska, and Wisconsin, recently came into possession of her uncle John Smith's journal.

John Smith, an early motiviator for a Durham School, later became Marion County Sheriff.

"Some days he would write, 'nothing much happened,' 'the sun came up,' 'the jury is deciding if so-and-so is crazy,' etc." she said with a chuckle.

According to handwritten diaries John Smith kept, he was sheriff of Marion County in 1895, '96, '97 and '98. According to this diary of 1899, there was a smallpox epidemic, and because of many families being quarentined, Smith had the responsibility of delivering supplies to those families. He records May 16 through May 31 and June 1 through June 21 of 1899 as delivering those supplies. He collected 31 dollars for those services.

But Smith had a heavy duty regarding the smallpox epidemic, and he not only had to issue the quarentines on homes, and deliver supplies, but there was a grudge against the people of Hillsboro, whom local folks blamed for spreading the smallpox disease. According to this diary, Smith pleaded with Durham residents to 'give up the bitterness toward Hillsboro and let by-gones be by-gones.'

Eldest Citizens

Leah Hamm. At age 85, she is one of Durham's senior citizens.

Irwin Geis -- He shops for all those Durhamites unable to travel far.

George Herbel, long time member of the Durham Baptist Church.

SENIOR CITIZENS

One aspect of a town's Centennial is the celebration of the people who have preceeded us in building the community. Durham has seen the passing of two such people recently. Katie Becker and Amelia Smith were two ladies deeply involved in the day-to-day life of Durham. They represent the type of person who can bind and hold together a small rural town in its struggle to exist. The stories of Amelia and Katie may not be as exciting as some of the early tales of Durham history but they symbolize the type of people who helped Durham achieve its 100 years.

Katie Becker, longtime worker in the community, passed away in March, 1987; one of Durham's eldest residents.

And where we love is home,
Home that our feet may leave,
But not our hearts.
The chain may lengthen,
But it never parts.   Oliver Wendel Holmes